The Cotton Kings

The Cotton Kings

CAPITALISM AND CORRUPTION IN
TURN-OF-THE-CENTURY
NEW YORK AND NEW ORLEANS

Bruce E. Baker and Barbara Hahn

OXFORD
UNIVERSITY PRESS

OXFORD
UNIVERSITY PRESS

Oxford University Press is a department of the University of
Oxford. It furthers the University's objective of excellence in research,
scholarship, and education by publishing worldwide.

Oxford   New York
Auckland   Cape Town   Dar es Salaam   Hong Kong   Karachi
Kuala Lumpur   Madrid   Melbourne   Mexico City   Nairobi
New Delhi   Shanghai   Taipei   Toronto

With offices in
Argentina   Austria   Brazil   Chile   Czech Republic   France   Greece
Guatemala   Hungary   Italy   Japan   Poland   Portugal   Singapore
South Korea   Switzerland   Thailand   Turkey   Ukraine   Vietnam

Published in the United States of America by
Oxford University Press
198 Madison Avenue, New York, NY 10016

© Oxford University Press 2016

Library of Congress Cataloging-in-Publication Data
Baker, Bruce E., 1971–
The cotton kings : capitalism and corruption in turn-of-the-century New York
and New Orleans / Bruce E. Baker and Barbara Hahn.
pages cm
ISBN 978–0–19–021165–3 (hardback : alk. paper)
1. Cotton trade—United States—History—19th century.   2. Cotton trade—
United States—History—20th century.   3. United States—Commerce—History.
I. Hahn, Barbara, 1967–   II. Title.
HD9075.B35 2015
381'.413510973—dc23
2015018313

1 3 5 7 9 8 6 4 2
Printed in the United States of America
on acid-free paper

To Isabel and Rose—B.E.B.

For my mother and my sister, and Jerry—B. H.

CONTENTS

ACKNOWLEDGMENTS

P IECING TOGETHER A COMPLEX story is always a story in itself. This one began when I (Bruce) was annotating a set of letters about the South by William Garrott Brown, and ran across a reference to another man named William Brown in New Orleans who cornered the cotton market in 1903. When I could not find an article or book about this, I started looking up contemporary newspaper articles to find out who that other William Brown was. I quickly realized there was a story to tell here, and just as quickly realized that I could not tell it by myself. I was a labor historian, a social historian; I had no understanding of markets and commodities and such. Fortunately, I had a friend from graduate school who did know about those things. So the first thanks here needs to go to Barbara Hahn for agreeing to work with me on this project. We have had a lot of fun with it.

Daniel Hammer at the Historic New Orleans Collection first alerted us to the existence of the William P. Brown Papers and used that word historians love to hear: "unprocessed." Mary Lou Eichhorn, also at the HNOC, helped us identify an encyclopedia entry for Brown supplied by his descendents. Bettye Brown of the Columbus-Lowndes Public Library sent important material on William P. Brown's early days. Claudia Freeman at Cadwallader, Wickersham, and Taft provided an important document. The very helpful staff at a number of libraries and archives made the research possible and enjoyable, especially Tulane University's Special Collections and the British Library (including the now-defunct newspaper library at Colindale).

Some near and distant members of William P. Brown's family and their friends helped us with important clues and missing links: Stephen Clayton, Yvonne Collier Gwin, and Paul Hays especially. William B. Rudolf was equally helpful in understanding the career of Frank B. Hayne and offering the use of a great image that ultimately did not find a place in the book. Crorey Lawton provided contacts, hospitality, enthusiasm, and a photograph. Jack Becker and Amy Kim at the Texas Tech University Libraries, and Brittany Moses in the History Department, provided useful help finding and scanning images, on short deadlines and with considerable goodwill. In Leeds, Larra Anderson also helped. Emmett Sullivan worked his visual magic on a few recalcitrant images.

At the end of my (Barbara's) first trip to New Orleans, shuttling on the streetcar between the French Quarter and Tulane, not yet recognizing Brown's house (or knowing anything about it), I fell into conversation with some people who have hosted me on every trip to the city I've made since—Karen Duncan and Kelley Dodd, on Algiers Point, who so many times opened their home and their neighborhood and friends and the city to me. Thanks also to Deede Chatelain and Dennis Santopietro around the corner, whose taste for the history of New Orleans inspired many fun evenings—and mornings and afternoons.

Anyone who has known either of us for the last four or five years has heard us talking about cotton endlessly, but we are particularly grateful for several opportunities to present our work before our peers and get useful (sometimes difficult) questions and suggestions. We first discussed this at the 2011 annual meeting of the Association of British American Nineteenth-Century Historians (BrANCH) at Cambridge, where we benefited from feedback from John Killick, who has studied cotton much longer than we have. The Business History Conference was a congenial and invigorating environment, thanks to Walter Friedman, Ken Lipartito, and Susie Pak. Regina Blaszczyk kindly invited Bruce to speak at a workshop at the Victoria and Albert Museum. Thanks to Thomas Kuehn for arranging for Bruce to speak at his alma mater, Clemson University, and to the University of Michigan Economic History Workshop for reading and discussing a draft with Barbara. When the federal government shutdown affected USDA crop reports in 2013, History News Network provided us with a platform to explain why that was important to traders and farmers.

At least one of us did not really know anything about most of this when we started, so it is a good thing there were generous scholars to point us toward the basics of unfamiliar fields. Thanks to R. Emmett Sullivan, Alex Barber, Mary Baumann, and D'Maris Coffman for specific things they will hopefully recognize in our final story.

Back when we thought this was still going to be an essay, not a book, we were fortunate enough to get helpful feedback from three of the best readers we could have hoped for: Paul "The Economist" Rhode, Scott Nelson, and Bill Link. David Weiman gave us useful feedback on a full draft of the book.

Historians need places to read and to write; there are too many unwelcome distractions waiting to ambush you at the office and too many welcome distractions at home. There are worse places to read Congressional committee hearings than the Atrium Café at the John Radcliffe Children's Hospital in Oxford late in the evening. Any British historian will have done some reading or writing in a pub, so thanks to the Fox and Hounds in Caversham, the Nag's Head in Reading, the Happy Man in Englefield Green, and the Angel in Corbridge. Important discussions and inspired writing also took place at the Euston Tap in London.

B.E.B.—Many circumstances have changed for me since I first read about William P. Brown: a new job, moving to the other end of the country, moving across the border. I appreciate old colleagues who worked in the same building at Royal Holloway, University of London, and I have enjoyed settling in to Newcastle University. But most important of all these changes has been getting to know my daughter, Rose, who arrived during the early stages of the research and has grown alongside it. It may be a few years yet before she is ready to read about futures trading, but her joyfulness infuses every page. She and her mother have put up with me hiding away to write, and I treasure every moment I have spent with them away from this project.

B. H.—Friends and companions eased the passage of this book to print. My first thanks go to Bruce Baker for involving me in what turned out to be the most fun book to research and write. I also thank Bruce for his patience and good cheer over the many years of working together. Meanwhile, Clifford Herbstman first suggested this should be a book instead of an article so that he, a nonacademic, could access and read it. Philip Reekers and Tom Nies in Cincinnati, and Cordelia Barrera, JulieAnn Carlton, Renee Lane, Randy McBee, and Julie Willett in Lubbock entertained many conversations about the topic. Eric Chiappinelli was unfailingly supportive and also taught me what that means. I'm grateful to all.

The Cotton Kings

Introduction

The history of the bull speculation in cotton of
1903 will never be fully written, because, though
the men who influenced it are very interesting,
their operations are interwoven with bloodless
statistics and tiresome technicalities.
  —Edwin Lefèvre, *Saturday Evening Post*, August 29, 1903

T HIS BOOK IS AN ATTEMPT to prove the business journalist
Edwin Lefèvre wrong. There are indeed bloodless statistics in
this story, and technicalities that could glaze even the most
attentive of eyes, but still the history of cotton **futures** trading at
the beginning of the twentieth century is an exciting one. It fea-
tures dramatic commercial confrontations where millions of dollars
were made and lost in a day. It contains corruption, intrigue, and
the abuse of power at the highest levels of government. It is a story
of men and their wives, of the social ties that link people together
and the networks they create. It is also a story of conflict. Grand battles in the marketplace determined the results of long campaigns,
nourished by careful logistics and the supply chains connected by
the associations necessary to support the contest. It is an economic
drama, enacted on stages from cotton fields and country stores to
the cotton exchanges of New Orleans, New York, and Liverpool
and the boardrooms of banks. It is a tale of prices and transactions
around the rings of trade.

Every history book is of its time. In the second decade of the
twenty-first century, as we write this book, many Americans feel they
are subject to economic forces beyond their control. Rich and powerful men trade complex financial instruments and gain fabulous
wealth, while average people struggle to get by. Critics of today's
economy compare it to the rampant inequality of the late nineteenth century when robber barons could manipulate the economy
to their own benefit. Other critics object to the remedies that were

applied in the early twentieth century, finding government regulation of markets anathema and insisting that markets work best when
governed least.

This history challenges both of these facile views of the past.
There are indeed some men in these pages who became very rich
by using shady financial practices that impoverished the masses, but
there are also men who used the markets to become very rich in a
way that happened to help many others in the process. The problem
is not the rich men, but the means by which they got their wealth.
Cheaters prospered, but so did honest transactors. Left to its own
devices, the market had become increasingly corrupt and increasingly inefficient. Institutionalized practices prevented prices from
accurately reflecting the relationship between supply and demand.[1]
The market—in this case the cotton futures market—worked better
when placed under federal regulation.

This story has a hero: William Perry Brown. Born in rural
Mississippi, Brown was smart, confident, and hard-working. These
traits carried him to New Orleans and made his fortune, along
with his reputation as "about the coolest man on the exchange
floor."[2] This story also has villains—unscrupulous cotton brokers in
New York who lied to poor farmers so they could buy cheaply the cotton watered with the farmers' sweat, rogues who stole information
and cheated the market, corrupt politicians who traded favors for
their friends and abused their power.

The Cotton Kings offers some challenges to received wisdom.
Ronald Reagan's assertion that "government is the problem" has
echoed through American culture of the late twentieth and early
twenty-first centuries. By contrast, this story argues that regulation
works—that the job of markets is not simply to make money for individual participants but to make prices reflect supply and demand,
and that rules need to be applied equally to all participants for this
to happen. Self-regulation by market participants may be corrupted
when some hold more power than others, which often happens. The
specific examples of self-regulation and its failures explored here are
cotton exchanges, which began as private institutions designed to
facilitate business transactions. For a while, they improved the market's efficiency. But as the economic conditions that brought them
into being changed, the New York Cotton Exchange (NYCE) altered
its practices to protect the vested interests of its members, and these
changes undermined the efficiency of the market. The brokers of
the NYCE thrived on price volatility that sunk well-run firms. They
pushed the price of cotton down relentlessly, immiserating millions

and skewing the nation's regional distribution of wealth. Part of the reason that the South was the nation's number one economic problem by the 1930s was that the NYCE had for decades cheated its cotton farmers of a fair return on what they produced.

The Origins of Cotton Futures Trading

Before the Civil War cotton was the nation's major export, equaling in value all other exports combined, but the system for marketing it was remarkably old-fashioned. Cotton factors, based in the major port cities of the South, handled most business transactions for planters. The planters sent their cotton to the factors, and the factors found the best place and time to sell it, earning a commission, usually 2.5%, on the sale of the planter's cotton. Factors also bought plantation supplies—food, bagging, tools, shoes, clothing, and so on—and forwarded them on to the planters, taking another commission from these transactions. These relations between planters and factors were remarkably informal, with few written contracts and surprisingly few legal disputes; the system worked because of the mutual trust developed between individual planters and individual factors over time.[3] That arrangement did not survive the Civil War, however; the role credit played in cotton production and marketing changed. The collateral for an advance before the war was often a planter's slaves, who could be sold quite easily if necessary. Once slaves were no longer available as collateral a new basis for advancing planters supplies and money was needed, and, after a period of experimentation, this replacement was the crop lien. Lenders could advance supplies secure in the knowledge that they had first claim on the growing crop. The lender became not a distant factor but a local storekeeper, whose chain of credit ultimately reached Wall Street.[4]

The system that replaced the antebellum factors was shaped directly by wartime practices. Textile manufacturers in the North had needed steady supplies of cotton to fulfill government contracts, but with the cotton supply from the South disrupted, they had been reluctant to take on the risk themselves. An opening was created for traders who could find ways to buy cotton when and where it became available and arrange to deliver it to those who spun it when they needed it. These traders were not factors, with long-established relationships with both growers and spinners, but cotton brokers.[5] These independent dealers were poised to become central to the cotton trade in the coming decades.

The rise of cotton brokers phased out the personalized nature of the antebellum cotton trade. Technological change furthered this process by overcoming the obstacles of distance and time. In 1866 the transatlantic cable made it possible to communicate immediately between America, where most of the world's cotton was produced, and Britain, where most of the world's cotton was spun. With this technological improvement, price information could for the first time travel to the most important cotton market—Liverpool—much more quickly than the goods themselves. What had been contracts for the **future delivery** of actual goods became futures trading, a trade in information and risk.[6] Improved communication had an equally profound effect on the cotton trade within the United States. When conditions or events affected the crop, they could be known instantly in the regional exchanges where cotton was bought and sold but also in the two key American cotton exchanges, New York and New Orleans.

Futures trading can be fiendishly complex, but it rests on simple ideas. A **spot** transaction is one in which the buyer and seller execute a trade on the spot—money changes hands and ownership of the cotton transfers from seller to buyer. Spot trading deals in particular lots of cotton—these specific bales of a particular **grade**. Futures contracts, on the other hand, are binding contracts that are agreed on at one time and executed at a specified time in the future. Under the rules of the cotton exchanges a buyer has an absolute right to demand his cotton on that date, and likewise the seller has an absolute right to demand his money. Brokers are free, of course, to sell a contract and transfer that obligation to another party. The buyer and seller are also free to cancel a contract, usually with some money changing hands, but only if both parties agree. A futures contract does not deal with a particular bale of cotton—it may well be entered into before the cotton is planted—but rather it gives the buyer the contractual right (and obligation) to buy a certain quantity of cotton at a certain price and gives the seller the contractual right (and obligation) to sell a certain quantity of cotton at a certain price.

Very few futures contracts were made in expectation of actual delivery, but rather in the expectation of closing the contract in exchange for a payment, rather than cotton. If the cost of spot cotton on **tender day**—the day a contract for delivery came due—were higher than the contract, then the seller owed the buyer the difference; if the price were lower, then the reverse. This meant that futures contracts were a device that allowed every transactor's assessment of the future supply and demand for the commodity to influence the

price of the contracts. They allowed information from a wide
of sources to shape the price of the goods. Yet it was the contr
right and obligation of delivery that tethered those guesses to the
real world of commerce in actual goods and made the information
about the future state of the market a valuable good in its own right.[7]
It may seem self-evident, but futures trading allows traders at every
stage of the production of cotton and cotton goods to plan for the
future. No amount of planning can completely avoid the unpleasant
effects of unknowable future events, but futures trading cushions
those effects and reduces price volatility.

Prices and Places

In the period this story covers it was commonly understood that certain markets "set prices," but which market—Liverpool, New York, or
New Orleans—would set the price of cotton? Liverpool, for example,
was for a long time considered the price-setter for cotton. So much
demand emerged there, seeking its supply, that it was the place where
a price would rise or sink depending on variations in that demand
and how much supply was available to meet it. In contrast to the
market at Liverpool, a country storekeeper might buy cotton from a
dozen tenant farmers on the land of two planters: there both buyer
and seller, storekeeper and farmer, had little influence on the price
and had to settle on a price made far away. Compare those transactors to the largest group of cotton mills in the world, their capacity and their prediction of what their customers needed in the way
of finished goods. Because they consumed so much of the world's
cotton, the cotton mills' demand and their perceptions of supply
would shape the price in ways that would filter down to the country
store. If a Lancashire mill closed due to labor unrest, demand for
raw materials dropped, and so did the price. Liverpool was the site
of the cotton exchange through which most of the world's cotton
flowed, headed toward those mills in Lancashire. To the people of
the period, supply and demand at Liverpool self-evidently set the
price of the staple.[8]

Nowadays the concept of the price-setter has been battered.
Economists now argue that the invisible and inexorable workings of
the market influence prices wherever trades occur—the exact same
forces affect the price at the country store where the farmer sells his
crops as on the cotton exchange in Liverpool. However, in the late
nineteenth century this spread-out price situation may have been
true in the abstract, but was not true in practice. Information about

demand from the mills of Lancashire filtered through their orders for raw materials in Liverpool, and information from Liverpool had to physically reach New Orleans for it to have an influence on the price there. Likewise, information had to reach the country store if the merchant and the farmer were to know the value of the commodity one had produced and the other wished to market. That physical arrival of information became possible with telegraphy and the transatlantic cable, though information about the market for cotton was something that could be manipulated—and, with it, the price of the good.

Futures trading not only allowed people to plan ahead and ease the impact of price volatility, but it also communicated information about prices, and indicated the market's prediction of supply and demand in future months. A lower price in the future indicated that the value was dropping, and better to avoid buying expensively now in the spot market when you could buy more cheaply what you needed later. Without buyers, the spot price dropped. In this way future prices shaped spot prices. Information about the future price, developed in the markets where exchange members traded futures, influenced the prices of spot transactions at country stores across the South. Cotton farmers were subject to economic forces beyond their control. They begrudged middlemen the money made by trading the goods produced on the farm, and they resented the fact that prices made far away and for future delivery structured the prices for goods they sold at the local store.

The Threat to Futures Trading

Farmers therefore fought against futures trading, because they usually did not understand how it helped them and understood all too well how it hurt them. In Germany, for example, futures trading was banned outright from 1896 to 1908.[9] In 1890 an Ohio Republican in the House of Representatives, Ben Butterworth, introduced a bill that aimed to satisfy agrarian interests by eliminating altogether the speculation in agricultural commodities.[10] For several years Americans had seen markets for agricultural products, especially wheat, influenced not by the old-fashioned laws of supply and demand but by the manipulations of traders who never actually saw a bushel of wheat, a pork belly, or a bale of cotton. In Chicago, speculation in the future price of wheat had become particularly dissociated from actual delivery of the grain, and around the country would-be traders placed bets on future prices in **bucket shops**, where anyone could walk in off the street with no intention of actual delivery.[11] Agrarian interests such as the Farmers' Alliance thought the Butterworth Bill would prevent speculators with no interest in the land or its products from gambling with agricultural commodities they did not actually own, just for the sake of making a profit on shifting commodity prices.

Those who actually dealt in futures contracts saw things differently. Getting rid of all futures trading, as the Butterworth Bill set out to do, would destroy the agricultural economy, they argued, especially where farmers depended on credit from year to year. The law meant that if a merchant or banker gave a farmer an advance on the future delivery of his crop—as had been standard practice—that would still be legal, since the farmer of the growing crop would have the right to sell it for future delivery. However, the transaction would stop there, with the local banker or merchant unable to sell that contract on. He would have to wait until the crop was harvested to get his money.[12] Rather than empowering the farmer, the bill's opponents argued, the Butterworth Bill would "crush out the small dealers and place the farmer at the mercy of the large capitalist, who can buy cash grain; but they will buy at such a price that they can hold it until Gabriel blows his horn without sustaining a loss."[13] That price would be low—lower than the price of future deliveries, according to this analysis, and almost always less than the products could bring around the world, since futures trading was an important mechanism for conveying information and setting prices in multiple and far-flung locations.[14]

Besides, observers pointed out, banning futures trading would prove especially damaging to southern cotton farmers, who depended on crop liens more than midwestern grain farmers. Unlike **future contracts** for grain, which were mostly traded in Chicago, cotton futures were a global business. Banning their use in the United States would only mean that the major cotton markets of Europe (Liverpool, Bremen, and Le Havre), unimpeded by American laws, would take over. Since more cotton farmers would have to sell as their crop came to market between September and December, the European buyers could push the price as low as they liked.[15] As the editor of the New Orleans *Daily Picayune* wrote, "If Western farmers desire to try dangerous experiments let them do so and welcome, but cotton interests can well afford to leave well enough alone."[16]

The Butterworth Bill did not become law, but it serves as a good marker. The end of slavery and the systems of finance it had supported had temporarily devastated the American cotton trade, but by the last decade of the nineteenth century, southern farms were producing more cotton than ever. All that cotton, however, had brought poverty, not wealth, to those who grew it, and it was clear that problems in cotton futures trading were somehow to blame for that. Over the next twenty-five years many actors struggled over how (or even whether) futures trading in cotton would be conducted and how the cotton futures market would affect the supply, demand, and price of cotton and thus the fates of millions.

CHAPTER 1

New Orleans and the Future of the Cotton Trade

William P. Brown

AMERICA'S NATIONAL MYTHOLOGY HAS A special place for the self-made man, the boy from the humble background who overcomes adversity to not only survive, but to thrive, the person who embodies the rags-to-riches story. This story is embedded just as thoroughly in the stories of the New South. A region devastated by war, with its economic foundation knocked away, had to start over from scratch and reinvent itself. Within a few decades its farms were producing more cotton than ever, its industrialists had begun to challenge the dominance of New England's textile mills, and the region had found new ways to prosper—all on the basis of hard work and good sense, without sacrificing that ineluctable southern graciousness and gentility. Sometimes there is a man who fits perfectly into his time and place, and William P. Brown was such a man for the New South.[1]

The man who would ultimately control the world's cotton supply began his life about as far from the action and the big city as could be imagined. Eight days after Lincoln was elected president, William Perry Brown was born in the community of Caledonia in Lowndes County, Mississippi. Just north of Columbus and a couple miles from the Alabama state line, Caldeonia was a fairly prosperous plantation community on the Buttahatchee River. Brown's

Figure 1.1 William Perry Brown was the most powerful cotton futures trader on the
New Orleans Cotton Exchange in the first decade of the twentieth century. From *The Book
of Louisiana: A Newspaper Reference Work* (New Orleans Item, 1916). Courtesy of The Historic
New Orleans Collection, Gift of Mrs. Niels Jacobson.

father had moved there from South Carolina and had married the
daughter of a local farmer. Before Brown was six months old, war
had come to the South, though it never quite reached Columbus
and Lowndes County. Tragedy on a more personal level affected
ten-year-old Brown and his younger siblings when his mother died.
By the age of fourteen, Brown had begun to look beyond the farm.
A local merchant named J. Warren Gardner took Brown under his
wing and introduced him to the world of business at his dry goods
store in Caledonia. Tragedy struck again in 1877 when Brown's
father was killed by a runaway mule. At this time he likely left the vil-
lage of Caledonia for the opportunities of Columbus. By 1880 Brown
was working as a clerk for Sol Lichtenstadter, a New York-born merchant. People began to notice his ambition, his business aptitude,
and his fondness for taking risks; they called him "Poker Bill." When
Lichtenstadter went out of business Brown went into partnership

buying cotton with Hunter Sharp, son of Confederate general and Columbus newspaper editor Jacob H. Sharp. Brown opened his own dry goods store, and by the end of the decade he was also a wholesale dealer in groceries and dry goods.[2]

In these early years, in country stores and small-town wholesale establishments, Brown was gaining the skills that he would later use as a cotton broker on the global stage. Any dry goods clerk had to keep track of stock, knowing almost instinctively how much coffee was left and when to order more bottles of "Southern Liver Regulator, for all bilious diseases or disorders arising from torpidity of the liver."[3] Country merchants usually charged different prices for the same goods depending on whether payment was by cash or credit (and, no doubt, for other reasons), so they did not put the price on the items themselves but instead used a code to indicate what it cost them. A merchant familiar with this would find it easy to use the elaborate cipher that was standard in the cotton trade, a code for transmitting numbers precisely without worrying whether a telegrapher accidentally transposed a couple of digits.[4] As a wholesaler in Columbus, Brown would also have had to watch trends to see which goods were selling faster or slower, consider carefully the best mode and the cost to transport goods to his warehouse and to customers' retail stores, and finance purchases and sales. All these lessons could be applied when he was trading cotton in Columbus alongside his other business, and they continued to be useful when he made cotton the focus of his career.

Also important to Brown's skill set was his interest in poker. The modern game of poker evolved in New Orleans in the early nineteenth century from a French game, *poque*, with Persian influences. Its crucial feature was betting against the other players on the basis of the cards held—bluffing. The steamboats that brought cotton and other goods down the river to New Orleans took poker upstream, and the game was commonly played by southerners by the 1830s. No doubt Brown's idle moments in Mississippi stores provided the perfect opportunity to hone his skills at the card table.[5] "There were some good poker players in Columbus," recalled one resident years later, "but there wasn't a man who could hold his end up in a game with young Brown. It didn't make any difference to him whether he was playing in a quarter limit game in the back room of a drug store or a limitless game with the leading financiers in a room of the hotel. He never failed to cash."[6] When Brown was bidding for control of the world's cotton supply in 1903, it was neither coincidence nor local color that led journalists to remark upon his reputation "through the Mississippi delta as one of the best poker players that ever handled a card."[7] He also "owned the finest lot of fighting chickens in the state," suggesting that he tempered the coolness of the poker player with an appetite for blood.[8]

As a successful wholesale grocer and local cotton buyer Brown could no doubt have settled down, bought an impressive home, and enjoyed life as a leading merchant in Columbus. But he had mastered the dry goods business and began to look for a new challenge. Before long he moved to Ruston, in northern Louisiana, and quickly built a substantial business as a dealer in spot cotton. For a man interested in brokering cotton in the 1890s, north Louisiana between the Red River and the Ouachita River was the place to be—much more than the Mississippi–Alabama border, which had been full of possibility for cotton farmers of his father's generation, before the Civil War. Once the Red River had been cleared of logjams and made navigable in 1873, bales from north Louisiana and East Texas could come down to New Orleans by steamship much more easily. Texas substantially increased its cotton production in the 1890s. From Ruston, Brown appears to have moved to New Orleans in 1894 when he found a bride there. Upon his arrival he went into the cotton business with Daniel Grant, who had only come to the city the year before. Three years later, Grant left New Orleans and Brown began trading as W. P. Brown and Company. He soon hired three of his younger brothers to manage local operations in several interior towns in northern Louisiana, east of Shreveport. He was building a network from the center of the cotton world just as things were about to get exciting.[9]

New Orleans and the Changing Cotton Trade

At the end of the 1880s, New Orleans was just beginning to stir. The Crescent City had few paved roads outside the central business district, and inadequate underground drainage meant that open gutters ran full whenever it rained hard. Businessmen had to pick their way carefully, paying children pennies to lay planks across particularly treacherous mudholes. There was a streetcar system, but it went only as fast as the plodding mules that pulled the cars. By the beginning of the twentieth century, however, the streetcars had been electrified, giving more distant neighborhoods and suburbs easy access to the center of the city. A massive underground drainage system had tamed the mud, and new houses and modern office buildings were springing up to replace outdated or outworn

Figure 1.2 Steamboats carried cotton from the rich farms along the Mississippi River system to be sold in and exported from New Orleans. From *The Picayune's Guide to New Orleans* (1903). Courtesy of The Historic New Orleans Collection.

structures. In those same years, New Orleans was increasing its capacity for handling cotton. Storage and shipping facilities could only handle about 400,000 bales at a time in the early 1890s, but by 1898 they could accommodate close to 700,000 bales. The Illinois Central Railroad built the Stuyvesant Docks stretching along twelve blocks of the river in 1898 and hauled a million bales into New Orleans that season.[10]

The system of cotton sales from before the war, in which factors marketed the crop for planters and extended credit to producers, changed dramatically as sharecroppers and tenant farmers sought credit at local stores. Now brokers would handle the marketing of the crop once it left growers' hands. Since the cotton trade no longer relied on personal relationships between planters and factors and between factors and spinners, institutional structures took their place. A buyer need not know and trust the broker who bought his cotton if the broker belonged to a trustworthy organization that vouched for him and provided rules for the transaction that the broker would use. Spinners who bought cotton needed to go where they knew they could find the goods that they sought. More importantly, brokers needed a place to meet with one another and strike deals. These were the purposes behind the cotton exchanges that sprang up across the geography of the cotton trade in the 1870s: in

New York City in 1870, in New Orleans and Mobile in 1871, in St. Louis and southern cities from Charleston to Galveston by 1874.[11] In the hands of clever brokers telegraphy helped to integrate all these cotton markets, which meant that price changes in one would influence prices in the others. With information moving to markets faster than goods, brokers could begin to do more than just spot transactions. They could make contracts for future delivery with some confidence that they were accepting a correct price according to what the conditions of the market were likely to be at some point in the future. Before telegraphic communication this would have been too risky, nothing but foolish gambling. But the development of formal cotton exchanges and improvements in communication created the possibility of a market in cotton futures. By 1868, modern futures contracts became an important part of the business in New York and New Orleans cotton markets.[12] The New York Cotton Exchange (NYCE) began trading futures when it opened in 1870, and the New Orleans Cotton Exchange (NOCE) followed suit in 1881. These were the only two cotton exchanges in the United States to operate a formal futures market, though Chicago's Board of Trade did a roaring business in grain futures. The institutions needed elaborate sets of rules to make futures trading work, and the NYCE and the NOCE

Figure 1.3 The interior of the New Orleans Cotton Exchange, pictured here in 1879, was a busy place with traders discussing market conditions, reading newspapers and crop reports, making deals, and posting the latest information on a large blackboard. From *Frank Leslie's Illustrated Newspaper,* Feb. 1, 1879.

were best equipped to do that. In addition to the futures markets of the United States, the cotton exchanges in Liverpool, Bremen, and Le Havre also established futures markets. These cities were far from any cotton fields but near to the places where the bulk of the world's cotton was consumed in the mid-nineteenth century.[13]

The rules of the cotton exchanges in New York and New Orleans governed the trade in cotton futures among their members. Anyone trading on the exchange had to be a member of the exchange, so there were committees on membership and only a limited number of places available. Trading had to be done on the exchange premises during regular hours. The exchanges had provisions for penalizing traders who tried to take advantage of a day's price trends by continuing their trading "on the curb" after hours. Like other self-regulating organizations, the ultimate sanction was exclusion; a trader could lose his membership on the exchange for violating the rules of the exchange or fraudulently breaking a contract or indeed "any proceeding inconsistent with just and equitable principles of trade."[14] In an open market where anyone may trade, such rules carried no weight. The regulations of the exchanges worked because both institutions controlled membership and trading privileges with considerable care.[15]

Most importantly, the exchanges developed a standard form for a futures contract and provided rules governing how such a contract was to be fulfilled. The standard contract at NOCE is a good example. A standard contract was for 50,000 pounds of cotton in "100 square bales." The contract did not stipulate what **grade** of cotton had to be delivered; that was entirely up to the seller. As long as he delivered cotton that was within the range of grades accepted on the exchange, he had fulfilled the contract.[16]

The contract created a binding obligation on the seller to deliver cotton and on the buyer to pay for it. That might seem obvious, but it was significant. Most often, a buyer and seller would agree not to complete a contract. Instead the two would settle the contract based on the difference between its value and the price of actual cotton. But if push came to shove the contract was enforceable, and brokers who failed to honor contracts risked their membership in the exchange, never mind potential legal action. Because most futures contracts were made but never completed, the number of bales of cotton that traded in the futures market vastly outstripped the number of bales that actually existed. But since a futures contract relied on the possibility of delivery, an exchange where futures contracts were delivered benefited from substantial traffic of actual, physical

---

CONTRACT

New Orleans,........................., 189...

    In consideration of one dollar in hand paid, receipt of which is hereby acknowledged ....have this day sold to (or bought from) .... 50,000 pounds in about 100 square bales of cotton, growth of the United States, deliverable from press or presses in the port of New Orleans, between the *first* and *last* days of .... next inclusive.

    The delivery within such time to be at seller's option, in not more than two presses, upon five days' notice to the buyer.

    The cotton to be of any grade from Good Ordinary White to Fair inclusive, and if stained, not below Low Middling, at the price of .... cents (................) per pound for Middling, with additions or deduction for other grades, according to the quotations of the New Orleans Cotton Exchange existing on the sixth (6ᵗʰ) day previous to the day on which delivery is due.

    It is distinctly understood and agreed that no cotton shall be tendered or received under this contract of a less market value than Good Ordinary White, and that the receiver shall have the right to refuse all sandy, dusty, red or gin-cut cotton; sandy and dusty cotton being defined, under this contract, as cotton lessened in value more than 1/8c. per pound, by reason of sand or dust.

    Either party shall have the right to call for a margin, as the variations of the market for like deliveries may warrant, and which margin shall be kept good.

    This contract is made in view of, and in all respects subject to, the rules and conditions established by the New Orleans Cotton Exchange, and in full accordance with Rule 25 of said New Orleans Cotton Exchange.

(Signed)..

Source: *By-Laws and Rules of the New Orleans Cotton Exchange, Embracing All Rules Governing the Spot and Future Contract Cotton Business in the New Orleans Market. Including Revisions Up To November 29ᵗʰ, 1894* (New Orleans: L. Graham & Son, 1894), 45–46.

Figure 1.4 The New Orleans Cotton Exchange followed a standard format for all trades in cotton intended for future delivery. The standardized contract, and its enforcement by the New Orleans Cotton Exchange, made possible the market for cotton futures.

cotton. If a broker had a contract to fulfill, he had to be able to buy the actual bales of cotton to deliver; futures trading depended on spot trading.

    An exchange with both a sizeable futures market and a sizeable spot market was able to carry out several functions that served the interests of everyone in the cotton trade, from the farmer all the way to the tailor in China buying a bolt of cloth made in Lancashire from Alabama cotton. The most important of these functions was **hedging**. Hedging in a futures market, at its most basic level, means that a trader makes a further transaction in the market in order to decrease the risk of the original transaction. Very few contracts bought and sold as hedges actually were completed, but they allowed traders to continually adjust their market **position**. For the hedger, futures contracts provided a means of eliminating risk of loss due to changes in the price of cotton. Merchants hedged cotton the minute they bought it from the farmers, and spinners hedged as soon as they took an order for yarn. These hedges made the market run more smoothly, and the sheer volume of trades took into account the continual changes in anticipated supply and demand that made prices more accurately reflect market conditions.[17]

Futures trading also shifted some of the risk inherent in anticipating future supply and demand from the buyers and sellers to speculators. When the system worked smoothly, speculators were betting that their analyses of information about market trends—their predictions of price—were better than those of their competitors and would allow them to make a profit; the collective effect of multiple bettors and speculators brought the best possible information into the market. In this way futures trading made prices more accurately reflect the real conditions of supply and demand than if there were no speculation. This sunny assessment assumed, though, that the information influencing the market was presented in good faith and was available equally to all.[18] When a futures market worked properly, only those who wanted to take risk did so and price volatility should be decreased as a result. Farmers should be happy to know what their cotton would bring, and spinners could price their own goods for future delivery with confidence, knowing what they would have to pay for their raw materials.

A cotton **squeeze** in New Orleans in April 1890 demonstrates how the futures market worked and how traders could use contingent external events to drive up prices. In January 1890, the price of spot cotton in New Orleans stood at 10.0 cents per pound. Cotton prices slowly increased throughout the spring of 1890, with **spots** gaining 69 **points** (a point is a hundredth of a cent) from the middle of January to the beginning of March and then a further 25 points by the middle of that month to 10.94. As cotton prices were rising, however, so too were the waters of the Mississippi River and its tributaries. By the last week of March, the river was flooding Memphis. The quantity of cotton coming in to New Orleans from the countryside was already low—contributing to its rising value—and the danger the flooding posed to the new crop pushed spot prices to 11.25 by April 17. Floodwaters covered the Illinois Central Railroad, cutting off the main route from Memphis to New Orleans, then the Louisville and Nashville Railroad at Michoud (now part of the famous Ninth Ward). Lake Pontchartrain began to wash over the rear of the city by April 23.[19]

Meanwhile, cotton traders in Liverpool began to realize that spring just how little of the old cotton crop was left, pushing prices still higher.[20] In New Orleans, some observers believed that " 'futures' have been oversold to a greater or less extent" and "some difficulty is being already experienced in filling contracts."[21] When **tender day** came on April 26, those who had promised to sell notified buyers that they intended to deliver over 8,000 bales of cotton. They expected the buyers to cancel the contracts rather than actually pay for and take delivery of the cotton; this would mean more cotton available on the market and lower prices. Instead, the notices were accepted (or **stopped**), the cotton was delivered and paid for, and the price of cotton continued to advance. There was little cotton in New Orleans, and not much in the countryside. With the railroads flooded, it would be that much harder to get cotton to New Orleans in time to satisfy a contract before the end of the month. **Bull traders** were able "to engineer a sort of squeeze," leaving **bears** "at their wit's ends to bring about a turn in the tide," according to a New Orleans newspaper.[22] Spot cotton at New Orleans rose as high as 11.69 before, like the floodwaters, slowly subsiding.[23] This episode may have taught New Orleans brokers some of the elements they would eventually use to **corner** the market: timing was everything, and local conditions could be leveraged when world markets provided the right conditions.

Business in New Orleans

Floods would prove useful to William P. Brown as he expanded his networks, and it is time we returned to his story. The New Orleans business community had historically been a very fractious group. This was not unusual in the rapidly expanding nineteenth-century American cities: bankers often had very different economic interests than storekeepers, storekeepers than wholesalers, cotton brokers in the cities from rural merchants and factors of international concerns. In New Orleans, this diversity in the affairs of trade was further complicated by historically important differences in the city's population of business actors. The city had only joined the United States with the Louisiana Purchase in 1803, and for nearly a century before that time the port, tied as it was between the Mississippi and a large interior lake, had been one of the commercial centers of the continent for several competing empires. American merchants who had arrived in the city in the antebellum decades had little in common with the longer-established "creoles," whether of French or Spanish heritage, and those distinctions persisted. When the French Quarter and the American side of town had distinct municipal governments, the name "neutral ground" became a common designation for the median strip of Canal Street that divided them. The ethnic, cultural, and historical distinctions in this city's so-called business community created contending groups.[24]

William P. Brown seems to have had an uncommon knack for joining established networks. He had been doing this since he was a teenager, going to work for Caledonia's preeminent merchant and then parlaying that into a better job in the bigger town of Columbus. But he outdid himself when he married Marguerite Braughn of New Orleans. Certainly he had a romantic side—at their wedding in 1894, he gave his bride a diamond brooch in the shape of a daisy, the meaning of "marguerite" in French—but sentiment aside, he married very well.[25] Marguerite's father was Judge George H. Braughn. Like Brown, Braughn was only fourteen when he began to make his own way in the world, moving from Cincinnati to New Orleans. He studied law, fought for the Confederacy, and was elected as a Democrat to the first Louisiana Reconstruction legislature in 1868. He was appointed to the bench of the Superior Court in 1875.[26] When he died in 1889, all the courts in the city adjourned, and "fifty honorary pall-bearers, including judges of the courts, officials of the city, and members of nearly every club and association in the city" carried him to rest in Metairie Cemetery.[27] Braughn himself knew a thing or two about networks. In 1872, he had been among the founders of Rex Organization, a parading krewe of Mardi Gras, a haven for slightly less hardline opponents of Reconstruction, especially businessmen.[28]

Rex may well have been where Brown met his ally in his later speculative adventures, Franklin Brevard Hayne. Like Brown, Hayne was a cotton broker and transplant to New Orleans. Born in Charleston in 1858, Hayne came from one of the most illustrious families of South Carolina. When he was fifteen, he went to work for a prominent Charleston cotton firm, Watson and Hill. Soon Hayne was ready to strike out on his own. In 1883, with $2,000, he went into business with another well-bred Charlestonian, Hugh de Lacy Vincent in Montgomery, Alabama, where the two young men were junior partners of an established cotton broker,

Daniel Partridge. Vincent handled business in Vicksburg, with branches around the Mississippi Delta, and two years later Hayne moved to New Orleans to manage the firm's business there, which required joining the local cotton exchange, the NOCE. Within just five years, Vincent and Hayne had become significant players in the New Orleans cotton world. In 1896 Hayne, like Brown, married into the New Orleans business establishment. His wife, Emily Poitevent, was the daughter of John Poitevent, the founder of Mississippi's largest lumber company and a prominent New Orleans businessman in his own right.[29]

At the turn of the century, William P. Brown and Frank B. Hayne were cotton brokers in one of the two national centers of the trade, a once-great city that was beginning to rise again in national prominence. A few years later, they would become the most important players in the entire cotton business. In the meantime, as the century turned, the cotton bulls still had lessons to learn.

CHAPTER 2

The Value of Information

THE WORLD WHERE WILLIAM P. BROWN and Frank Hayne found themselves in the mid-1890s—the world of cotton centered on the New Orleans Cotton Exchange, at the corner of Carondelet Street and Gravier Street—was a world ruled by information. Buying and selling cotton relied on knowledge about the market, about supply and demand, so that both buyer and seller could settle on a price. As a broker once put it, "We suppose that prices are governed by the actual relation of supply and demand, but they are not. They are governed by what people think is going to be the relation of supply and demand."[1] Accurate information, however, was hard to find. The people who knew the cotton market best were usually people with interests in the market, brokers who held specific positions that would be affected by changes in supply and demand. When they shared information with others, they would use it to shape perceptions of supply and demand and thus benefit from other people's actions in the markets. However, the New Orleans Cotton Exchange had as its secretary one of the few men in the world who collected information without participating in the trade. His name was Henry G. Hester, and his encyclopedic knowledge of cotton production provided New Orleans brokers with a crucial advantage in the marketplace.

Hester had begun his career as a newspaper reporter on the financial and market beat, and he worked hard to provide regular and up-to-date reports for his newspaper. In 1871, twenty-four-year-old Hester accepted an offer to serve as the secretary and superintendent of the NOCE—a position for which he had not even applied. He held the job for fifty-six years. Hester's work lay in careful statistical computation, but at the end of the working day he knew how to enjoy life, his marriage and his clubs, a drink and a cigar. Ruddy-faced, short and stocky, he stayed well-groomed and tailored into his eighties. His reputation for rectitude circled the globe. In the twentieth century, his weekly compilations of mill takings and cotton brought to market, "Hester's Report," went out to subscribers every Friday. He made his career in information, not the market: he "never owned a bale of cotton in my life," as he said. In his capacity as secretary of the Exchange, he sent and received more than a hundred telegrams a day. Though he described his work as simply knowing that "two plus two makes four," years of experience had taught him just how much weight to attach to the figures that arrived on his desk from the **gins**, the mills, the farmers, and the crop reporters of the interior.[2]

Hester had the best infrastructure for gathering information about cotton in the South, but others whose opinions on the cotton futures market carried the most weight were participants who had positions and made money within that market.[3] Their success in the trade, combined with their circulation of information, also served to increase their power in the market, making their statements that much more significant. At the beginning of the twentieth century, the federal government was still looking for ways to supplant self-interested market operators and provide more accurate market information in cotton.

Cotton Futures and Information

A futures contract is a derivative, which adds to the complexity of trading in futures. Buying and selling spot cotton—an actual physical commodity—is tricky enough. Both buyer and seller need to know something about supply and demand for the commodity in order to agree on a price that is advantageous for both. If the seller underestimates the demand, he might accept a price that is lower than he could get. Likewise, if the buyer underestimates the supply, he might agree to a price much higher than he really needs to pay. Information about supply and demand is crucial to determine the price of a good in a market. Futures contracts add the element of time. In such a deal, both buyer and seller must know something about supply and demand not only at the moment of the transaction; they also must have some information about supply and demand in the future. With cotton futures contracts trading as far

Figure 2.1 Henry G. Hester, the first secretary of the New Orleans Cotton Exchange, was a central figure in the national cotton trade from the 1880s to the 1930s. From Meigs O. Frost, *Hester Says* (Theo. H. Harvey, 1926). Courtesy of The Historic New Orleans Collection.

as twelve months ahead, getting good information became critical. The broker who could figure out how much cotton would be needed in six months' time or the size of next year's crop held tremendous power in the market and could leverage a modest investment into a fortune.

Demand for cotton was relatively easy to figure. A variety of sources published annual statistics on American cotton consumption.

Cotton Movement and Fluctuation had been published by the New York brokerage of Latham, Alexander, and Co. since the end of the 1860s. Since the mid-1880s, A. B. Shepperson published his annual *Cotton Facts*. Demand generally increased steadily due to factors that were readily observable and quantifiable. A new mill in Alabama, for instance, would have a certain amount of capacity, usually expressed in the number of spindles in operation. Each spindle could consume a certain amount of cotton; if there was an unlimited demand for the cloth produced, it was possible to figure out the maximum amount of cotton a mill would consume. Well-informed brokers paid attention to news of mill openings and had a good sense of how much cotton could be consumed in the next several months. Some factors limited consumption, of course. Labor unrest might bring spindles to a standstill. Transportation could be disrupted or unrest in a market could stifle demand or make it impossible to get products to their markets. The Boxer Rebellion in China in 1900 worried American cotton manufacturers—the Taiping Rebellion had gone on for fourteen years—but this rebellion was over within a matter of months.[4] Of course, if market demand for cloth dropped, spindles would stand idle.

Supply was harder to calculate. In the early years of the twentieth century, cotton was being grown in more and more places around the globe. As late as 1910 the United States still produced over 60% of the world's cotton, and the cotton crop of the American South was the most important for several reasons.[5] Cotton from most other sources might enter niche markets, or have a relatively low or uneven quality, or was simply too scarce to have a major effect on price. Cotton from India had "a short, coarse fiber, and can not be utilized in the manufacture of finer counts of yarn." Yields per acre averaged little more than half that of the United States, and even as World War I began the Indian government was trying, slowly, to improve the quality of seed used so that Indian cotton would be more attractive to European markets.[6] Egyptian cotton, on the other hand, was very high quality, but Egypt produced only about a tenth of what the United States grew, and that went exclusively for fancy goods.[7] African production outside Egypt was negligible, less than 3000 bales in 1903.[8] Despite other countries' production, the important number to know was how many bales of cotton would be produced in the states from Virginia to Texas.

Many factors affected cotton cultivation in the United States in any given year, and they were not very easy to know. The most basic question was: how many acres were planted in cotton? Related was the question of yield: how many bales of cotton would each acre produce? Imagine the vast Cotton Belt, covering 700,000 square miles from Virginia, across to Missouri, out to Texas, and down to Florida. How was it possible to know how many acres were planted to cotton compared to the year before?[9] Guessing that acreage had increased by 5% rather than 4% had real effects when multiplied by the huge number of acres involved. Yield was not constant across the region, either. In 1900, for instance, Texas produced twice as many bales per acre as Florida.[10]

Even knowing how much cotton was being produced did not mean knowing the amount supplied to the market. Any number of things could decrease the size of the crop or its quality, and many of these could happen suddenly. What looked like a good crop in May could simply dry up if a drought hit, losing as much as 80%, so cotton brokers paid close attention to the weather. Cotton harvest began as early as mid-July in the southernmost parts of the Cotton Belt, but most cotton started being harvested by the beginning of September and continued into the new year, depending in part on when the cotton was planted (which itself could be delayed by excessive rain or cold in the spring).[11] If cotton bolls freeze before they open to reveal the fiber within, the bolls turn black, do not open, and shrivel up. Too little rain in the summer was bad, but too much rain in the fall was worse. The same part of the country that produced most of the cotton was also the most susceptible to hurricanes and other tropical storms, which tended to arrive in the early autumn just before harvest. Floods at any time of year could wash away the growing crop, and what cotton was spared would be damaged and dirty, diminishing its value substantially. Somehow the successful futures trader had to be ready for all of this, or at least be able to figure out just how much of an effect an early freeze in southwest Georgia or flooding in August on the Red River in Louisiana might have on how much cotton came to market that season. Even with good weather, insects could strike throughout the growing season, turning lush fields nearly barren almost overnight.

For the farmer actually raising the cotton, spot price mattered most—he sold a physical commodity. After futures trading began in the 1880s, however, spot prices paid to farmers depended on future prices. Bear traders could easily predict a large crop and push down future prices, and that would depress the spot price. After all, if a cotton buyer for a mill sees in September that the spot price is 12¢ but the price of future delivery—a May contract, for example—is only 9¢, why would he buy any more cotton at 12¢ than he absolutely needed at the moment? He could buy contracts for May delivery for a lower price and save the cost of storing the cotton until May—what the trade called "carrying charges." This was the practice of most US and European manufacturers. English mills, on the other hand, which produced short runs of goods to meet specific orders, often bought the raw materials they needed in the spot market, but used futures to hedge the price they paid against the value of contracts made for their finished goods.[12] To keep the price of raw materials low, bear traders would predict a large crop early in the season. This would force down the price of future deliveries, which then drove down spot prices, allowing buyers to acquire low-priced spot cotton from its producers.

The farmer taking his crop to market in the fall had many incentives to sell quickly, especially in a bear market, with prices headed lower. If further crop predictions came in with a larger number they were likely to drive futures prices down further, dropping spot prices down again, and further diminishing the return he would get for his wagon full of cotton. If the cotton farmer had deep pockets, he could hold the cotton until later in the season and see if the price went back up eventually. He could—but in reality most cotton farmers produced on credit and therefore lived with debt, and what they owed increased each month. The sharecropping and tenant farming structures that emerged in cotton production after the Civil War always relied on credit relations. Cotton farmers therefore needed to sell sooner rather than later to avoid losing money to usurious interest rates at the crossroads store (and likewise with the crossroads merchant, who owed his wholesalers). Most debts came due at the end of the calendar year. For this reason farmers had to operate on an annual agricultural cycle, and since the Civil War bear brokers had learned how to use the timing of that calendar—and self-interested information—to push prices down, impoverishing farmers while enriching themselves.[13]

More often than not, by the time most of the cotton was **ginned** and sold by January, the jolly predictions of record-breaking crops from early in the season gave way to more sober numbers.[14] Suddenly, with a smaller crop to be marketed, the price of those future contracts for the latter months of the season shot up. That buyer confident of buying cotton at 9¢ on the spot market in May worried that the limited supply would push the spot price up quite high by that time and was now willing to pay more for the security of a future contract for that May cotton, whether for actual delivery or as a hedge. As the date of delivery approached and the spot price began to rise to meet the future price, the bears who had bought cotton or contracts at 9¢ in September could sell it for a few cents more, often making huge sums of money in the process. This motivated bear operators to predict large crops every year, buy cotton cheap, wait for the real (smaller) size of the crop to become clear, then sell at rising prices. This was the standard operating procedure of the bears.

Who to Believe?

For a long time, the crop reports that made prices came from commercial sources—brokers with interests in the market, rather than disinterested institutions such as the federal government or Henry Hester in New Orleans. Farmers selling their cotton had to rely on those buying it for the most important information that would affect the price. While European consumers, especially in Britain, dominated the cotton textile trade, brokers from Liverpool had long dominated the business of crop reporting, gaining credibility over decades. The most prominent of these was Thomas Ellison. An influential observer and statistician of the cotton trade since the late 1850s, Ellison began publishing monthly reports on cotton production in 1864, and by the 1880s he was the world's leading authority on cotton.[15] Another British broker with a strong following in the United States became well known for "making 'car window' estimates, his programme being to make a flying trip through the cotton belt, observing the appearance of the fields as he goes along." Despite what might seem a haphazard approach, he "acquired some notoriety as a successful guesser."[16]

With so many crop estimates coming in from people with an obvious bias, better information from disinterested sources could only help southern cotton producers. The federal government stepped in to fill the gap. At first, government crop reporting originated in the Department of Agriculture. Ever since the USDA was formed in 1862, gathering and disseminating crop statistics had been part of its job. Over the years, the Department's Bureau of Statistics had developed a network of correspondents from across the cotton belt who regularly sent information to Washington giving estimates of the amount of cotton planted and the current condition of the crop. These correspondents included planters reporting on their own plantations, gin operators, county correspondents covering all or part of a county, and salaried state-level statisticians. The various sources of information came in to Washington and were tabulated and compared to the data from the last census. The statistician, using a methodology known only to himself, gave each bit of information the weight he thought it was due to create an overall estimate of the crop.[17] It was, as one southern senator noted in 1902, "pure guesswork from start to finish."[18]

In October 1899 the Department of Agriculture hired two full-time field agents to investigate cotton production directly, which enabled the quick assessment of the effects of sudden events such as the 1900 Galveston hurricane. In 1900 the USDA compiled a comprehensive list of cotton ginners to add to its rolls of correspondents.[19] By this time the Department's Bureau of Statistics produced reports on acreage and condition in May, analyzed crop conditions from June through September, and began to estimate the season's yield in November. Its state-by-state report on the season's total yield appeared in early December.[20] Still, even with this profusion of reports, extensive network of reporters, and reasonably sound track record, the public did not fully trust the Department of Agriculture estimates. Since they simply compared acreage and yields to those of the year before, a figure that started out quite soundly, based on census data, could get distorted, as slight errors each year compounded. The census came about too infrequently for the Department of Agriculture to correct its figures as regularly as it would like, leaving its crop reports open to criticism.[21]

The USDA's primary obligation was toward the farmers themselves. The statisticians in the crop reporting service hoped that if farmers had accurate and unbiased information on crop size, especially through the crucial fall harvest season, they would be empowered to insist on fairer prices and not be fleeced by cotton buyers using bogus numbers. The last thing officials wanted was to provide information that brokers could use to manipulate the market, so the Department tried to insure that its crop reports were available to everyone on an equal basis. When the Department's monthly crop report came out, it was released to everyone at exactly the same time via telegraph.[22] This insured that no broker could get the crop reports early and use inside information to make trades with others who did not have access to the information yet. Postcards with the latest crop report were in the mail to about 2,750 post offices across the cotton states within four hours after the report was released by telegraph.[23] Most issues of the Department of Agriculture's monthly newsletter about crop reporting reminded readers that "postmasters are requested to display conspicuously in their offices the crop report cards sent to them each month for the information of the public," and asked readers to report postmasters who did not do so to the Department of Agriculture.[24] This was crucial, since most post offices in the rural South were located in country stores, the same stores where a substantial portion of the cotton crop first passed out of the hands of the farmers who grew it.[25]

The Crisis in Crop Reporting

However, the Department of Agriculture's efforts to spread good acreage and condition information proved relatively weak, as the 1899–1900 season would show. Henry M. Neill, a prominent broker with offices in Liverpool and London as well as New Orleans, used his reputation and his knowledge of the cotton trade to push the price around mercilessly. Although, unlike Henry Hester, Neill traded in the market and thus could benefit if people believed his predictions, his claims were well-regarded, and the government reports could not compete.[26] The "carefully collected information published by the Department during this period [did not have] the influence on prices that it should have had," lamented a USDA statistician.[27] The 1898–1899 crop had set records at 11.4 million bales.[28] The following year's crop opened very low on September 1, 1899, at 5.94 in New Orleans for middling upland.[29] But the September 1899 crop report from the Department of Agriculture was grim, predicting between 9 million and 9.5 million bales, and giving the crop's condition the second lowest rating in twenty-five years.[30] Two days later, however, Neill issued a circular affirming the prediction he had made in mid-August that the cotton crop would be 12 million bales.[31] If he were short of the market, such a large prediction would work to his advantage. If he represented anyone with an interest in low prices, the prediction would benefit those bears.

Neill played this game for the next four months. The Department of Agriculture kept foretelling gloom and doom, eventually trimming the prediction back as far as 8.9 million bales. Each time Neill, "as if to break the force of such announcement," insisted on a crop of at least 11 million bales.[32] Despite the government reports, prices in southern markets rose only slowly during the selling season, hitting an average of 7.50 in New Orleans in January.[33] By that time, with farmers' cotton nearly all sold, Neill's ridiculous claim of 11 or 12 million bales rapidly became unsustainable. The short crop—ultimately reckoned by Hester (secretary of the New Orleans Cotton Exchange) at just under 9.5 million bales—and surging textile manufacturing in the South pushed the price to 10.25 in July 1900.[34] Southern farmers who sold in October lost out on $17.10 (the price of a hundred pounds of Gold Star roasted coffee or three pairs of patent leather shoes) for each bale they had produced.[35] Manipulating prices had profound and practical effects on cotton farmers across the South.

Sometimes traders were able to use the regularity of government reports to manipulate the price of the staple. Rumors about what an imminent announcement would report could be circulated to create a "temporary price disturbance" that the broker could use to his advantage. For example, the Agriculture Secretary, James Wilson, thought this had happened in October 1901, when the New York Cotton Exchange buzzed with the idea that the upcoming report would indicate a crop in good condition. However the report, when it officially appeared, showed a condition six points below the imagined number. This caused a sudden drop in the price of cotton by five dollars a bale, delivering profits to brokers who had sold short. At other times cotton dealers claimed that the reports were inaccurate, or that corruption in the USDA had allowed the figures out early, so the information they contained already influenced the price in the market. Constant criticisms like these devalued the impact of the crop reports the government collected and distributed.[36]

Maybe more information would help—or so some political advocates of the cotton farmers argued. The federal government could overcome problems like these by fighting self-interested information with more reports from more sources. The census seemed like an obvious place to turn. As the nation had grown over the nineteenth century, it began to seem increasingly useful to establish a permanent Census Bureau, rather than recreating and then dismantling the complex bureaucracy of information-gathering and record-keeping every ten years. Many observers also realized that a permanent Census Bureau could perform many important statistical functions in the periods between the constitutionally mandated decennial census,[37] including crop reporting. If the census office existed on a permanent basis, the statistical expertise of its staff and the nation's records could be employed more often and more regularly to aid its citizens.

In the Census Office's annual report of November 1901, the chief of the manufacturing division suggested that Congress should authorize the Office to make an annual report on the cotton crop based not on information from farmers, but on a canvass of cotton ginneries. This would solve the problem of the compounding errors in the USDA's figures by providing a definitive, annual statement of cotton production.[38] The suggestion came just as Congress was beginning to consider a bill to establish a permanent Census

Bureau. Part of the debate in the Senate about the permanent Census Bureau turned on its role in providing up-to-date information on the growing cotton crop, which the Census Bureau's machinery of enumerators would be well placed to do. James Wilson, the USDA Secretary, opposed the plan because reports from the cotton gins would appear too late to affect the price already paid to farmers. One Senator questioned its utility, exasperated that cotton farmers were swayed by commercial information when Department of Agriculture crop reports were readily available.[39] A Mississippi senator set him straight on the value of Census Bureau data, arguing,

> If they have two sources of information—one the Agricultural Department and the other the estimate made by certain companies—they must judge from those two; but if you have the Agricultural Department and then a report from the Census Office, under the authority of law requiring them to investigate this matter, the planter, who is the seller, and the purchaser will have a better opportunity to judge of the amount of the cotton that has been produced during the year and a better opportunity to judge whether cotton will go up in price or whether it will fall.[40]

After considerable wrangling, a law creating a permanent Census Bureau and requiring that the Bureau collect statistics on cotton production from ginners was enacted on March 6, 1902. The Census would publish weekly bulletins from September through January of each year.[41] At last, the weight of federal government machinery was in a position to overwhelm the flood of information provided by cotton brokers who predicted crop sizes that would help only themselves.

This moment marked a high point in one approach to regulating the cotton futures market—an approach that relied on "sunshine," or transparency and good information, to tie prices more tightly to market conditions of supply and demand.[42] The federal government now had two increasingly sophisticated bureaucracies that were collecting and aggressively disseminating the best possible information about the cotton crop. No longer would brokers on the exchanges and farmers at the local cotton gin have to rely on self-interested informants like Henry M. Neill or the fellow who made car-window estimates. The problem of information asymmetry, the government hoped, had been solved. Everyone buying and selling cotton would have equal access to information and could

take positions based on their own analysis of how that crop information would affect prices. What federal officials had not quite
counted on, however, was that in creating such valuable information they had created something worth stealing. Good information alone could not fix a bad market if the rules of the market,
set by its participants, facilitated skullduggery—as would shake
the cotton world in 1905 and 1906. For the moment, however, the
regulators' belief that good information could regulate the market would have its day.

However, information on its own remained inert. While good
information was necessary to make markets and prices reflect
actual conditions of supply and demand, it was not really enough.
Old ways of operating, especially the fixed arrangements of the
agricultural calendar and the scope it provided for bears to manipulate prices, persisted into the new century. Men had to make use
of the available information if they wanted to move prices and
shock the trade and the government into new ways of doing business. William P. Brown, Frank B. Hayne, and other New Orleans
cotton men who wanted to make money in the market almost
immediately found opportunities to take advantage of the new
sources of information. With new and better information about
the crop as it came to market they would boost the price of cotton,
corner the market, and briefly own all the cotton in the world, to
destroy the long-standing power of the Liverpool and New York
bear brokers who kept prices low.

CHAPTER 3

Building a Bear Trap

E VEN WITH MULTIPLE GOVERNMENT BUREAUS supplying better information, bear brokers in New York were still able to use bad information to distort the market, insuring that supply and demand themselves did not quite function to set price. Economic change is usually gradual. What was needed was a coup that would take the power to set prices out of the hands of the New York bears. Men in New Orleans, bulls who wanted to make fortunes by raising the price of cotton to reflect actual conditions of supply and demand, knew that they needed to corner the market to squeeze the bears who made money by keeping prices low. They needed to break pessimistic assumptions that cotton prices would always stay low and that the bears could not be challenged. But cornering the market took an array of resources and skills, as well as nerve and knowledge. The skills had to be developed and practiced, and the resources needed to be marshaled. The bull pool's assets included not just money but also buildings and institutions, a Mardi Gras krewe and an old local bank, their wives, and their friends and connections. The bulls gathered these actors together behind their purpose. They knew the mistakes they had to avoid because before the corner of 1903 turned the cotton world inside out, others had attempted the feat.

Peter Labouisse and the 1895 Fiasco

Peter Labouisse's failure taught the bulls what not to do. In 1874, Peter Labouisse (1846–1902) had married Marie Pauline Rathbone, whose father was a banker and financier and whose sister had also married a well-known member of the Cotton Exchange.[1] The family was an old one in New Orleans and played a significant role in the cotton brokerage community of the city after the Civil War. With the rise of futures trading in the last decades of the nineteenth century, New Orleans cotton men had begun to recognize that the price was too low. They could see that New York brokers had become bears who usually made their money on the short side of the market and who developed trading methods that depressed the price of the staple. The changing New York market provided opportunities for bulls, who sought higher prices, to make money on the other side of the market.

Cornering the market might make an individual a fortune, but it was also a mechanism for affecting the price—one that played off the efforts of bears to keep prices low even when supply was small and demand was large. The trick for a bull was to buy contracts that promised future delivery, until more was bought than would physically exist. Bears would sell those futures contracts at low prices in order to depress spot prices. Then, when time came for delivery, those who had promised to sell without having the cotton in hand—a **short position**—would need to buy in order to deliver. They would pay anything to acquire the cotton they had long ago promised for future delivery (or to settle their contracts), and thus the spot price would rise. To run a corner, buyers must actually pay for the cotton that is delivered on contracts—until everyone has to buy it back from them. Of course, it was possible to buy those contracts on credit, or a small **margin**—a deposit in promise of future payments. No matter the size of the margin, however, to corner a market requires considerable funds, and Labouisse did not have enough. He tried to pyramid his profits into further purchases, but this scheme would instead speed his downfall.

Labouisse also mistimed his efforts. A small crop and circumstances—a late storm and lots of worms, and the perennial and probably deliberate miscalculations of bear operators—coaxed Labouisse to attempt a corner in October 1895. The 1894–1895 crop had been huge. Although consumption was rising, with a crop of 9.9 million bales the price of cotton slumped to five cents a pound early in 1895—below the seven cents it cost to produce it. Farmers convened in New Orleans, Jackson, and Atlanta to discuss their plight and agreed to reduce their acreage—according to state officials, perhaps 20% fewer acres of cotton were planted in 1895 than the year before. Then, just as the plant was nearing harvest, it began to rain. The crop was already running late around Rome, Georgia when heavy rains in late August and early September slowed the fruiting of the plants, which were full of sap. Weeds began to fill the fields. At the same time, there were so many worms in the Yazoo and Mississippi deltas and up the Red River that in New Orleans, suppliers of worm poison could not keep up with the orders. By the end of September, predictions for the new crop lay between just 7.5 and 8 million bales. Prices rose from 6.50 cents in August to above 8 cents, and contracts for future deliveries likewise promised high and steady prices into January.[2]

On Thursday, October 10, however, the USDA predicted a crop condition that was 5% better than expected, and prices dropped more than a dollar a bale, though large orders from New Orleans managed to rally the market from the break occasioned by the government report. Yet as usual, contradictory information kept coming: Texas had only half the usual crop, Georgia had less than expected, and the quality of the whole received poor ratings. These reports inched the price back up, as did the purchases made in New Orleans. By October 14 New York newspapers had begun to see, in those orders from New Orleans, Peter Labouisse's scheme to corner the market.[3] Prices jumped a dollar a bale, the highest price in years. The leap "induced heavy general **profit-taking** sales, but the demand was far in excess of the supply, and prices steadily advanced up to noon." Spot cotton in the interior towns near New Orleans sold for high prices as short sellers bought bales to meet their engagements.[4] Before too long spot cotton stood higher around New Orleans than in the city itself, while the market price in New Orleans rose above that of Liverpool (once the cost of getting it overseas had been subtracted). Observers found this condition "anomalous" and unnatural—a sign of speculation, not market forces.[5]

Rising prices in small towns had international effects. The New York *Evening Post* editorialized that "speculation" had raised the price of cotton "to a point which prevents its exportation," ending gold imports and threatening the economy.[6] Large portions of the country's cotton crop found markets overseas, in the textile mills of Lancashire, for example. With a world and a nation on the **gold standard**, exports of the staple would bring gold back as payment, increasing a nation's money supply. The new high price, however, "made exporters timid." If they bought while the price was high and then the corner collapsed, they would own contracts worth less than they had paid.[7] If foreign importers shrank from paying a higher price, then their gold would not enter the country's coffers, and would not increase the cash of the United States.[8] Farmers had for years been protesting the limits in the money supply, organizing into the People's Party, listening to leaders describe the Cross of Gold on which they felt crucified. The Populists understood that the gold standard kept prices low, since the limits it placed on the quantity of currency in circulation had a deflationary effect on prices. Now, even as their product was bringing higher prices, the gold standard was still working against them, inspiring buyers to wait and thus restricting the money available for circulation.

Then, in the third week of October, the anticipated collapse of Labouisse's corner happened. Sharp breaks on successive days lowered the cost of January contracts from 9.44 to 9.00 on Friday, 8.51 at the close of Saturday, down to 8.07 on Monday, October 21. The volume of trade was higher than it had ever been. Curb trading, outlawed by the exchanges, was being investigated, as brokers desperately tried to adjust their positions to the changing conditions, even after the closing bell had sounded.[9] As the price swooned, the pyramid financing of the bulls magnified their losses. Labouisse and the bulls had tried to use rising prices to increase their winnings. As the prices rose, the contracts the bulls held would be worth more than when they were made. This was not actual money in hand, of course, but the prospect of more money when the contracts matured. The bulls used these paper profits to get credit to use as margins for still more purchases. "The majority multiplied their original holdings several times by this means," a very risky move.[10]

As the prices fell, Labouisse faced layers of problems. The new contracts would be worth less than he had thought, so he lost money there. Worse than that, the falling prices meant that the projected profits from the earlier contracts also evaporated, but Labouisse had already borrowed against these paper profits. The profits disappeared; the debts did not, as "losses came much faster than gains." As one observer wryly noted, "Speculators who had their margins multiplied by twenty on their brokers' books learned something of division yesterday."[11] Efforts to boost the price by buying collapsed as the "New Orleans bull clique" **liquidated** its holdings. The New Orleans firm of Emmett and Buech was reported to have failed, and several other large houses seemed on the brink. The downfall took only a few days. By October 23, the cotton market had gone still. Trading was very quiet. It was over.[12]

Despite Labouisse's failure, his attempted corner provided valuable lessons. Efforts to raise the price of cotton might promise profits to farmers, but the voices of world finance would protest, arguing that higher prices would destroy the economy.[13] Moreover, the rise and fall of prices demonstrated that the price of cotton reflected manipulation of information, rather than simple supply and demand. Then again, using profits from rising prices to finance future purchases had damaged the chances of the bull pool. So did its timing: demanding delivery or settlement of low-priced contracts worked poorly in the fall, as supplies increased and the harvest began to reach the market, even when the crop was small and poor in quality. A New York broker, interviewed in the aftermath, knew it: "It is one thing to undertake to corner cotton in October, when the volume of receipts is enormous, and another to take up a bull campaign in the spring of the year, when the crop has been taken up and is out of the way, stocks then being very small."[14] Farmers usually sold their crops starting at harvest and ending by January in order to pay their debts to landlords and merchants. Bears had used this calendar for years, predicting large crops to keep the price low as farmers sold out. Now the calendar could be turned to advantage by the bulls, as crops sold in January made their way to market by the spring, creating a shortage in summer time before the new crop came in. Eventually, this summer shortage would prove useful to bulls.

1900 Corner in New Orleans Spots

The lessons of Labouisse's fiasco were not lost on William P. Brown. By the dawn of the new century, he knew exactly how the cotton market worked. His business associates in New Orleans appreciated Brown's keen grasp of the intricacies of the market and his gambler's instinct for when to take a risk and when to withdraw. The next few episodes in his career raised the blinds on his bets, demonstrating even bigger aspirations—to reshape the entire cotton market. Before he could corner the world's cotton and permanently boost its price to match his view of market conditions, he needed a few more things. Most of all he needed a stake, a pot of money he could leverage into the financial support needed to buy all the cotton in the world. While so far the trade had earned him (according to local papers) "a cool $600,000," a minor triumph in September 1900 provided him with the money to begin.[15]

Cornering **spots** in this period was relatively straightforward: more of a squeeze applied as supplies ran short at the moment contracts for delivery came due. During the season of 1899–1900 Henry M. Neill and his bogus crop estimates yanked future prices up and down.[16] What Brown realized, though, was that this volatility of price created an opportunity. Both Brown and Hayne made some money that summer as prices fluctuated, manipulated by faulty information and actual supplies. When Henry Hester released his official report on the 1899–1900 season at the beginning of September 1900, it showed that the crop had been 1.8 million bales smaller than the year before, while consumption of cotton by southern mills had increased by nearly 200,000 bales in the same period. The **visible supply** of American cotton at the beginning of September 1900 was less than half of what it had been a year before, and the quantity of new cotton coming to market in August 1900 was also well under the average. These dour figures pushed the price of cotton up during the week after Hester's report came out. Rumors of a corner on September and October contracts in Liverpool contributed as well to the rising price.[17]

Then, on Saturday, September 8, 1900, one of the most devastating hurricanes in American history struck Galveston, killing thousands and wrecking the city.[18] For a few days, it was unclear what the effect had been on the Texas cotton crop. When the New Orleans Cotton Exchange opened on Monday, Brown saw his chance and coolly took it. Buying up all the available cotton in the New Orleans spot market—3,300 bales—Brown successfully cornered the New Orleans market briefly, raking in over a million dollars when he sold.[19] Brown had his stake and was ready to move into a much larger game. The key would be to use his money and connections to create a network of even more powerful elements, a collection of people and information, banks and money, institutions and buildings, expanding with every success—a network that would eventually include farmers eager for higher prices, southern spinners willing to pay the new rates for their raw materials in exchange for less volatile prices, and correspondents in the country who would send him regular reports on the crop and the weather and the market in their neighborhood. He started in New Orleans, where he found more cotton men to array on his side.

Betting on Information

Brown and his fellow New Orleanians had begun to realize that they had better information about crop size than others did. Brokers who began their careers in the country, as did Brown and Hayne, probably gleaned more information from government reports and the newspaper coverage of disasters than city dealers who may never have met a cotton farmer. When a flood came, Brown and Hayne knew to consider how much cotton along a particular river grew in the batture between the river and the levee, or whether the crop stood beyond the reach of high water. Was an outbreak of worms in Tallapoosa County, Alabama, more significant than one in Tuscaloosa County, Alabama? New Yorkers were unlikely to possess this level of detail regarding growing conditions. Neither were men whose networks in the trade stemmed from the manufacturing side of the business. Knowing crop size was a vital part of being a successful cotton broker, but the granular information that Brown made part of his network could be acquired only on the ground. Henry Hester, secretary of the NOCE, maintained an extensive network of telegraphic correspondents across the cotton belt and thus provided superior information to the city's brokers, the members of the exchange. Nonetheless, the brokers often disagreed as they discussed the crop in the ground and as it made its way through the country stores and cotton gins. As these men shared news with one another about the crop's size, they also began to make their own predictions.

By 1901, New Orleans cotton brokers were betting amongst themselves on what they called "crop guesses." They would bet on the size of the whole crop for 1901–1902, as realized on a particular date. Brown gave respected NOCE member George A. Hero, for example, a hundred dollars for the right to call a bet of a thousand dollars on the size of the crop up to March 1, 1902.[20] These men were playing more than trading—challenging one another to put money behind their claims about the crop. Some bets were as small as ten dollars, while one contended for sixty dollars worth of suit cloth. Some of the bettors made state-by-state assessments—Brown apparently used state-level figures for the crops produced between 1898 and 1900 as part of his calculations. They also looked ahead to how weather later in the season would affect the crop: one bet included the clause "if no killing frost before Oct. 25 add 30000 bales if none before Nov. 4th add 50000." Initial wagers were usually deposited with Julius Weiss & Co., who paid 3% interest on the deposit, payable to the bet's winner. Always, these local brokers agreed about who represented the final authority: "Hester's figures to decide."[21]

These crop guesses indicate the readiness of New Orleans cotton men to stand behind their views of the market. Their confidence in their opinions added to the advantages that, by the beginning of the twentieth century, the city had accumulated—advantages that Brown was ready to build into a foundation to support his ambitions. The institution within which they operated provided one set of advantages: the New Orleans Cotton Exchange was a very active trading floor, with a respected set of rules and practices for the trade in futures contracts, and it was part of the network Brown and Hayne were creating. The Exchange was a mediator that linked actors, a point of attachment in the social realm, a path through which the circulating fluid that is society flowed. The Exchange translated and modified the deeds of its members, while at the same time those deeds modified it and distorted it into new forms. Even as its rules and location shaped the activities of its members, their actions shaped and strengthened the institution.[22]

For example, members of the Exchange traded within a set of bylaws defined by the membership and, as one of only two cotton markets in the United States with rules facilitating futures trading, these regulations aided the business of the Exchange's members. The Exchange also collected market information and supplied it to its members—another benefit provided by the institution. Its superior information came from its telegraphic correspondence, which tied it to those producers and

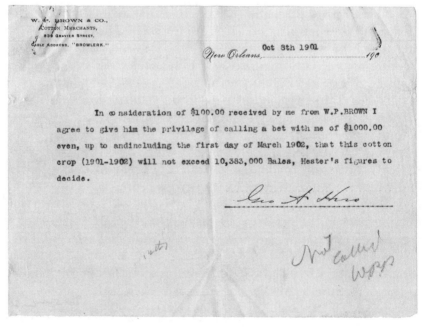

Figure 3.1 By the early twentieth century cotton brokers in New Orleans had the best information about the market, and they used this information in informal bets with one another like the one recorded here between William P. Brown and George Hero. From William Perry Brown papers and Braughn Family papers. Courtesy of The Historic New Orleans Collection, Gift of Yvonne Brown Collier.

middlemen across the South who sent data to Hester. Along with just facts, these producers often sent their actual cotton. Because Exchange members actually received cotton, the Exchange itself could provide better information about the quality and quantity of cotton on the market. New York had ceased to be a significant spot market for cotton; huge deals were done, but not many actual bales of cotton came near the Hudson River. New Orleans, on the other hand, remained a spot market and a site for delivery on contracts—bales arrived regularly on the banks of the Mississippi.[23] Because the NOCE maintained a spot market alongside its growing futures business, its dealings in futures were influenced by what was happening in spot trading, rather than mere speculation. This improved its information. Thus the Exchange supported the business of its members, whose deals returned information about the cotton supply to the institution.

Nonetheless, these structural advantages growing from the interactions between the New Orleans Cotton Exchange and the transactions of its brokers were not enough to overcome the inertia that kept New York in charge or to break the bears' power to lower cotton prices. Since the end of the Civil War the "monied metropolis" had dominated the trade, the result of its control of finance, transatlantic shipping, and communication. New Orleans brokers

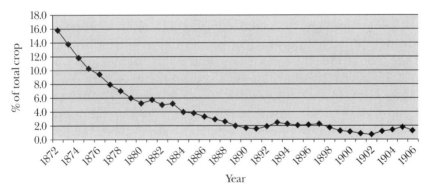

Figure 3.2 Spot Cotton Sales in New York City (as a percentage of the total crop)

As the quantity of spot cotton actually sold in New York declined in the late nineteenth century, traders found it ever more difficult to know exactly what buyers and sellers would pay for the various grades of cotton. This ambiguity made it easier for members of the New York Cotton Exchange to manipulate values and unlink prices from conditions of supply and demand. Figures for the total crop and **spot sales** in New York come from United States, Bureau of Corporations, *Report of the Commissioner of Corporations on Cotton Exchanges, Part 1* (Washington, D.C.: GPO, 1908), 248–249. The equivalent figures for New Orleans can be found in the "Annual Review of the Commerce of New Orleans" published in the New Orleans *Daily Picayune* on September 1 every year.

needed something more than confidence, something more than their Exchange, its information and its physical trades, more than steady improvements to their position in the marketplace, more than railroads and links to shipping, to change the price of cotton and the way that price was made. They needed a coup. To cut off the head of the trade, the New York bears, they needed to unite behind their common purpose, and they needed both finance and infrastructure to do so. The bets among the city's cotton brokers illustrate an emerging network. For Brown and Hayne, the next step was finding the funds to buy cotton and building the structure to link money and men behind their goals.[24]

Banks and Buildings

The two men occupied different positions in the hierarchy of New Orleans cotton brokers. Frank Hayne stood right in the center. He had served on the Board of Directors of the New Orleans Cotton Exchange early in the 1890s and again in 1901 to 1903. Brown's position was more marginal, physically and organizationally. Although he was a member of the exchange, he served on none of its committees.[25] His offices with Daniel Grant had been in the 900 block of Gravier Street—several blocks from the Exchange at the corner of Gravier and Carondelet. His bets with other brokers, the crop guesses with which the men occupied themselves, were transactions outside the Exchange—wagers, games unrecognized in the ring of trade, not serious business. At the end of his partnership with Grant in 1897, however, Brown moved closer to the action, into a building at 839 Gravier, only a few doors down from the Exchange.[26] With the fortune won in the aftermath of the 1900 Galveston hurricane, he bought a property directly across the street from the Exchange, the Equitable Building at 806 Gravier.[27] Rumors flew that he would construct a ten-story skyscraper there, a structure to hold his new enterprises that would tower over the Exchange itself. Among his new ventures, in 1901 he began to incorporate the city's banks into his network.[28]

Brown's physical moves bringing him closer into the orbit of the Cotton Exchange mirrored his role in the financial community. Real money would be necessary to corner the cotton market. Using paper profits to buy more cotton could hardly weather a storm of dropping prices. Brown and Hayne therefore took another step toward cornering the world market in cotton by adding local banks to their array of resources. These institutions would provide the capital they could leverage into the sums necessary to buy all the cotton in the world. Because the city's banks had shareholders and directors, gathering the city's banks brought more actors into the network, thus meaning more allies to support the campaign for higher cotton prices. Befitting an important cotton market, New Orleans also had a significant banking community.

During the city's rise as an entrepôt in the 1830s, its financial sector had contributed capital and credit to the economic development of the southwest. The city's banks had suffered several reverses thereafter, including supporting the Confederacy, which contributed to the capital shortage that afflicted the entire postbellum South.[29] The New Orleans Clearing-House, organized in 1872, had helped the banks work together, "checking distrust in times of panic."[30] In late summer 1896 four of the national banks in New Orleans failed, largely because of the exposure of $600,000 worth of embezzlement at the Union National Bank. That bank was reorganized in 1901, bringing New Yorkers such as John Jacob Astor and Stuyvesant Fish in as directors alongside New Orleans stockholders and directors, including William P. Brown. With correspondent firms in New York, Chicago, London, Paris, and Berlin, the Union National Bank represented a small link in a powerful network of worldwide finance.[31] The limited capital of the Union National Bank, $600,000 in capital in 1901 and another $100,000 surplus, was nowhere near enough to corner the market. Brown and Hayne, therefore, put together a "small coterie of local business men," who together raised rapidly a million dollars in assets for a new company called the Southern Trust and Banking Company, which then bought the Union National and, by May 1902, the Hibernia National Bank, which had a capital and surplus of $800,000.[32]

Because the Hibernia was a well-regarded institution with a long history in the city, the new consolidated firm kept its name while changing the business to the Hibernia Bank and Trust. As a trust company, the institution had no need to maintain cash reserves against its deposits the way a national bank did.[33] Such trusts could keep as much cash in reserves "as their own sweet wills suggest," and depositors had less access to their money—giving the trust more freedom to spend or invest its resources and those of its customers.[34] By September 1902, the Hibernia had nearly quadrupled its capital and surplus to $3 million. During 1902 the banks of the city had increased their capital, surplus, and deposits by 25 percent. The whole conglomeration commanded more than ten million dollars—enough money to buy 200,000 bales of cotton at ten cents a pound.[35] Just as importantly, Brown and his partners had reached their position quietly and rapidly, while Wall

Street lay sleeping. They considered hiring a manager from New York, but—perhaps to keep their activities hidden from New York—they found a Chicago financier to serve as president.[36]

When Brown's new skyscraper was complete it was the largest building in New Orleans in terms of floor space, and the Hibernia Bank and Trust took up residence in his structure.[37] With this bank, and the men who contributed to its formation, Brown corralled at least some members of an historically fractious business community into a network that provided "a working capital for this city."[38] This New Orleans elite meant to operate on a national—even international—stage, though they cut their teeth on local ventures. Several of them found

Figure 3.3 William P. Brown consolidated banking resources in New Orleans in 1902 to provide capital for his attempt to corner the cotton market. As a symbol of this new power, he built a skyscraper for the Hibernia Bank and Trust Company in 1903. From *New Orleans Daily Picayune*, Sept. 1, 1903. Courtesy of Texas Tech University Library.

themselves on the same side of some contentious local issues—in favor, for example, of concessions in October 1901 that would have let the Illinois Central Railroad build a big grain elevator above the Stuyvesant docks, an action opposed by the Levee Board. One of the board members of the Southern Trust who supported the improvement was Abraham Brittin, one-time president of the City Council and regular officer in the New Orleans Cotton Exchange. Several officers of the railroad were named as directors of the Union National Bank—both the president of the railroad, Stuyvesant Fish, and its financial officer E. H. Harriman—thereby tying into Brown's network the city's most important transportation link with the rest of the nation.[39]

Contributors to the banks that composed the Hibernia Bank and Trust included not only William P. Brown, who brought $190,000 to the deal (making him the largest stockholder in the venture), but also Frank Hayne and his business partner, Hugh de Lacy Vincent, who contributed $60,000 apiece to the new banks. Brown was publicly lauded as "the father of the project." He had known such "home money" would be needed; banks united behind his purposes, he said, had been "a pet project of mine for a considerable time." He had spent a year and a half setting up the deal and discussing it with men of capital who could be roped into his goals. As he explained, "when we were ready to organize, the business meeting did not take more than thirty minutes to create a million dollar company."[40] He had the city on his side. With sufficient financing and superior information, with the institutions of the Exchange and the Hibernia Bank and Trust, with real estate at the center of the cotton trade, the network stood ready. Brown needed only to wait for the right circumstances to create a corner.

Setting the Bear Trap

Conditions became favorable for a corner because, as Brown seemed to know better than many others, demand had been rising while supply had begun to struggle to keep up. The 1902 crop had been large—at 10.6 million bales, nearly 10% more than the year before—but still considerably smaller than consumption, straining the visible supply. While some buyers had hoarded the fiber, creating a reserve of "invisible cotton" that high prices could coax to market, Brown calculated that demand was beginning to regularly outstrip supply, especially in years when circumstances damaged the crop and reduced its quality or slowed its passage to market. He predicted that 10.75 million bales would be produced in the 1902–1903 sales year, but figured consumption in 1903 would reach 11.25 million bales.[41] He had about thirty brokers on his side, ready to support his campaign by purchasing cotton as the prices rose. He kept accounts of the purchases he made on their behalf, buying contracts for future delivery—sometimes selling as the price rose, but mostly to apply those profits to purchases of future months' contracts.[42]

Brown was not alone in his calculations. The government bureaucracies that collected disinterested information also distributed that information publicly. More than one man realized that with demand outpacing supply, bears could not force low prices forever. As a result, the 1903 season witnessed three separate bull campaigns that eventually culminated in the complete corner. It began in the fall. In late 1902, Theodore H. Price began buying contracts for January delivery, when the cost of those contracts dipped sometimes below eight cents a pound.[43] After all, in November 1902, the usual bear strategy meant that "the greater part of the cotton trade reached the conclusion that the crop would be a large one" with the predictable depressing effect on the price. Those who disagreed saw an opportunity.[44] With "the effective use of printer's ink and telegraph wires," Price was able to "disseminate ideas favorable to the market," raising the value of his holdings. When the price reached 8.5 cents in January, he got out.[45]

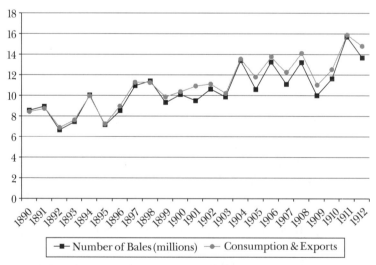

Figure 3.4 US Cotton Production vs. Consumption + Export

Domestic consumption plus cotton exported regularly exceeded production of the fiber. Under these conditions, the price should rise to reflect the scarcity. Bear traders, however, kept prices low with rumors of big crops until farmers had sold out their year's production. Source: Department of Commerce, Bureau of the Census. *Bulletin 125. Cotton Production, 1913*. Washington, D.C.: GPO, 1914, p. 29, Table 15.

As Theodore Price was selling out his positions, a second group of bulls was buying, persuaded that the price could go higher. The new bull campaign was led by Daniel J. Sully, who was born in Providence, Rhode Island, and married the daughter of a textile manufacturer. On a salary of $75 a week, Sully traveled south every October and February for his work.[46] According to newspaper reports, the "young cotton king" had developed a theory—that the best and earliest seed was regularly bought by cotton-seed oil producers, leaving only late-blooming, less vigorous strains for farmers to plant.[47] In addition, he claimed, a wet freeze he had observed in February 1899 had damaged the seed supply in ways that would affect the harvest in 1903.[48]

Some would later claim that "a clique of New England mill owners backed [Sully] in his first venture," indicating that every bull needed a network. With the support of other cotton men, and armed with his theory predicting the size of the crop, he bought a seat on the New York Cotton Exchange, started a firm called Daniel J. Sully & Co. with some partners, and began buying cotton. His tangled arrangements with other brokers included Zerega & Co., a Liverpool firm that bought on consignment and paid their bills through George H. McFadden, the most powerful spot cotton dealer in the country. Sully also had Harris, Gates & Company on his books, and F. W. Reynolds as well—a firm capitalized principally by himself, his father-in-law, and other employees and members of the Daniel J. Sully & Co. firm. He also had an operative in New Orleans, who would manage purchases there and report on doings on the Exchange.[49] His predictions proved correct. In May, the London *Daily Mail* reported that he cornered the market. When the price that month reached eleven cents, he sold out his positions, pocketing two million dollars in profits for himself and his backers and fellow bull brokers.[50]

As the cotton bulls made one fortune after another, a fictional futures trader entered the public discourse. Frank Norris's *The Pit* was appearing in the *Saturday Evening Post*, in serial form, between September 1902 and January 1903. When it was published in book form, it sold 95,000 copies in its first year. It told the story of a bold bull trader in the wheat futures markets of Chicago who got richer by the day until eventually he began to see the possibility of a complete corner. His efforts ruined his physical and mental health, as well as his marriage. He also failed to run a complete corner on wheat and as a result lost his fortune. Though the novelist sympathetically sketched his speculator, the futures trade in which he engaged seemed rackety and dangerous. A morality play for the public about the dangers of speculation, about misguided bulls and their attempts to corner commodities, *The Pit* was wildly popular. The cotton bulls were playing a role familiar to the American reading public, who disapproved of their activities. Yet this did not discourage the bulls from trading.[51]

While Sully was selling out his positions in May, Brown was still buying. He had been in the market as long as Price and Sully, but more quietly. With cash from the consolidated banks of New Orleans and his allies at the ready, by August 1902 Brown had begun to buy contracts for delivery of cotton in July 1903. These contracts came from the bears who offered future delivery at low prices, betting that the price would drop. By holding some of his contracts as the price rose in May, selling others to realize profits from the rising prices and then buying even more at the new higher prices, Brown began to give the impression of an overambitious bumpkin who would eventually realize he had left it too late to get out. Brown's very appearance—ruddy faced with dark red hair and moustache—contributed to the impression.[52] "The new bull leader is a big, strongly-built man," observed a New York newspaper, "with heavy shoulders, big arms, weather-beaten face and shrewd dark eyes" who "looked just a bit out of place among the metropolitan brokers."[53] Many thought Sully clever for unloading his holdings on Brown in mid-May. By then, everyone wanted to sell to Brown to get in on the action; his very appearance on the New York exchange could stimulate the price of future deliveries.[54] As tender day approached at the end of May, sellers started to see that Brown had no intention of cashing out.[55]

Those who sold just as Brown was buying pushed prices down. Throughout the month of May, the New York bears kept up a steady liquidation, delivering cotton and demanding payment, forcing spot prices lower and straining the resources of the New Orleans bulls. "It was no unusual thing to see spot cotton from South Carolina unloaded in New Orleans," delivered there in fulfillment of futures contracts, "and immediately reloaded and sent back to its original shipping point" for use in the Piedmont textile mills.[56] In the middle of the month, as Sully sold out, prices dropped between eight and nine **points** in the week ending May 15. Even the New Orleans market "had a waiting appearance" as prices floundered. Yet in New York the next Monday, Brown seemed serene. Prices spiked again on Wednesday, but the next day the bears drove July and September **options** down 26 points.[57]

Sully meanwhile was planning at the end of May to sail for Europe in early June.[58] Whether to calm the runaway market for "the best interests of the cotton industry of the country," as he claimed, or to prevent the price from rising after his successful bull campaign came to an end, Sully switched sides and took on the bear role.[59] He worked in the second half of May to prevent cotton prices from rising. He called Brown's margins "wherever they happened to be in the brokerage houses of his friends."[60] His allies agreed. George H. McFadden, the powerful spot cotton dealer from Philadelphia, and James Stillman, the president of National City Bank (the forerunner of Citigroup), worked to "bring the 'bull crowd' to a standstill and instruct the general calling out of margins through brokers."[61] To **call margins** this way meant that Sully and his friends were demanding that Brown deposit up to five dollars a bale for the purchases he had made on credit, on the margin. According to the rules of the New York exchange, contracts could be made between buyers and sellers without any deposit. Any party to the contract could, however, demand a good-faith payment on a contract made on the margin, as long as he matched that payment with his own deposit.[62] This would prevent his opposite number, his fellow transactor, from overextending himself and using credit to drive up the price artificially—as Labouisse had done.

Regardless of Sully's goals, calling Brown's margins tied up his money—the money he would need to pay for cotton as it was delivered, in order to effect the shortage that ran the corner. At least half a million dollars had to be deposited in the trust companies that the New York Cotton Exchange had designated for this purpose.[63] Brown kept his cool: "My brokers could put up any amount required of them." Calling margins, he contended, would strengthen the market by eliminating the "small traders, who always sell at the wrong time and thus sometimes depress prices when there is really no other cause for it. I am still a bull purely on considerations of supply and demand."[64] To demonstrate the depth of his pockets to the other bulls who might be thinking about selling out and taking their profits before it all fell apart, Brown "turned a trick" and shifted from buying nearby options to buying contracts for the next crop year, 1903–1904. That bluff signaled to everyone that the bull campaign was still going strong: "This flank movement caught the Northerners entirely by surprise, and pandemonium broke loose on the Exchange."[65]

Nonetheless, long-time bear brokers on the Exchange had significant resources, and they kept selling short. By the end of the

Table 3.1 Cotton Futures Prices, 1902–1903

1902	September Prices		October Prices		November Prices		December Prices		January Prices		February Prices		March Prices		April Prices		May Prices		June Prices		July Prices		August Prices	
	Low	High	Low	High	Low	High	Low	High	Low	High	Low	High	Low	High	Low	High	Low	High	Low	High	Low	High	Low	High
Sept. 5	8.34	8.75	8.28	8.78	8.10	8.63	8.22	8.65	8.22	8.66	8.19	8.52	8.16	8.55	8.18	8.50	8.20	8.55						
Sept. 12	8.22	8.55	8.18	8.46	8.18	8.41	8.12	8.42	8.15	8.42	8.09	8.29	8.07	8.27	8.17	8.29	8.09	8.29						
Sept. 19	8.50	8.78	8.39	8.80	8.34	8.80	8.35	8.80	8.36	8.78	8.22	8.63	8.19	8.64	8.45	8.60	8.21	8.65						
Sept. 26	8.66	8.84	8.62	8.86	8.58	8.84	8.62	8.86	8.65	8.92	8.45	8.67	8.43	8.68	8.44	8.64	8.44	8.66						
Oct. 3	8.61	8.73	8.59	8.71	8.65	8.75	8.72	8.84	8.75	8.90	8.56	8.67	8.54	8.67	8.54	8.66	8.54	8.68						
Oct. 10			8.45	8.72	8.46	8.75	8.54	8.83	8.60	8.90	8.43	8.70	8.42	8.72	8.49	8.70	8.43	8.74						
Oct. 17			8.29	8.54	8.31	8.61	8.40	8.71	8.48	8.80	8.32	8.49	8.28	8.61	8.37	8.62	8.28	8.60	8.31	8.50	8.35	8.40		
Oct. 24			8.32	8.50	8.34	8.48	8.41	8.62	8.50	8.72	8.29	8.44	8.31	8.45	8.38	8.42	8.33	8.46	8.37	8.43	8.32	8.45		8.27
Oct. 31			8.29	8.50	8.29	8.48	8.42	8.59	8.51	8.66	8.27	8.40	8.26	8.43	8.26	8.41	8.28	8.41	8.31	8.31	8.26	8.39	8.16	8.27
Nov. 7					8.06	8.32	8.12	8.47	8.17	8.55	7.97	8.27	8.01	8.32	8.08	8.21	8.03	8.32	8.15	8.25	8.04	8.31	7.94	8.15
Nov. 14					7.87	8.10	7.90	8.22	7.90	8.29	7.83	8.12	7.84	8.13	7.90	8.12	7.87	8.16	7.95	8.06	7.91	8.17	7.80	7.92
Nov. 21					7.98	8.33	7.95	8.35	7.92	8.35	7.85	8.20	7.85	8.25	7.87	8.25	7.88	8.26	7.92	8.20	7.92	8.29	7.83	8.06
Nov. 28					8.25	8.40	8.24	8.44	8.22	8.48	8.18	8.34	8.13	8.39	8.14	8.39	8.15	8.40	8.19	8.37	8.19	8.42	8.02	8.25
Dec. 5							8.17	8.38	8.13	8.37	8.04	8.26	8.05	8.29	8.19	8.29	8.05	8.30	8.10	8.26	8.06	8.32	7.88	8.13
Dec. 12							8.19	8.38	8.18	8.37	8.12	8.27	8.10	8.32	8.22	8.31	8.12	8.36	8.18	8.32	8.14	8.37	7.98	8.21
Dec. 19	7.95	8.01					8.30	8.57	8.30	8.59	8.21	8.34	8.23	8.38	8.25	8.36	8.26	8.42	8.29	8.40	8.27	8.43	8.10	8.28
Dec. 26	7.92	8.00					8.46	8.59	8.49	8.61	8.28	8.34	8.30	8.40	8.34	8.34	8.31	8.40	8.31	8.39	8.30	8.40	8.16	8.22
1903																								
Jan. 2	8.00	8.17	8.04	8.27			8.50	8.69	8.53	8.82	8.35	8.73	8.38	8.79	8.49	8.74	8.39	8.80	8.54	8.80	8.39	8.82	8.21	8.67
Jan. 9	8.09	8.30	8.09	8.18					8.49	8.78	8.53	8.74	8.55	8.78	8.60	8.75	8.55	8.80	8.55	8.73	8.56	8.80	8.44	8.64
Jan. 16	8.11	8.31	8.07	8.20					8.52	8.78	8.51	8.75	8.59	8.85	8.65	8.84	8.61	8.90	8.62	8.84	8.61	8.91	8.44	8.68
Jan. 23	8.20	8.31	8.03	8.19					8.68	8.78	8.65	8.75	8.71	8.85	8.74	8.85	8.76	8.90	8.77	8.87	8.76	8.91	8.55	8.68
Jan. 30	8.18	8.31	8.05	8.17					8.68	9.00	8.62	8.87	8.66	8.91	8.72	8.92	8.71	8.95	8.72	8.90	8.71	8.93	8.50	8.72
Feb. 6	8.19	8.29	8.19	8.30							8.68	8.83	8.71	8.97	8.75	9.00	8.79	9.03	8.78	8.86	8.77	8.96	8.58	8.75
Feb. 13	8.33	8.52	8.26	8.56							9.00	9.41	8.98	9.44	9.08	9.46	9.06	9.53	9.00	9.40	9.00	9.40	8.77	9.07
Feb. 20	8.44	8.85	8.40	8.65	8.20	8.48	8.33	8.45			9.36	9.92	9.31	9.95	9.38	9.93	9.40	9.94	9.30	9.81	9.27	9.78	8.98	9.48
Feb. 27	8.64	8.98			8.31	8.56	8.30	8.52			9.84	10.10	9.73	10.14	9.73	10.10	9.70	10.12	9.55	9.85	9.49	9.90	9.18	9.57

Mar. 6	8.76	9.08	8.46	8.72	8.38	8.60	8.33	8.59			9.61	10.26	9.66	10.16	9.60	10.17	9.45	9.94	9.40	9.92	9.12	9.60
Mar. 13	8.69	9.02	8.39	8.69	8.35	8.59	8.31	8.58			9.56	10.05	9.56	9.95	9.54	10.02	9.37	9.77	9.32	9.80	9.05	9.52
Mar. 20	8.85	8.98	8.52	8.67	8.45	8.57	8.44	8.53			9.73	10.01	9.76	9.93	9.68	9.95	9.54	9.80	9.53	9.80	9.30	9.54
Mar. 27	8.74	8.98	8.40	8.68	8.30	8.57	8.29	8.53			9.79	9.95	9.82	9.93	9.80	10.00	9.64	9.78	9.63	9.82	9.32	9.52
Apr. 3	8.60	8.75	8.33	8.47	8.26	8.36	8.25	8.37			9.61	9.87	9.63		9.65	10.07	9.53	9.65	9.46	9.70	9.15	9.34
Apr. 10	8.71	8.88	8.44	8.60	8.33	8.43	8.32	8.43	8.34	8.40			10.08	10.31	10.04	10.44	9.67	9.99	9.68	9.99	9.32	9.51
Apr. 17	8.75	8.89	8.49	8.59	8.39	8.47	8.34	8.45	8.35	8.38			10.23	10.47	10.24	10.63	9.85	10.22	9.84	10.20	9.43	9.58
Apr. 24	8.70	8.99	8.45	8.72	8.35	8.60	8.34	8.60	8.48	8.58			10.15	10.33	10.10	10.40	9.77	9.94	9.71	9.99	9.36	9.62
May 1	8.90	9.06	8.61	8.75	8.53	8.63	8.49	8.64	8.55	8.60			10.50	10.57	10.40	10.60	10.02	10.16	9.98	10.17	9.60	9.75
May 8	8.90	9.08	8.62	8.78	8.55	8.67	8.53	8.69	8.55	8.70					10.50	11.01	9.91	10.35	9.88	10.22	9.59	9.86
May 15	9.09	9.56	8.75	9.01	8.67	8.90	8.65	8.89	8.67	8.89					10.90	11.44	10.42	11.03	10.18	11.00	9.85	10.76
May 22	9.30	10.14	8.84	9.59	8.77	9.55	8.74	9.54	8.75	9.55					11.10	11.98	10.70	11.36	10.63	11.36	10.36	11.05
May 29	9.74	10.14	9.30	9.70	9.28	9.53	9.16	9.54	9.18	9.54							11.02	11.29	10.92	11.34	10.58	10.86
June 5	10.01	10.22	9.49	9.77	9.35	9.62	9.34	9.62	9.34	9.62							11.08	11.20	11.13	11.35	10.65	10.80
June 12	10.00	10.87	9.46	9.96	9.30	9.84	9.31	9.80	9.34	9.75							11.06	12.17	11.13	12.30	10.67	11.81
June 19	10.76	11.37	9.98	10.58	9.78	10.45	9.72	10.31	9.72	10.30							12.10	12.20	12.10	12.35	11.69	12.00
June 26	10.76	11.99	10.00	10.57	9.78	10.18	9.71	10.10	9.72	10.07							12.31	12.31	12.10	13.20	11.69	13.00
July 3	11.38	11.97	10.10	10.51	9.78	10.10	9.75	10.08	9.70	10.03	9.71	9.75					12.58	13.06	12.55	13.06	12.41	12.95
July 10	10.16	10.52	9.60	10.30	9.50	9.92	9.46	9.94	9.44	9.86	9.45	9.80							11.15	12.55	11.00	12.55
July 17	10.25	10.72	9.63	9.90	9.48	9.68	9.46	9.67	9.43	9.60	9.42	9.61							11.80	12.40	11.50	12.21
July 24	10.40	10.95	9.65	10.10	9.50	9.88	9.50	9.87	9.46	9.83	9.47	9.81							12.18	13.75	11.85	12.75
July 31	10.47	10.90	9.76	10.03	9.64	9.83	9.60	9.85	9.60	9.85	9.61	9.86							12.40	13.60	11.84	12.49
Aug. 7	10.31	10.88	9.78	10.09	9.64	9.90	9.61	9.88	9.61	9.88	9.64	9.88									11.30	12.05
Aug. 14	10.35	10.89	9.77	10.08	9.32	9.84	9.61	9.81	9.63	9.81	9.64	9.80									11.45	12.44
Aug. 21	10.56	10.88	9.87	10.05	9.70	9.83	9.67	9.85	9.68	9.86	9.67	9.80									12.10	12.30
Aug. 28	10.81	11.36	10.01	10.55	9.82	10.34	9.79	10.30	9.81	10.31	9.83	10.28									12.19	12.37
Aug. 31	11.28	11.80	10.55	10.82	10.27	10.48	10.22	10.45	10.22	10.41	10.21	10.39									12.20	12.30
Sept. 4	10.98	11.68	9.95	10.60	9.69	10.38	9.68	10.36	9.62	10.30	9.62	10.29			9.68	9.90						
Sept. 11	10.58	11.03	9.60	10.00	9.50	9.79	9.50	9.83	9.49	9.80	9.48	9.80			9.50	9.81						
Sept. 18	10.75	11.48	9.72	10.10	9.66	9.99	9.69	10.01	9.70	9.98	9.74	10.00	9.50		9.75	9.99	9.43	9.80	9.77	9.95		
Sept. 25	10.80	11.53	9.43	10.05	9.34	1.13	9.34	9.84	9.32	9.82	9.33	9.83	9.33	9.61	9.41	9.83	9.57	9.70	9.44	9.84		
Oct. 2	11.16	13.20	9.28	9.62	9.30	9.63	9.34	9.63	9.34	9.64	9.36	9.66	9.24	9.59	9.42	9.71	9.34		9.50	9.70		
Oct. 9			9.01	9.44	9.07	9.46	9.10	9.50	9.10	9.51	9.14	9.52		9.35	9.20	9.60		9.35	9.25	9.63		

(continued)

Table 3.1 (Continued)

	September Prices		October Prices		November Prices		December Prices		January Prices		February Prices		March Prices		April Prices		May Prices		June Prices		July Prices		August Prices	
	Low	High	Low	High	Low	High	Low	High	Low	High	Low	High	Low	High	Low	High	Low	High	Low	High	Low	High	Low	High
Oct. 16			9.10	9.57	9.12	9.63	9.18	9.73	9.17	9.73	9.40	9.75	9.20	9.79	9.25	9.81	9.26	9.83	9.37	9.79	9.28	9.84		
Oct. 23			9.33	9.87	9.34	9.85	9.45	9.94	9.43	9.93	9.51	9.90	9.49	9.98	9.65	10.00	9.54	10.01	9.67	9.94	9.56	10.00		
Oct. 30			9.79	10.40	9.78	10.25	9.84	10.38	9.79	10.33	9.82	10.32	9.82	10.35	9.88	10.32	9.87	10.37	10.00	10.25	9.88	10.36		
Nov. 6					10.12	10.81	10.25	10.93	10.15	10.87	10.20	10.86	10.20	10.90	10.35	10.86	10.27	10.92	10.31	10.81	10.27	10.92	10.15	10.66
Nov. 13					10.68	11.20	10.70	11.32	10.72	11.33	10.72	11.22	10.76	11.43	10.78	11.43	10.78	11.45	10.81	11.34	10.79	11.34	10.60	11.15
Nov. 20					10.84	11.16	10.84	11.24	10.83	11.25	10.89	11.22	10.88	11.32	10.90	11.32	10.88	11.32	10.95	11.32	10.89	11.30	10.64	10.99
Nov. 27					10.90	11.15	10.92	11.18	10.99	11.25	11.06	11.20	11.04	11.32	11.08	11.22	11.04	11.31	11.06	11.11	11.05	11.29	10.77	10.96
Dec. 4					11.33	11.33	11.17	12.55	11.21	12.60	11.25	12.52	11.30	12.73	11.32	12.63	11.33	12.71	11.50	12.68	11.32	12.67	10.93	12.35
Dec. 11							11.81	12.41	11.91	12.49	12.09	12.55	12.11	12.60	12.23	12.58	12.16	12.60	12.21	12.56	12.15	12.59	11.87	12.27
Dec. 18							12.04	12.97	12.13	13.05	12.25	13.15	12.29	13.25	12.35	13.30	12.35	13.36	12.46	13.39	12.35	13.42	12.07	13.10
Dec. 25							12.57	13.45	12.66	13.51	12.81	13.58	12.87	13.81	13.05	13.75	13.02	13.91	13.05	13.84	13.04	13.92	12.68	13.47
1904																								
Jan. 1							12.87	13.82	12.73	13.88	12.99	14.00	13.01	14.18	13.05	14.20	13.05	14.26	13.03	14.24	13.04	14.27	12.60	13.90
Jan. 8									12.45	13.42	12.73	13.55	12.70	13.74	12.80	13.75	12.80	13.95	13.13	13.87	12.90	13.96	12.42	13.50
Jan. 15			11.25	11.60					13.10	13.65	13.33	13.62	13.38	13.96	13.53	14.00	13.61	14.19	13.61	14.18	13.63	14.25	13.20	13.73
Jan. 22	12.45	13.37	11.40	12.62	12.20	12.20	11.98	12.10	13.50	14.55			13.69	14.75	13.80	14.85	13.91	14.95	14.06	14.98	13.98	15.03	13.50	14.37
Jan. 29	13.05	14.30	12.48	13.09			12.40	12.55	14.35	15.87	14.95	16.03	14.59	16.45	15.13	16.55	14.78	16.79	14.85	16.86	14.87	16.91	14.21	16.11
Feb. 5	12.60	14.35	11.80	13.00	11.70	12.40	11.40	12.55			14.50	16.75	13.75	17.04	14.16	17.10	13.99	17.46	14.28	17.27	14.08	17.55	13.25	16.15
Feb. 12	11.53	13.10	11.00	12.07	11.50	11.50	10.65	11.50			12.50	13.60	12.30	14.20	12.50	14.29	12.69	14.51	13.00	14.31	12.80	14.62	12.15	13.90
Feb. 19	11.70	12.25	11.07	11.50	10.95	11.25	10.80	11.25			13.10	13.62	12.54	13.90	12.88	13.65	12.85	14.26	13.02	14.19	12.95	14.28	12.40	13.76
Feb. 26	12.05	12.65	11.38	11.90	11.35	11.60	11.17	11.55			13.68	14.05	13.40	14.39	13.78	14.39	13.75	14.73	13.93	14.66	13.80	14.71	13.40	14.30
Mar. 4	12.62	13.74	11.82	12.65	11.76	12.00	11.55	12.36					14.30	15.78	14.53	15.88	14.63	16.08	14.73	15.94	14.42	16.00	14.15	15.44
Mar. 11	13.35	13.99	12.38	12.99	12.13	12.69	12.02	12.70					15.49	16.30	16.00	16.33	15.80	16.65	15.81	16.48	15.66	16.65	15.08	16.03
Mar. 18	11.50	13.99	11.50	12.98	11.92	12.76	11.50	12.70					13.02	16.32	13.00	16.35	12.65	16.62	13.50	16.58	12.80	16.65	12.90	16.01
Mar. 25	11.96	12.72	11.33	12.00	11.25	11.90	11.22	11.90					13.10	14.50	13.18	14.60	13.15	14.87	13.45	14.19	13.45	15.01	12.97	14.48

Date																												
Apr. 1	12.50	13.07	11.80	12.35	11.95	12.14	11.64	12.12	11.90	12.15							14.44	14.97	14.55	15.00	14.50	15.28	14.81	15.36	14.71	15.50	14.20	14.90
Apr. 8	12.50	13.10	11.80	12.33	11.70	12.19	11.62	12.15	11.62	12.15									14.24	14.92	14.39	15.28	14.71	15.32	14.60	15.38	14.11	14.87
Apr. 15	12.25	12.83	11.66	12.14	11.57	12.00	11.51	11.96	11.53	12.00									13.80	14.61	13.71	14.78	13.94	14.67	13.93	15.02	13.40	14.47
Apr. 22	12.13	12.50	11.60	11.92	11.52	11.76	11.47	11.75	11.46	11.75									13.62	13.88	13.57	14.20	13.75	13.98	13.90	14.43	13.30	13.86
Apr. 29	11.75	12.16	11.22	11.62	11.16	11.49	11.10	11.46	11.08	11.46									13.50	13.55	13.29	13.72	13.49	13.68	13.53	13.96	13.07	13.52
May. 6	11.77	12.15	11.28	11.65	11.22	11.35	11.16	11.49	11.17	11.52											13.20	13.72	13.33	13.78	13.40	13.89	13.13	13.61
May. 13	11.74	11.90	11.28	11.44	11.20	11.32	11.17	11.32	11.21	11.31											13.15	13.51	13.38	13.57	13.35	13.69	13.08	13.34
May. 20	11.27	11.88	10.85	11.39	10.78	11.31	10.77	11.29	10.82	11.30											12.66	13.47	12.70	13.53	12.78	13.69	12.38	13.31
May. 27	11.05	11.37	10.68	10.99	10.65	10.90	10.60	10.90	10.63	10.90											12.45	12.83	12.53	12.94	12.54	13.12	12.16	12.62
June. 3	10.27	11.25	9.83	10.87	9.80	10.75	9.76	10.80	9.79	10.79											12.43	12.73	11.13	12.70	11.23	12.88	10.87	12.40
June. 10	9.84	10.42	9.50	9.98	9.47	9.75	9.42	9.92	9.47	10.00													11.04	11.74	11.08	11.97	10.63	11.54
June. 17	9.81	10.75	9.55	10.14	9.45	10.03	9.48	10.07	9.53	10.13													11.20	12.17	10.93	12.48	10.50	11.90
June. 24	9.45	9.92	9.30	9.71	9.31	9.58	9.37	9.72	9.37	9.74													10.35	10.95	10.29	11.18	10.10	10.74
July. 1	9.57	9.95	9.40	9.75	9.39	9.66	9.40	9.73	9.41	9.76	9.52	9.60											10.46	10.46	10.06	10.75	10.10	10.65
July. 8	9.59	9.90	9.31	9.68	9.30	9.57	9.30	9.64	9.32	9.65	9.39	9.74													10.18	10.87	10.12	10.90
July. 15	9.56	10.09	9.40	9.72	9.40	9.60	9.38	9.65	9.40	9.66	9.48	9.65													10.47	10.99	10.42	11.00
July. 22	9.74	10.16	9.48	9.92	9.44	9.79	9.44	9.86	9.47	9.93	9.53	9.82													10.41	10.67	10.35	10.70
July. 29	9.75	10.09	9.56	9.92	9.56	9.78	9.53	9.84	9.56	9.87	9.63	9.91													10.15	10.34	10.05	10.38
Aug. 5	9.50	10.01	9.50	9.86	9.49	9.86	9.46	9.90	9.48	9.91	9.53	9.94	9.69	9.71											9.86	10.28	9.65	10.25
Aug. 12	9.81	10.07	9.62	9.90	9.58	9.76	9.57	9.84	9.58	9.85	9.65	9.92	9.69	9.89	9.77	9.77											9.98	10.25
Aug. 19	9.69	9.97	9.53	9.76	9.50	9.67	9.49	9.75	9.52	9.75	9.57	9.79	9.64	9.84	9.59	9.71											9.96	10.16
Aug. 26	9.97	11.06	9.76	10.95	9.72	10.90	9.72	10.91	9.73	10.91	9.81	10.95	10.84	10.92	10.17	10.86											10.25	11.00
Aug. 31	10.60	11.25	10.50	11.16	10.63	11.01	10.50	11.16	10.51	11.16	10.60	11.15	10.64	11.23	10.74	10.98											10.79	11.04

The price of cotton was the basis for the economic conflict between the bears who kept prices low and the bulls who worked to raise the price. These prices show the success of the bulls as they cornered the market in summer 1903. From *Cotton Movement and Fluctuations* (New York: Latham and Alexander, 1902-1907), volumes 30 and 31.

week, they seemed to have succeeded. On Thursday, May 21, the price of July dropped 55 points, to 10.70, under an "avalanche of selling orders."[66] More sellers than buyers meant prices sunk. By Friday, Brown was visibly worried. He "began the day well by dodging the bears," bidding up prices on near months, but when he tried to take some profits on August and September contracts, he weakened the market, and prices sagged. "Beset by bears," Brown "ran around the floor trying to shake off the huggers who were dogging him about prepared to stop any effort at kiting" the prices higher. He conferred at one point with the president of the Exchange, then sent "quite an avalanche of telegrams."[67] Nonetheless, May's price kept sinking, reaching a low of 10.63.[68] That weekend, newspapers were reporting Brown's failure. "Brown Quits New York Cotton Pit ... Market Quieting Down," ran the characteristic coverage. "Short Was Brown's Reign" headlined the article in the Cincinnati *Enquirer.* The Atlanta *Journal* grieved: "Brown, of New Orleans, Folds His Tent and Quietly Steals Away. Cotton Men Wonder But Cannot Explain." The newspaper had the facts straight: after trading closed on May 22, Brown left New York for New Orleans. His failure seemed imminent.[69]

CHAPTER 4

Cornering Cotton

BEARS MAKE MONEY BY PUSHING prices down. As a result, they work to make people think that the price is going down. In May 1903 they were trying to demonstrate that the price of cotton was being raised artificially by bull operators who were manipulating the market—that five cents or eight cents was a natural price reflecting supply and demand. Anyone with a **long position** who believed them—who believed that the price was going down—would want to sell as soon as possible in order to get the higher price, and those sales would further push down the price. Moreover, the physical reality of the cotton exchanges helped them out. With lots of people crowded around the **ring** selling, a buyer can wait, knowing that some seller who wants to stand out from the rest of the crowd will eventually nudge his price down just a bit. When the buyer buys at that lower price, other sellers follow the first in order to make their sales, and the price slides down. That was what happened on Thursday, May 21, 1903. May cotton had surpassed twelve cents on Wednesday, but large selling orders cabled from Liverpool dropped the price 36 points before New York opened on Thursday. By the end of Thursday May had dropped to 11.60, a forty-point decline in a day. July dropped 55 points, to close at 10.70, while August "slumped off" 51 points to 10.47. September closed at 9.65, October at 9.27, and December at 9.10. The future looked grim.[1]

Brown stayed cool. "Declines always make the market healthier," he told the New York *World*. "Cotton prices will go still higher." However persuasive the bears' warnings might be temporarily,

Figure 4.1 This illustration from a New York newspaper depicts William P. Brown calmly surveying the floor of the New York Cotton Exchange, just when he was about to corner the world market in cotton futures. From *New York Evening World*, May 19, 1903.

Brown had his eye on supply and demand and knew these must push prices higher, so long as he could continue his bull campaign. Arrayed against him were not only the bears of the New York Cotton Exchange. The dry goods trade was disrupted: cotton brokers were buying finished goods, as the price seemed sure to go up, and mills saw more profit in selling their raw material than in manufacturing it.[2] The high price of raw cotton had effects well beyond the cotton trade. The "Wall Street contingent," reported the evening *World*, had discovered that bulls had $50 million tied up in the campaign and decided to liquidate this "menace to the money market."[3] Speculators on the stock exchange were selling off their stocks in order to shift their money into cotton.[4] Bankers and capitalists who supported them began to worry about their money. It was reported that "the losses were sensational," but to Brown, Friday's drop in price and liquidation of cotton contracts represented merely "a general filtering process which is always occurring," as people took their profits and got out of the market.[5]

Nonetheless, Brown retreated from the battle in New York when he secretly hopped a train for New Orleans at the end of the week. He had not failed, however. He disembarked "among friendly bankers" and prepared to "manage his battle."[6] Perhaps his telegrams from New York had paved the way for discussions with business partners, the bankers and brokers of the Crescent City he had worked into a network behind his scheme. He returned to town to explain in person the situation and confirm that the financing was still in place to pay for it. Luckily, his "New Orleans friends ... stood ready."[7]

On Monday, May 25, he renewed his campaign in the New Orleans Exchange, giving any bears lingering in the NOCE "a touch of the horn."[8] Summer prices once again began to rise as he pushed the price of August deliveries to twelve cents a pound.[9]

The scope of Brown's resources and ambition was becoming clear. Rumors of a "world-wide corner" had begun to appear in New Orleans papers.[10] By the first few days of June, the trade awaited the USDA's first report of the 1903–1904 season, expecting that it would support the bulls' position. When it came out, the report said the condition of the crop was well below average. Though the acreage was a bit larger than the year before, the quality would be much below middling—the same as the year before.[11] All observers predicted another "flurry" in the cotton market.[12] The weather, too, looked bad for cotton. Then, June floods along the Mississippi damaged the crop in the ground and "the railroad tie-up due to floods" slowed its passage to market.[13] The Texas crop was maturing on average two to four weeks late, the fields were full of weeds, and, even with the weather improving and rain falling where the crop needed it, it was too late. There would be no sudden rush of good quality cotton to hit the market early and relieve the position of the bears. Under these conditions, a squeeze might become a corner.[14]

Though one reporter characterized Brown's activities as a game of two cities, the speed of telegraphic information and the market integration it permitted meant that a true corner required control of worldwide markets—including Liverpool, the long-standing price-setter. The slump in mid-May looked as though it had domestic origins, but in fact the drop had originated in Liverpool "due to **realizing**" at high prices the cotton held in England.[15] The sales of hoarded cotton did not relieve the upward pressure on its price and, by May 23, Liverpool had sold British manufacturers the cotton its brokers had on hand. With less than half the cotton available than was needed in the mills, New York papers predicted that European textile firms would have to close due to the shortage. As the May story began to repeat itself in June and prices again began to rise worldwide, some sources thought that Sully must still be in charge, working with Brown. Perhaps his trip to Europe was not a vacation, but a mission to manipulate the price in the Liverpool market.[16]

The bulls did not need to use manipulation to raise the price of cotton. In a short crop year, it required only pockets deep enough to meet New York speculators as equals. With consumption increasing and production often unable to keep pace, Brown led the bulls in his understanding that "cotton is going up on its merits." According to his own account of the 1903 corner, "manipulation has had but little to do with advance in prices." Poor cotton coming to market had "awaken[ed]. . . foreign spinners . . . to the quality of what cotton is left from last year's crop."[17] The late arrival of the new crop also contributed considerably to the shortage in the mills—a gap Brown and Hayne had spent years preparing to exploit, creating the banks and coordinating their investors in support of this goal.[18]

Rumors and resources played a role in the game of speculation as it continued through June: did the bulls have twenty million dollars at their command? Or only a quarter of that sum?[19] It was possible that what money they could not raise in New Orleans or New York "they borrowed very readily from the plethoric purses of the French."[20] Some said that "the money kings of New York" would deliver to Brown his July purchases when June's tender day approached—some 200,000 bales of "actual cotton . . . stored in this city along its water front"—unspinnable trash cotton that had been in New York warehouses for years, discouraging anyone from demanding delivery of actual cotton. One New Orleans broker complained that New Yorkers would hardly recognize proper cotton if they saw it since they were so accustomed to dealing in "sticks and leaves done up in the shape of cotton bales."[21] Receiving these useless bales would require the immediate payment of ten or twelve million dollars.[22] Its poor quality meant that Brown would necessarily lose dollars a bale on it and likely land himself in deep financial trouble.

June's prices took much the same shape as had May's: a steady upward price trend—punctuated with a mid-month drop, fought off the same week—leaving the bulls again in control. Rumors of a complete corner of the season's cotton gained credence. With Brown ready in New Orleans, Frank Hayne went to New York to be on hand for tender day, June 25. When it came time to deliver the cotton promised for July delivery, it became a question of quantities: how much money did the bulls hold, and how much cotton could the bears deliver? The cotton would arrive, and it had to be paid for. If the New York bears could keep delivering cotton longer than Brown and Hayne could keep paying for it they would win, forcing Brown to buy his way out of the contracts rather than buying cotton. Brown and Hayne stood in the pits, awaiting the battle of money-versus-cotton as July deliveries came due.[23] Would the bulls' finances support the campaign? The *New Orleans Picayune* had no doubt: "The whole campaign has been so skillfully managed that it is reasonable to assume that this little detail of finance has been worked out successfully."[24]

Indeed the bulls held their ground, proving they had more money than the bears had cotton. When June 25 arrived, those who had sold cotton to the bulls lined up in both cities to hand over their notices that they intended to deliver the cotton, demanding their money. Brown and Hayne paid each contract, Brown taking in approximately 36,000 bales that day in New Orleans, while Hayne in New York "**stopped the notices**" of 95,000 bales, spending nearly six million dollars to do so.[25] When Brown was done, he still had money left. He returned to the ring and called out offers to buy cotton at an even higher price, the unheard-of figure of fourteen cents a pound. No one took his contracts. "The plain inference," crowed the *New Orleans Picayune*, "is that the cotton is not to be had."[26] New York newspapermen, doing the math, indicated that by tender day the bull clique's profits had reached ten million dollars. July and August looked no better for the bears. If they could find cotton to deliver as they had promised, they would have to buy it at the higher market prices and receive for it the low price specified in their contracts. But by the end of August, there was no more real cotton available. The new crop was late in arriving at the ports, the mills were closing for lack of raw materials, and Brown himself had physical possession of all remnants of the last year's crop (whether 200,000 bales or less than half that, no one knew). Some speculators had needed to wire Liverpool for "real cotton" to be shipped back to the United States to deliver to Brown and Hayne and their associates. A bale rumored to be from the 1872 crop actually finally came to market, indicating how greatly demand outstripped supply.[27]

By the end of August, the corner was complete. The world's cotton mills held less than ten days' supply of their raw materials, and Brown owned the only cotton available to meet their demand.[28] As September began, the bulls' position only improved. Men could not find cotton anywhere to meet their contracts for delivery and settled instead. They sometimes paid higher than cotton prices for release from their contracts, since defaulting on a contract on the exchange could result in expulsion. "For the first time in the history of cotton selling on a world-wide basis the market is absolutely cornered," wrote an *Atlanta Constitution* reporter. The corner on September cotton alone made Brown between seven and eight million dollars in profits.[29]

On September 1, 1903, the day the *New Orleans Picayune* published its annual review of trade in New Orleans, Brown took out a half-page ad declaring "Cotton Is King And New Orleans Its Capital."[30] It marked the moment when the New Orleans exchange set the price of the staple and became the new cotton capital of the

United States. Cotton hit eighteen cents a pound, and those who had bulled it to that height declared that fifteen cents would be the floor in the future. Just seven years earlier, cotton had brought only a third that price.[31] Tripling the price in a few short years signaled not only that demand outpaced supply, but also that a new market dictated the flow of the staple, produced the information that influenced its price, and thus set the price it could command. As one writer noted that September, "the developments of the past year have finally demonstrated the supremacy of the New Orleans cotton market as the dominating power in fixing the value of the South's great basic product in the various marts of the world."[32]

Figure 4.2 William P. Brown celebrated his success and the triumph of New Orleans with this newspaper advertisement. From New Orleans *Daily Picayune*, September 1, 1903. Courtesy of Texas Tech University Library.

Effects of the 1903 Corner

The 1903 cotton corner had worldwide implications, starting in New Orleans and rippling outward. Unlike Peter Labouisse, who challenged the bears of New York and came crashing back to earth, Brown and Hayne rode back to New Orleans as conquering heroes. Brown did what he tended to do when he won big: he called in the architects. With the new electric streetcars running along St. Charles Avenue, the Uptown neighborhood was now less than half an hour from the cotton exchange. By the beginning of September 1903, Brown had bought the lot that sat at the corner of St. Charles Avenue and Valence Street and stretched all the way back to Carondelet Street. He knocked down the mansion that was already there and hired the architectural firm Favrot and Livaudais to design him the grandest house in the city. He wanted a home that would stand out and remind all who passed of the power and wealth of the man who built it.[33]

At a cost of more than $150,000, at a time when a perfectly decent family home could be built for under $5,000, Brown's mansion rose in splendor. It had nine bedrooms, a billiards room, a bowling alley, and flame mahogany throughout. Its Richardsonian Romanesque style set it apart from the other admittedly impressive houses on the street. Built of limestone, which was foreign to the region, its huge stone shapes evoked medieval European cathedrals.[34] Ever the romantic, Brown even included an architectural homage to his wife. Like the diamond brooch he gave Marguerite at their wedding a decade earlier, the stained glass window on the landing of the grand staircase featured a bouquet of marguerites, the daisy that was a sort of icon for Brown, the Mississippi hillbilly who lived in the finest house in New Orleans.[35]

Frank B. Hayne already had a perfectly good house. His recognition came in a more transient, if no less impressive, form. New Orleans had ways to celebrate its leaders and their accomplishments, a public culture expressed in the celebrations of Mardi Gras, the Fat Tuesday carnival before Lent. On February 15, 1904, a yacht called *The Stranger* made its way up the Mississippi River, an impressive flotilla arrayed in its wake. As it landed near Jackson Barracks, the 120 guns of the *USS Texas* thundered a salute, soon lost in a cacophony of steamboat horns, factory whistles, church bells, and the cheers of tens of thousands of voices. From the Isles of the Blest had arrived the Emperor of Joy, Rex, the King of Carnival. Sitting atop his royal throne on its wheeled pedestal, His Gracious Majesty made his way past the crowds to City Hall, where the mayor handed over the keys to the city to the most important man in New Orleans: Frank B. Hayne.[36]

Figure 4.3 With some of the money he made on the 1903 corner, William P. Brown built this unusual stone-clad mansion on the corner of St. Charles Avenue and Valence Street. Photograph courtesy of Crorey Lawton.

Figure 4.4 Frank B. Hayne, William P. Brown's partner, was honored for his role in the 1903 cotton corner by being made King Rex of Mardi Gras in 1904. Here he is seen arriving in New Orleans by yacht for the parade along Canal Street. From *Times Picayune/Landov*.

The motto of Rex Organization is *pro bono publico*—"for the public good"—and few acts by Rex members could have done more good for the public, especially the southern public, than Hayne and Brown's cornering of the cotton market in 1903. While they made millions of dollars for themselves, the benefit extended well beyond the builders Brown hired for his mansion. By cornering the market and disrupting the bears' long-term control, they did what Brown said they would do: they pushed cotton prices higher, permanently. This benefitted not only the brokers on the exchange, but also the farmers who produced the fiber.

Contemporaries noticed particularly the positive effects this had on black southerners. Katherine Coman, the Wellesley College economist, argued in 1904 that "the cotton corner of the year just past was the means of putting thousands of negro farmers in full possession of the land they tilled."[37] Land ownership, long desired by the freedpeople and their descendants, finally came within reach of many. Bull traders may have been vilified by some, an interpretation supported by Frank Norris's *The Pit*, but others knew better. One commentator a decade later argued about Brown that "in ten years he either gave or saved the South two billion dollars," and that judgment seems about right.[38]

While New Orleanians were cheering Hayne, and poor cotton farmers became a little more secure, the same could not be said of mill operatives in New England. Many New England mill owners saw the high price of cotton as a blessing in disguise. They used the cost of cotton as an excuse to stop production in mills that had been experiencing labor trouble since the spring. Rather than admit to locking out workers, employers at the end of July could simply say that "the combination of an overstocked market and the high price of cotton" forced them to close their doors.[39] By the middle of August mills from Maine to Rhode Island sat idle, putting around 20,000 operatives out of work. Thousands more still had jobs, but their hours were cut to save money. The industry sputtered through the rest of August and into September, some mills resuming production while others ceased. After the mills in Fall River closed for Labor Day, they did not bother reopening. Over 12,000 workers had an extended and unwelcome holiday. Following as it did the massive strike in Lowell that spring, and a dawning awareness that the South's cotton mills were beginning to challenge New England, the 1903 cotton corner revealed new signs of weakness in New England's traditional industrial base.[40] The center of the industry was shifting, as was the center of futures trade in the staple. Southern spindles were influencing demand, just as the New Orleans Exchange had raised the price.

The Global Effects of the Cotton Corner

The disruption caused by the 1903 cotton corner touched on some of the period's most important debates over global trade and the effects of industrial turmoil. Lancashire mills could not get the cheap cotton they had learned to rely on and even shipped back what they had already bought. The resulting "cotton famine" echoed the 1860s, with spindles sitting motionless, 80,000 mill hands idle, and as much as £2,000,000 in wages unpaid. Many gave up and moved to Canada to try farming instead. The mill owners responded to the rising price with short work schedules; in June 1903, Lancashire mills agreed to operate only Tuesdays through Fridays. One manufacturers' representative calculated the capital cost of idle machinery at £40,000 per week. The situation in Lancashire was worse than in America or the rest of Europe partly because the market for its cloth was already soft. As a result, spinners had not bought any extra cotton and were caught short when the corner happened, unable to support idle workers on half-wages as had happened in America. More spinners joined organizations designed to protect their interests; the proportion of firms involved in such associations rose from 42 to 60% of the Lancashire total between 1903 and 1905.[41]

With the mills unable to keep their doors open and pay their labor, many workers suffered wage cuts of 30 percent. Their unions tried to make up the difference, which strained their resources to the breaking point. The massive unemployment in Lancashire, and especially the coordinated efforts by spinners to deal with high prices by cutting back hours and pay, became part of the debate that led to the Unemployed Workmen Act of 1905, a cornerstone of modern unemployment insurance.[42] In Westminster, a Member of Parliament for Dublin asked the Secretary for the Board of Trade "whether he will confer with President Roosevelt respecting [the corner and] suggest a conference with the various Governments which have considered the subject of future options, with a view to propose the introduction of international legislation to control gambling in food-stuffs and other produce."[43]

The Lancashire cotton famine also became entangled in Britain's debate over tariff reform. Protectionists thought that using a protective tariff to favor products from the British Empire—including cotton—might increase prices, but that increase would be balanced by the greater stability protection would bring to markets. The stability would alleviate the problems of periodic unemployment that had become part of the free trade system since 1849.[44] Speaking at the Free Trade Hall in Manchester, an MP acknowledged that "no doubt Lancashire has had, and is now having a difficult time and a cloudy time," but he argued that it was due not to free trade but "various doings in the United States."[45] A writer for *Blackwood's Magazine* thought that was disingenuous at best, self-serving cant from mill owners who professed to take care of their workers but were content to let them suffer the effects of periodic cotton shortages caused by free trade. "No protectionist regime," he wrote, "could possibly have reduced Lancashire to a more dangerous and humiliating dependence not only on foreign cotton-growers but on foreign speculators than she occupies at this moment after sixty years of *laisser* [sic] *faire*."[46]

The 1903 cotton corner and the resultant cotton famine in Lancashire made the British cotton industry, among others, rethink its reliance on American cotton. So long as Lancashire spinners could count on New York bears to hold down cotton prices, and could get enough cotton at these low prices, everyone was happy—except for the cotton farmers in the South, of course. But when 5-cent cotton became 14-cent cotton, Lancashire's manufacturers sought a new strategy: organization and diversification. They joined together into protective associations and recruited continental cotton manufacturers to their cause. As a writer in the *Christian Advocate* pointed out, "the recent great cotton corner in America has caused a permanent fright in Europe."[47] Manufacturers in Normandy and other parts of France had to curtail production and worried that American exporters would be able to charge what they pleased, disrupting their attempts to market cotton goods at competitive prices. A German official worried about the effects of a cotton famine on his country and suggested a European conference on the matter.[48]

Seeing another bad year coming in 1903–1904, an influential Lancashire industrialist floated the idea of getting all European spinners to run on short time. He took the lead in March 1904 by calling a meeting of representatives of the cotton industry from across Western Europe. At the meeting in Zurich that May they formed the International Federation of Master Cotton Spinners' and Manufacturers' Associations to deal proactively with the problems the industry faced with supply.[49] The British Empire had plenty of land suitable for cotton, the Federation argued, especially if cultivation could be encouraged by a protective tariff. The Manchester

Chamber of Commerce viewed Africa as a viable source to supply cotton to the region's mills. These conferences and conclusions did not go unnoticed in the United States. James Wilson, the US Secretary of Agriculture, warned that the corner "threatens our control of the cotton markets of the world." Britain had just "dammed the Nile [so] that its fructifying waters may be systematically released to develop its ancient cotton lands."[50] France was likewise considering how it could boost cotton production in Sudan, Dahomey, and Madagascar.[51] While imperialists in European cities were thinking about how they could produce more cotton in their colonies, the farmers of the US South were thinking of how they could produce less, and they had help.

CHAPTER 5

Of Weevils and Wool Hats

THE SPECTACULAR EVENTS OF THE summer of 1903 showed that the New Orleans bulls had learned a lesson Peter Labouisse had not: timing is everything. For years the bears had taken advantage of the crop calendar and the farmers' need to close out accounts by the end of the year to push prices down with inflated predictions of crop sizes. Now the bulls had learned to use another part of the crop calendar—the summer months when one crop had all come to market and the next was still growing—to catch the shorts and squeeze them until they squealed. With a relatively precise knowledge of demand, crop size, and visible supply, the bulls stood ready to take full advantage of any fleeting disruptions to the market caused by natural forces. But rivers could not be counted on to flood, as they had in 1903. The bulls needed some other mechanism to suppress supplies coming to market, and here they had two potential groups of allies: farmers and boll weevils.

The "wool-hats"—one of the many derogatory nicknames for farmers in the late nineteenth century, a disproportionate number of which seemed to comment on farmers' fashion sense or the condition of their skin—and the weevils were, of course, enemies. Farmers also had good reason to mistrust the cotton trade as a whole. Getting the weevils to trust the bulls was not necessary and probably futile. The weevils had a single-minded drive to suppress cotton supplies no matter what happened on the exchanges. The farmers were another matter. If they could be persuaded to help the bulls by strategically limiting cotton supplies, the bulls could push prices higher more reliably and everyone would win—except perhaps the bears. The New Orleans bulls, led by William P. Brown, used the farmers' mobilization against the weevil to draw the farmers into the bulls' network. While it did not pay immediate dividends, it completely changed the political landscape and set up the bulls' ultimate victory over the bears.

The Rise and Fall of Daniel J. Sully

The 1903–1904 season illustrated two important new lessons for the New Orleans bulls. First, Daniel J. Sully showed them again how not to corner the market. Second, the bulls learned that they needed some mechanism more reliable than flooding rivers to squeeze supplies and push up prices to what they thought was a more appropriate level. As these lessons developed in 1904, the course of cotton prices validated the bulls' basic approach, in which timing and the use of accurate information shaped price as much as did supply and demand. The bulls' triumph of the previous spring and summer continued to have effects well into the 1903–1904 season. The corner had scoured the market of cotton, liquidating both the visible and invisible supply. Uncertainty about the size of the 1903–1904 crop led to uncertainty about prices.

A few days before Christmas 1903, the Manchester *Guardian* noted that while the US government had predicted 9,962,039 bales from the 1903–1904 crop, word from New Orleans was that ginners were reporting a total of only 9,500,000 bales.[1] According to Brown, when interviewed about the spot price and his predictions for the future in early February 1904, "spinners have sold their output," and "jobbers and merchants have likewise sold their stocks down to a minimum on the belief that the crop was a large one; that prices would decline and that they would be able to buy cheaper in the future." According to Brown, spinners and merchants believed that the new crop would be large and its price would therefore necessarily drop. Brown suggested that this strategy by the manufacturers was based on a fantasy, and lower prices were unlikely to reappear anytime soon. Mills should "adjust their prices," he declared, and "mark their goods on the basis of 20-cent cotton." The high price of cotton that his corner had established the year before was "up to stay."[2]

High prices persuaded Daniel J. Sully to try another corner. Sully had made millions of dollars as a bull in May 1903. He had achieved considerable celebrity that spring: newspapers dubbed him

Figure 5.1 Daniel J. Sully won great acclaim trading cotton futures in the early twentieth century, but he never understood the market as well as Brown and Hayne. His failure in 1904 deranged the cotton trade. From St. Paul *Globe*, March 19, 1904.

the young Cotton King (though he was the same age as Brown) and printed his theory about seed deterioration.[3] Once he sold out his market positions in May 1903, with the price at eleven cents a pound, he had called Brown's margins in an unsuccessful attempt to tame the runaway market. Then he sailed for Europe early in June and, despite rumors about his role in Liverpool as the worldwide corner took shape, had apparently lost out on the bull movement crafted out of New Orleans. He had missed the most exciting action—the summer corner that lifted the price of cotton to fifteen cents. Back in New York in December, he bought his wife a Christmas gift: a

$300,000 six-story house (with twenty-five rooms and an elevator) on the newly developing Upper East Side.[4] A few weeks later, as the high summer prices showed some signs of persistence into the new year, Sully tried to reproduce the success of the New Orleans bulls.

Sully was a speculator, but he was never a cotton man in the same way as the New Orleans brokers. He had prepared for his bull campaign by diversifying, perhaps hoping to use profits from one field to support speculation in another. He bought seats on the New York Stock Exchange and the New York Coffee Exchange, the Liverpool Cotton Association and the New Orleans Cotton Exchange, and the Chicago Board of Trade. A big man in business, he was elected a director of the Merchants' Trust Company in December 1903.[5] Using his new celebrity as the Cotton King, he published an article in the *North American Review* justifying the bull position: high cotton prices were the product of supply and demand, not speculation. According to the Census Bureau's January 1904 report, Sully noted, the quantity of cotton ginned through December 13, 1903, was 400,000 fewer bales than up to that date the year before—when the high prices obtained by Brown and Hayne that fall should have "rushed" all the cotton to the market.[6] Thus even invisible cotton must be in short supply, he reasoned, and the high prices should continue through the spring.

Sully began to put together a new bull pool, and "tips circulated in Wall Street" that this network was "stronger than any before formed." According to the rumors, Sully's New York pool commanded between thirty and fifty million dollars, and united an unusual group of interests in the quest to keep cotton high: New England mills, speculating in the markets as the prices climbed, linked with New Orleans bulls and New Orleans banks that had profited so handsomely the summer before.[7] According to the reports, Brown would handle the New Orleans market while Sully worked in New York.[8] Nonetheless, as the last of the 1903–1904 crop began to reach the market in February 1904, the bears played the familiar short game, offering future deliveries at lower prices and thus trying to drive down the value of spots. They warned Sully that "if he did not desist he would find no mercy."[9] Even as bears drove down the price of future deliveries, Brown and Hayne "insist[ed] that the scare [was] unwarranted" and stood fast against the drop. They would not sell at the prices offered. As holders of spot cotton refused to sell until higher prices prevailed, and spinners from around the world were demanding spot cotton of their local factors, the price seemed bound to rise, not fall.[10]

The New Orleans bulls supported Sully into February, refusing to sell spots below 15.94. Brown had publicly predicted the price would yet reach 20 cents a pound.[11] But Sully had another holiday planned, a trip to Palm Springs in February. As his vacation neared, the price dropped in a "wide decline," which cost the New Orleans bulls heavily.[12] Sully blamed "too many shorts" unloading their contracts on the news of his plans to leave the market, and he cancelled his travel plans.[13] But the damage to his network was done. According to later reports, the New Orleans bulls felt that Sully had broken their agreement and "sold out on them." Crossing the New Orleans brokers was a bad idea. They understood the futures market and its monthly rhythms and did not need to wait long for "retribution."[14] On the afternoon of March 17, during a lull in trading, the superintendent of the New York Cotton Exchange read aloud a notice from Sully: "We regret that we are unable to meet our engagements and will therefore have to suspend." After a brief pause, the bears tossed their hats in the air and trading began:[15] "Coats were torn by frantic brokers in their mad efforts to unload their holdings and chairs and campstools were dashed into the **pit** to emphasize some wild broker's offer to sell."[16] Some observers estimated that 750,000 bales changed hands in the twenty minutes after the pronouncement, and the price dropped 250 points. Sully personally lost three to five million dollars in ten days. His liabilities were estimated at twice that.[17]

How could the young Cotton King have gotten it so wrong? Some newspapers reported a "hint of treachery" from New Orleans, where brokers sold while Sully was holding.[18] Indeed heavy sales originating in New Orleans helped lower the price, and in the Crescent City it was "pretty well understood that the local crowd have gotten even with Sully for their grievance."[19] Nonetheless, the continued bullishness of the New Orleans men quelled those rumors.[20] Some of the "best known cotton operators" indicated that it was the bears in New York instead who had "figured out the weakness of Sully's position" and driven down the price just far enough "to make it impossible for Sully to meet his margin calls."[21] Liverpool also held back "enormous supporting orders" long enough to require of Sully more money than he had. When the price on that exchange dropped thirty to forty points on his failure, its brokers were once again ready to buy.[22] Though reports from as far afield as Australia declared that Sully had written to the president of the Exchange to declare his troubles only temporary, his creditors refused his offer to settle his liabilities at forty cents on the dollar, the difference to be made up in two years. As a result, the "compulsory winding up of his estate" began.[23]

Sully's confidence and his steady nerve had given way to hubris, with the predictable result. In his hometown of Providence, Rhode Island, despite "great excitement" at the Chamber of Commerce, "there was no apparent regret that he had got into difficulties."[24] Philadelphia also rejoiced, noting that he "had no branch in this city ... had no bank accounts here," and the spot cotton interests of the city were not involved in the campaign.[25] The "deluge of his long cotton" that flooded the market when his affairs collapsed created "the biggest slump the market here had ever seen."[26] His failure shook more than just the American cotton market. Wheat, corn, and oats all dropped dramatically on March 18 as he liquidated his accounts on the Chicago Board of Trade.[27] The announcement of his suspension "convulsed Wall Street," and the lawsuits dragged on for years.[28] By April 1904, his failure was the butt of jokes: "I'm on my feet again," he told a business acquaintance, according to the "Man In the Street" column in the *New York Times,* but only because "I've sold my horses."[29]

Sully's firm went into the hands of receivers to make sure that all his creditors counted when dividing the assets of his firm. The bankruptcy proceedings revealed his affairs were a complicated tangle, in which he and his wife owned the majority interest in firms from whom (and for whom) he bought and sold in the first months of 1904. Like so many failures, it was not clear whether he was a liar or simply incompetent, bold or confused.[30] "After the failure" he "condemned his former associates in the cotton corner in strong terms," calling his friends "responsible for his troubles."[31] He lost his seat on the New York Stock Exchange. The new six-story house on Upper 62nd Street finally found a buyer in 1906.[32] Sully's failure broke only the heart of "Nig," the black cat who hung around the floor of the New York Cotton Exchange, who had been "always hailed as a sign of good luck by the bulls, who would bid the market up with great vigor whenever Nig came up to be petted and to purr." Without the young Cotton King around, she sickened and died a few months later.[33]

Sully's spectacular "skyrocket" and its destabilizing effects on the market reminded the public why corners were such bad things, bolstering the negative opinion of futures trading generated by Frank Norris's novel *The Pit.*[34] Sully's failure even had dire results for cotton farmers, along with a surging 1903–1904 crop. Farmers, likely influenced by the high price of 1903, produced nearly four million more bales than the previous season.[35] In December 1904, as the crop came to market, Brown urged the farmers to hold firm against the dropping price. He argued that ten cents a pound better reflected supply and demand than the costs below production emerging in early December—seven and a half cents in New Orleans, for example. Of all the bulls in the world, Brown knew how time changes everything. Low prices in the fall and winter might well give way to a spring and summer shortage if conditions were right. He urged farmers to hold their cotton, but they could not.[36] They needed the cash too much, however little their crop brought. Farmers were not yet in a position to help suppress supplies and force prices higher. Luckily for everyone, the weevils were.

Weevil Agency

The boll weevil had made its first appearance in the cotton-growing regions of the United States in 1892, spreading from Mexico into the vast cotton fields of the Gulf at the speed of 40 to 160 miles a year. The weevils' annual August migrations used wind to carry them further than their usual short flights; the hurricane that struck Galveston in 1900, for example, carried weevils deep into Texas. Farmers anticipating the weevil's arrival often made one last big crop. Then, tenant farmers and sharecroppers would leave the land, seeking new opportunities, disrupting long-established agricultural arrangements—oftentimes moving even before the pest appeared. The weevil wafted deeper and deeper into the Gulf and across the southwest, the postbellum centers of cotton production, as the twentieth century began. Town leaders and agricultural elites called meetings, the USDA and state agricultural societies sent educators, but the weevil infestation still spread. According to President Theodore Roosevelt, the State of the Union included "a serious menace to the cotton crop" by the end of 1904.[37] The boll weevil was an agent that brought cotton planters into the network of the bull traders.

Of course, weevils are but insects. What chance does a mere pest a quarter-of-an-inch long have of using its powers to effect historical change? To anthropocentric historians, weevil agency extends only so far as the beetles seek to live and to reproduce before they die. In order to survive, weevils eat the leaves of the cotton plant. Then, when the plant puts forth buds (squares), the weevils puncture the squares and lay their eggs inside. When the eggs hatch, the larvae eat the cotton fibers, grow into pupae, and then become adults. The bolls drop to the ground and release the adults.[38] According to evolutionary biologists, weevils were merely responding to their environment in their expansion from Mexico into the United States and their destruction of the cotton crop. That environment, however,

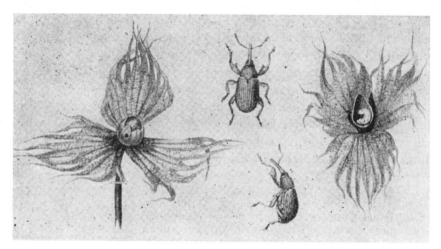

Figure 5.2 The boll weevil, a small insect that ate the cotton fibers in the boll before it was harvested, damaged cotton production and thus influenced prices as it moved up from Texas and across the South in the first two decades of the twentieth century. From Eugene Clyde Brooks, *The Story of Cotton and the Development of the Cotton States* (Rand McNally and Co., 1911), p. 326.

was the product of human effort and technology. The "cotton belt" had expanded throughout the nineteenth century as farmers tried to capitalize on expanding demand, and the wide miles of monocrop cotton provided a perfect home for weevils to pursue their goals. Human actions created conditions for weevils to thrive. Then the spread of the weevil called forth a response in humans that employed institutions and people, devices and objects and policies alike.

Humans were not the only things to act as agents and play a role in assembling the constantly shifting interactions even if they lacked conscious intention.[39] Buildings, of course, helped Brown corner the market. They represented his personal power and connections and helped to array New Orleans finance behind him for 1903. The weevil followed its own designs and, in doing so, played a significant role in the human history in which farm workers in the cotton belt sought better terms and more freedom, in which landlords sought to use rents to create profits, and in which merchants and middlemen and cotton brokers of the New Orleans Exchange cornered the market to raise the staple's price.

The agency of the weevil can partly be gauged by how much response it called forth from human actors—including not only the farmers but also brokers, including Brown, government scientists, and bureaucracies. State agricultural societies and the federal USDA all responded to the problem of the weevil with scientific experiment, the importation and testing of various insecticide measures, and new cultivation methods and sanitary efforts to prevent the bug from surviving the winter and increasing across the seasons. For farmers, the weevil inspired numerous actions. Farmers created a trove of folklore and music about the weevil and its impact on their lives. ("Well, the first time I seen a boll weevil/He was sitting on a square/And the next time I seen the boll weevil/He had his whole damn family there/They were looking for a home/Just looking for a home.") And some of them faced the problem with collective action. After becoming active in the Farmers' Alliance in the 1880s and the Populist movement in the 1890s, farmers had significant experience forming organizations, holding meetings, and calling on the government for help with their problems.[40] The threat of the boll weevil to the cotton economy of the Gulf stirred some of the region's farmers into familiar activist organizations.

Farmers' Movements

The Southern Cotton Association (SCA) was the latest in a long line of efforts to boost prices by limiting production.[41] While the SCA grew out of this general habit of southern farmers to talk about limiting production, its immediate antecedents were a series of regional conventions called to combat the boll weevil. Farmers from around Texas met in Dallas in December 1902, and then five hundred delegates assembled in Dallas in November 1903, to discuss how to respond to the weevil. Secretary of Agriculture James Wilson came down from Washington to lend his support. The first speaker at the convention outlined nicely the weevil's role as an actor in the cotton fields and its impact in the market:

> There are some good points about this insect. He is a first class bull in the cotton market, and we will never see any more six cent cotton as long as he is abroad in the land. His partner in price raising, Mr. Brown, takes profits and quits; but in the vocabulary of this little fellow there is no such word as "quit." We farmers have had convention after convention to curtail cotton acreage and reduce the crop, and each farmer rushed home and planted more cotton, thinking the other fellows would obey instructions and thereby raise the price. The boll weevil is doing for us exactly what we tried to do for ourselves and could not. I do not believe this insect would be a very bad investment if he was properly

distributed over the South. We would then raise an eight
million bale crop and get 15 cents a pound for it. What we
object to now is that Texas is doing all the reducing.[42]

At the same time this convention met in Dallas, representatives of
the New Orleans Cotton Exchange, the Shreveport Board of Trade,
and the North Louisiana Cotton Planters' Association persuaded
the governor of Louisiana to call a convention to meet in New
Orleans at the end of November 1903 to consider what action the
state legislature should take to prevent the boll weevil from devastating Louisiana's cotton crop as it had Texas's. The New Orleans meeting gave rise to an organization that called for a national boll weevil
convention. Governors of twelve cotton-producing states appointed
up to one hundred delegates apiece for this meeting in Shreveport
in December 1904.[43]

One of the delegates to the Shreveport conference was Harvie
Jordan, president of Georgia's Southern Cotton Growers' Protective
Association. He took a wider view of the problems facing the cotton farmers and was determined to do more than just battle bugs.
Taking up the point made at the Dallas convention, Jordan used
the Shreveport meeting as an opportunity to discuss further
plans: reducing the acreage for the next season and holding cotton off the market for better prices.[44] "The ruling spirit," wrote one
Georgia correspondent, "is that the boll weevil shall be killed and
the bears put to flight."[45] Local meetings were held across the South
in advance of another convention in New Orleans in late January
1905. Meeting in the same building that housed the 1884 World's
Industrial and Cotton Centennial Exposition, delegates from
across the South came to easy agreement on the policies to pursue and named Harvie Jordan the leader of a new Southern Cotton
Association.[46]

By mid-February 1905, enthusiastic farmers were reported to
be signing pledges to reduce both their acreage and the fertilizer
they applied. Holders of spot cotton—some of them likely its original growers—refused to deliver the goods for less than ten cents a
pound. They likewise stood united in their promises to "sign contracts to tie up the surplus part of the crop until next fall," creating
a summer shortage to keep the price high.[47] The SCA, like many
such organizations, used a network of organizers to travel the South
and drum up support for their program. A South Carolina cotton
farmer named Ellison D. Smith, later known as "Cotton Ed" Smith,
had attended both the Shreveport and New Orleans conventions

BRUIN'S SAD FATE.

Figure 5.3 This bear (trader), keen to get to the honey of low-priced cotton, found himself caught in a trap when the Southern Cotton Association organized to hold cotton off the market to increase prices. From the *Atlanta Constitution*, Jan. 25, 1905.

and become a fervent opponent of the bears in the cotton trade. Smith served as a field agent for the SCA, traveling his home state and further afield and gaining a reputation as "the most popular public speaker in South Carolina." This taste of public life convinced him to run for the US Senate in 1908.[48]

Southern farmers didn't have the money to hold their surplus cotton off the market, but William P. Brown did. Brown had heard farmers' angry pipe dreams about planting less cotton for years and had yet to see results. He knew that any successful approach to reducing cotton supplies had to encourage acreage reductions, but the farmers simply could not do that on their own. They had to pay their bills at the end of the year and could not wait for prices to rise. They needed allies in their network, partners to break the bind of the credit calendar that bears had used to keep prices low, supporters who could hold what cotton was produced off the market until spring or summer when prices would be higher. Even if hard-pressed farmers could not resist the temptation to plant a couple acres more than they had promised, waiting from the harvest glut until the summer shortage might well produce a higher price.[49]

Brown recognized the problem. Even before the New Orleans meeting, he had spearheaded a group of financiers in the cotton trade who were willing to "organize a fund, to be used in the purchase of cotton to be withdrawn from the market" with the goal of pulling 10% of the cotton off the market. That was more than enough to help the bulls.[50] At a meeting a week after the organization of the SCA, Brown, Hayne, and Abraham Brittin formed the Southern Planters' Commission and Holding Company in order to finance the SCA's plans.[51] If farmers had reason to thank Brown and the bulls for the higher prices after the 1903 corner, they now could see that these New Orleans bulls were on their side against the New York bears and would back the farmers' organization with cash.

Observers who listened to the SCA rhetoric about withholding cotton and minimum prices considered the organization a failure by the time it disappeared in 1908 because it had not succeeded in these goals. Populist politician Tom Watson attacked it for "running with Wall Street gamblers." That was precisely the point, except that it was Carondelet Street rather than Wall Street.[52] The SCA did not reduce cotton acreage and raise the price of cotton as Harvie Jordan thought it would. What it did do was to end the standoff between cotton farmers and cotton merchants in the South. Both groups wanted higher prices for cotton, and they knew they had to break the control of the New York bears to get them. The actions of the humble and hungry boll weevil provoked cotton farmers, yet again, into organizing, doing the work of mobilizing people and resources into a new social institution, the Southern Cotton Association. The New Orleans bulls saw the potential to draw this institution into an alliance, creating a broader social grouping of southerners of all economic positions interested in higher cotton prices. Where the farmers went, their politicians followed. Once they got political traction, these southern Democrats, especially "Cotton Ed" Smith, would implement legislation that would reform, but not destroy, cotton futures trading. But before the federal government could help cotton farmers, it would have to endure yet more humiliation at the hands of the more corrupt side of the New York market.

CHAPTER 6

Of Scandals and Sunshine

B Y 1905, THE COTTON FUTURES market had reached something of a deadlock. Neither bears nor bulls dominated, but
this did not mean that the market was working. It did not make
price mirror actual conditions of supply and demand. Perceptions of
supply could still be misused, and accurate information still needed
people with networks and resources to have any effect on the price.
The 1903 corner had marked the arrival of the New Orleans bulls
as a force to be reckoned with. These businessmen were capable of
turning the market in the direction they wanted it to go despite the
wishes of Liverpool or New York. At the same time, the weaknesses
of the long position in 1904 exposed just how tenuous was the bulls'
grasp on power. For a coup like 1903 to be possible, all the factors
had to be perfectly aligned, and that did not happen often. The federal government had done its best to make the market work better
for everyone by providing authoritative crop information, but its representatives still resisted any form of regulation other than sunshine.

"Sunshine" had been an important element of government regulation of enterprise since Charles Francis Adams had established
the Massachusetts Railroad Commission in 1869, and it remained
the guiding principle of regulation into the twentieth century.
Rather than trusting business to act in the best interests of society
or getting into the specifics of how a particular business operated,
this approach to regulation set up independent and impartial organizations that were granted the power to investigate the industries
they regulated. Bad practice and malfeasance would have nowhere

to hide once the state—and the people it represented—could bring information into public view.[1] It was another species of the disinterested information regarding supply and demand that government had been providing in the form of the crop reports disseminated by the Department of Agriculture and the Census Bureau.

Secretary of Agriculture James L. Wilson agreed that information made markets work better. A Scottish-born farmer from Iowa, Wilson had distinguished himself in the state legislature by chairing the agricultural committee and also requiring that railroads submit to state regulation. A farmer himself, he stood for the farmers; like so many of them, he saw all speculators as gamblers. From his perspective even bulls were gamblers, and they acted too late in the season to benefit the producer who sold out his crop in time to pay his bills.[2] For example, in August 1903, as the New Orleans bulls boosted the price of cotton, Wilson complained to the press that "infinite mischief is being done to the manufacturing industry and the cotton growing industry of the United States by this gambling movement."[3] He believed that futures trading involved only "fictitious produce," not real agricultural goods, and therefore was illegitimate by nature. His position reflected older views that all speculation was nothing but gambling on the price of a good.[4]

Popular opinion may have leaned the same way, but there were plenty of people in the South who disagreed. Manufacturers benefitted from hedging, and even some farmers' advocates knew what the bulls had done. A United States Senator pointed out that "Messrs. Brown and Hayne have done more for the producers in a few months than the Department of Agriculture has done in ten years."[5] For his own part, Brown was a southern gentleman and resented the insult of being publicly called a "common gambler." Poker Bill gambled, but when it came to the sophisticated markets of cotton futures, he was a legitimate speculator. When Secretary Wilson paid a visit to the floor of the New Orleans Cotton Exchange in late October 1903, Brown turned his back on the old man from Iowa and refused to shake his hand. Brown and his clique kept their faces turned to the ring, buying and selling cotton, pushing the prices ever higher.[6]

Further humiliations were in store for Wilson and the USDA. A pair of scandals in 1905 and 1906 showed just how vulnerable the cotton futures market still was to manipulation and chicanery. These scandals, in turn, convinced many that if the federal government really wanted to influence the cotton futures market, it would have to do more than just provide information about acreage and crop conditions. Rules in the cotton exchanges shaped the behavior of their members, but at the same time the members composed the exchanges. Their actions and transactions, their behaviors and their choices, and their committees and the rules they wrote shaped the institutions. In the New York Cotton Exchange, the congenial home of bear brokers intent on keeping prices low for their own profits, corruption crept in.

The 1905 Window-Shade Scandal

A scandal in 1905 destroyed the reputation for trustworthiness that the USDA had spent years trying to cultivate. It demonstrated that despite the best efforts of well-intentioned government officials, even sunshine could be corrupted. Government figures were intended to fight other numbers, produced by speculators, and the official statistics did not always win.[7] A trusted forecaster such as Henry Neill had long been able to "break the force" of government calculations, and claims that the administration's figures had been manipulated also undermined their effectiveness.[8] So too did any suggestion that some traders received the reports before others, as early information would give its possessors an unfair advantage and their actions might affect the price for all market players. The USDA worked hard to prevent this possibility. The Department insisted that state agents west of the Mississippi River telegraph their information to Washington in cipher and took pains to keep separate the various field reports that went into the final compilation, which took place just a few hours before distribution. Then the compiled crop reports went out first by telegraph rather than by mail so that places near Washington would have no advantage over more distant locations.[9]

Rumors of dishonesty were also a form of information, however, and on their own could create distrust in the government reports. Secretary James Wilson, in testimony before Congress in January 1904, denied rumors that crop reports had been leaked from his office, but similar rumors surfaced again in September when a New York cotton firm circulated a lucky guess about the crop condition that matched exactly the figure the government was to release a half hour later.[10] Responding to the September rumor, a USDA spokesman said, "It is very probable that some unscrupulous brokers, if any such there be, will make tempting offers to agents for 'inside information.' It places upon the agents a great responsibility, but I am sincere when I say that I believe that practically all of them are of a caliber to resist such temptation as may be placed before them."[11] Nonetheless, claims circulated that some traders had early notice of a report's contents, while every year allegations surfaced that a USDA employee had offered advance knowledge to someone. Stories like these undermined the effect of using transparency and information as a form of regulation.[12]

Wilson had faith in his statisticians, but even one dishonorable man could throw a wrench in the entire market mechanism. Edwin S. Holmes Jr., associate statistician in the USDA's Division of Statistics, helped the chief statistician prepare the crop reports. He also apparently knew the value of information. In August 1904 he met a New York cotton broker named Louis van Riper, who later attested that Holmes had offered to sell him information he tabulated himself using the state crop reports. For the next several months Holmes fed crop statistics to a go-between who relayed it to van Riper, who would make trades on the basis of the information before the state reports were compiled into the published version. Other traders were also involved in the scheme, including Theodore Price and F. A. Peckham, who gave Holmes a one-fifth interest in his cotton firm for a time—Holmes was not only selling information, he was trading himself. The men did other business together as well, investing in farmland, apartment houses, and a gold mine.[13] Even though the statisticians worked in a closed room, Holmes conveyed the information to the go-between by raising or lowering a window shade to signal whether the crucial numbers were higher or lower than had been anticipated.[14]

Soon Associate Statistician Holmes grew "immensely wealthy" and could be seen driving around Washington in a "stylish turnout."[15] It later emerged that the bean counter had not only supplied bear brokers with information but had manipulated the reports to suit their purposes. In order to fudge the numbers, Holmes tried to get his superior a job in the private sector so he could move into his position, but that plan failed. Nonetheless the Chief Statistician often made summer trips to Europe, which gave Holmes ample room to "juggle" the figures.[16] With his boss safely out of the country, Holmes was in charge of producing the June 1905 report, at the crucial period of the commercial year when the old crop was gone and the amount and timing of the new crop was the determinative factor in the market. Holmes followed the advice of his friends, adjusting the estimate a few times before official publication to make the June report "as bearish as they could make it."[17]

A former employee of van Riper told the whole story to the secretary of the Southern Cotton Association, who took the evidence to Washington. It was not easy to persuade Secretary Wilson, "an

Figure 6.1 The stylish buggy and fancy clothes of Edwin S. Holmes came from money he made by trading on inside information about the cotton market he acquired in his role as a statistician at the US Department of Agriculture. From the Atlanta *Constitution*, July 29, 1905.

old man, as honest as the day is long," of the corruption within his service, but after thorough consideration he suspended Holmes and brought in the Secret Service to carry out an investigation.[18] A broker with an office in New York but a wife from New Orleans alerted both the New York and the New Orleans Cotton Exchanges to the accusations. The NYCE president, Walter C. Hubbard, wrote to US President Theodore Roosevelt to declare himself "greatly shocked" by "the venality in the Department of Agriculture." When his letter was read at first call on the floor of the Exchange the members "cheered loudly."[19] Not all brokers were corrupt, and some had likely made trades on the basis of the manipulated information; unfortunately, when the Agriculture Department released a revised estimate to replace the falsified data, it relied on the existing reports, which the SCA secretary argued did not accurately represent acreage reductions that his organization had worked so hard to effect. He pointed out that Holmes had been "at his desk for several days after he knew that he had been found out" and could have discarded some crucial information. Some brokers even thought that the July figures were then also doctored in order to make up the difference caused by the fraudulent June report.[20]

Wilson explained to Roosevelt, in private correspondence, that he thought the imbroglio a family argument between two gamblers. Peckham's wife had deserted him for van Riper, who was jealous of the information Peckham was receiving from Holmes. Van Riper also felt that some of what Holmes told him was inaccurate.[21] Though Wilson had for years dismissed allegations of corruption in his statistical division and now made light of the evidence, he nonetheless announced new procedures for compiling the crop reports: no individual would have access to all the reports before the day they were compiled, and the telephones would be disconnected.[22] When it came time to put together the July report, Wilson locked all the staff in a room and kept the key in his pocket, with windows shut and shades pulled down to avoid the kind of signals Holmes had used. In the heat of a July afternoon in Washington, the statisticians were "wringing wet with perspiration" and had to "pound on the door some time before he [Wilson] let them out."[23] With these changes, and the departure of the disgraced Holmes, Wilson thought the scandal was finished. It had exposed the venality of speculators, but that need not tarnish the reputation of the USDA and its crop reporting.[24]

Wilson underestimated the damage done to the USDA's reputation, and, by extension, the reputation of the entire federal government in its attempt to rein in the power of business. No sooner were the results of the Secret Service investigation made known than rumors swirled that the Tobacco Trust had similarly manipulated tobacco crop reports, and perhaps all was not well with wheat and corn.[25] The Treasury also created a Committee on Departmental Methods, the Keep Commission, to examine the government's statistical work.[26] The Southern Cotton Association was far from satisfied. Wilson had argued that Associate Statistician Holmes could not be prosecuted since there was no applicable legislation banning the kind of insider trading he had performed, and he was right. Amazingly, it was not until the aftermath of the 2008 financial crisis that the sort of thing Holmes did became illegal in the commodity markets.[27]

The editorial page of the *New York Times* shifted the ground, writing, "The gravamen of this case is not in acting upon early information, but in corrupting a public officer and in falsifying sources of public information."[28] It was not an apple that was bad, but the barrel itself. Yet Wilson refused to give up the statistical work of the Department, knowing that the crop report "interferes with [bears'] full opportunity for exaggerating the volume of crops in the fall and buying them cheaply, then decrying the amounts in the spring when they want to sell." Discontinuing the crop reports would give the bears their "fat times" again.[29]

Harvie Jordan, president of the SCA, traveled to President Theodore Roosevelt's summer home in Oyster Bay, New York, to raise the issue with him, and the investigation then went to the Department of Justice. Roosevelt wrote to the attorney general that Holmes "is, in my judgment, a far greater scoundrel than if he had stolen money from the government, as he used the government in order to deceive outsiders and to make money for himself and for others."[30] Roosevelt may have been interested in placating southern planters for political purposes, and scandals such as this one threatened to undermine public trust in the federal government's ability to protect the public from the power of corrupt business practices. As the investigation proceeded, Holmes's boss, the chief statistician at the USDA since 1890, was forced to resign. Eventually Holmes was indicted for malfeasance in office and paid a $5000 fine.[31]

The window-shade scandal had several important effects on the relationship between the federal government and the cotton futures market. First, it undermined trust in the USDA as an honest source of unbiased crop information. For a number of years, especially since the 1899–1900 season, the USDA's position had been that accurate and timely information would empower cotton producers and prevent cotton brokers, especially the bears in New York, from driving the price down, a practice that enriched a few people in New York at the expense of millions of poor farmers in the South. The exposure of corruption that had gone unnoticed seriously damaged the USDA's reputation. Second, the experience drove a wedge between the SCA and the USDA. Wilson's initial determination to limit the scope of the investigation to Holmes's misdeeds, his defense of the Statistics office, his lack of interest in extensive reforms, and his own ultimately successful defense of his position gave the impression that the USDA was more concerned with its own reputation than with the interests of the cotton farmers of the South. Third, despite Wilson's reluctance, there was a fundamental shift in the way the USDA handled crop reporting for cotton. At first the response was further secrecy—the hot and airless room where sweaty statisticians compiled reports—but about a week later, after his Chief Statistician's resignation, Wilson changed the goal to "the entire absence of secrecy." From now on, "All reports coming to the bureau are to be placed at the disposal of the public . . . they will be announced from day to day, instead of being . . . periodical statements."[32]

In other words, the government response to the scandal was to use more sunshine as the way to make business operate fairly. No longer would the USDA try to beat the New York bears at their own game, using secret sources of information to produce oracular statements that were meant to overawe the public. Instead, the USDA shifted to more frankness and greater transparency in its provision of market information. It would become more of a clearinghouse for information as it came in. The USDA had staked its role in the market as the principal and most disinterested institution receiving detailed reports from around the cotton belt, transforming the crop into statistics by means of repetition and standardization, or having its correspondents fill out forms. Distributing the information immediately as it came in avoided the criticism that the USDA methodology was mere guesswork. It also marked a more confident stance for the federal government and the sunshine approach to regulation. The USDA believed it had the best information on the cotton crop, and that was enough. The market would take note of the correct data, supplied by disinterested sources, and respond accordingly.[33]

Ultimately, even if good and reliable information existed, it mattered little if the markets that used that information could be rigged. It mattered even less that only some brokers were corrupt if their self-regulated institution could bend to their wishes. While the bulls in New Orleans had succeeded in cornering the market once, their success did not effect any changes in the practices governing the NYCE that made it such a hospitable home for short sellers and bear trading. In the first few years of the twentieth century, the federal government put in place powerful mechanisms for compiling and disseminating what it considered to be the best possible crop information. Still, the New York Cotton Exchange remained powerful even as its position began to decline. A new scandal the next year would demonstrate in dramatic fashion the capacity for its corrupt practices to ruin men.

The 1906 NYCE Revision Committee Scandal

The 1906–1907 season began like any other, but a natural disaster turned into a commercial disaster because of shady practices at the NYCE. In the first week of September, correspondents for the *New Orleans Picayune* cheerily reported, "Cotton is opening rapidly in a greater portion of the territory and ideal weather permits a rapid harvest."[34] But on September 27, 1906 a hurricane made landfall at Biloxi, Mississippi, and moved inland up the Mississippi River valley. In addition to devastating the cities of Pensacola, Mobile, and Biloxi, the storm had disastrous effects on the cotton crop.[35] In Mobile, hundreds of bales simply floated down flooded streets and out to sea. As much as a third of the crop was still in the field, bolls open and ready to be picked, when the storm's winds plucked cotton from its bolls and bent stalks down into the mud. In many cases, the seeds in waterlogged bolls began to sprout. Estimates of the damage to the cotton crop in Alabama, Louisiana, and Mississippi ranged from 25 to 50 percent.[36] "A great deal of the cotton can be rescued from the mud," one newspaper reported, "but it will necessarily lose in grade."[37] Adverse weather could affect the market, as William P. Brown knew when he used the 1903 floods on the lower Mississippi River that wiped out thousands of acres of growing cotton as one of the tools to help corner the market. However, the 1906 storm did not wash the cotton away completely; it just damaged its quality.

Still, no one in the cotton trade worried too much about this since there was a mechanism for dealing with quality variations. A cotton futures contract was a **basis contract**; its price referred to cotton of middling grade. The seller had the option of delivering any grade of cotton, but if higher grade or lower grade cotton were delivered, the price paid would be different than specified in the contract. "The proper theory of a basis contract," one observer noted, "is that all grades shall be deliverable at prices which will make them commercial equivalents of each other."[38] The **difference** between the contractual price and the actual price paid for cotton received of a different grade ("on" meant that cotton was higher than middling, while "off" meant it was lower quality) was set by the exchanges in order to reflect the supply and demand of the various grades. By the beginning of the twentieth century, NOCE and NYCE used different methods to decide what the differences should be, with NOCE's method of **commercial differences** responding more quickly to changes in market conditions. The NYCE system of **fixed differences** only responded to changes in the market twice a year, in September and November. Brokers had learned to lower their prices to account for the likelihood that NYCE differences would have fallen somewhat out of line with the spot market. Establishing correct differences for futures contracts that matched the differences in the spot market in predictable ways was one of the most important things that made a futures market work fairly for everyone.

Figure 6.2 The New York Cotton Exchange was as lively as the one in New Orleans (see Figure 1.3), but it was the home of many of the bear traders in futures who made money by short selling. Its self-regulation resulted in corrupt practices that kept the price of cotton low. From *Harper's Weekly*, May 4, 1885.

What happened in the wake of the September 1906 storm exposed just how vulnerable the NYCE system of fixed differences was to exploitation by the New York bears. The storm hit in the last week of September, and by the first week of October, it was clear to the cotton trade that the 1906–1907 crop would have a lot of low-quality cotton and not much of high quality. They would need to price lower grades much lower since they would be in abundance, while the scarce higher grades would bring a greater premium. No one knew exactly what figures the NYCE revision committee would reach at its November meeting, but everyone assumed they would reflect this new reality. Trade continued on that basis.[39]

When the NYCE revision committee met on November 21, 1906, it confounded expectations. The differences the committee had set in September were revised, but only slightly—not as much as the storm had changed conditions in the spot market. For example, the NOCE commercial differences put low middling at 1.13 off, so that a delivery of low middling would be paid at more than a full cent per pound below the price stipulated in the basis contract; the NYCE revised its difference for that grade from 0.38 only down to 0.50. The results were disastrous. Some merchants who had bought contracts on NYCE to hedge lost $10 per bale. Buyers and exporters in Savannah lost around $1,000,000. The experience, claimed one, "has shaken the whole foundation of the cotton business."[40] The disruption to the cotton trade reached from brokerage firms, exporters, and banks right down to cotton farmers themselves. It reinvigorated the Southern Cotton Association after its 1905 plans to restrict acreage and push prices up had failed to make much of an impression on the markets.

With such a clear example of fraudulent practice, the SCA tried another way to bring the NYCE to heel. The SCA president Harvie Jordan and Rep. Leonidas F. Livingston of Georgia asked the postmaster general to issue a fraud order against the NYCE. A fraud order gave the postmaster general the right to refuse to deliver or send any mail from a business or organization involved in fraud, and the method had been used against lotteries and other ventures since the 1870s. The NYCE was no different than any other scam, Jordan and Livingston argued, since it was no longer a commercial spot market and since so much of the cotton actually delivered on future contracts was not suitable for spinning. The NYCE immediately threatened to sue both Jordan and Livingston for libel.[41] At the same time, the NYCE's president, Walter C. Hubbard, published an article—with a cheerful graph—showing southern cotton planters how well they had done in 1906, thanks to the revision committee of the NYCE. "The situation, in fact," Hubbard argued, "is developing in a way that tends to make some of the criticisms of the Exchange a little unwise."[42] Just in case those tactics failed, the NYCE did not have to go very far to get a good attorney to prepare its defense, if it came to that. Around the corner was the office of Cadwalader and Strong, one of the oldest and most powerful law firms in the country. A partner there went down to Washington a few days after the petition was filed to have a chat with the postmaster general and to stop in for lunch with President Roosevelt, presumably to suggest that the accusations against the NYCE were baseless.[43]

The postmaster general never issued the fraud order against the NYCE, so Livingston and another congressman from Texas next resorted to one of President Roosevelt's new bureaucracies, the Bureau of Corporations, headed by Herbert Knox Smith. In January 1907 the congressmen introduced a resolution to the House of Representatives calling for the Bureau of Corporations to investigate the NYCE, with the possibility of referring evidence of fraud to the Department of Justice for prosecution. The resolution as passed the next month expanded the scope to include New Orleans as well, and Herbert Knox Smith initiated a thorough investigation of the practices and effects of the nation's cotton exchanges that would continue for two more years.[44] The first three parts of Smith's report appeared in May 1908. Even in its incomplete form, the Bureau's analysis rendered a harsh indictment of the practices of the NYCE. With the exchange so thoroughly associated with the **short** interests, the fixed-differences system operated as just another tool in the arsenal of the bears.

The NYCE's system of fixed differences (adjusted only twice a year) and the large number of grades (many of them unspinnable) produced a situation where the **margin** between future prices and spot prices fluctuated widely and unpredictably. When the market was working properly, the price of future contracts converged toward the spot price as the date of future delivery drew near. Though prices would change from month to month, the margin between spot price and future price for the current month should remain constant. It was this constancy of the margin—called "parity"—that was predictable and that made hedging, the most important and constructive role played by the futures market, possible. While critics saw futures contracts as simply a form of gambling or a means of manipulating the market, they served a crucial and legitimate purpose in hedging against the risk of changing prices. If the margin between spot and future prices were subject to unpredictable swings, however, hedging actually became more dangerous than not hedging. Only the gamblers stood to benefit.[45]

Unpredictable margins between spot and future prices also prevented the useful function provided by speculation: allowing market information to shape prices. Fixed differences put all the power in the hands of sellers, allowing them to play the differences as set by the revision committee and deliver—or threaten to deliver—grades of cotton that were overvalued by NYCE's fixed differences and that could never actually be sold again for the price paid. The link between spot prices and future prices was broken. Good crop information of the kind Henry G. Hester, the USDA, and others had been trying for years to provide to the market could affect spot prices, but in the NYCE's system these spot prices were unable to have a normal and proper—and predictable—influence on future prices. The legitimate function of speculation was to use the best possible market information to make price predictions and act on them, accepting the risk that entailed. But in the NYCE's system, with price differences of the different grades settled occasionally by committee, all speculation became mere gambling.

And that was before considering downright corruption. Herbert Knox Smith's report stopped a hair's breadth from charging New York brokers with fraud over the November 1906 revision. The revision committee's failure to widen the differences between middling and the lower grades after the September hurricane threw so much lower grade cotton onto the market was, the Bureau of Corporations concluded, "improper." It caused future prices to plunge and caused "enormous losses to holders of contracts in the New York market."[46] Several members of the NYCE revision committee admitted that they had been short of the market or had been holding considerable quantities of low-grade cotton when they made the decision not to change the differences to reflect the new conditions. They reaped tremendous profits as a result. "While, therefore, it cannot be asserted absolutely that the action of any members of the committee were taken with such deliberate intent [to establish false differences]," Smith concluded, "the evidence at least condemns beyond question a system which makes such abuse possible, and, indeed, extremely probable."[47] Still, Smith stopped short of insisting that any crime had been committed. No prosecution ensued.

Smith's investigation contributed to the process of illuminating the futures trade and how its practices affected the market mechanism. Now, in its investigation of the practices of the cotton exchanges, the Bureau of Corporations had begun to recognize what worked: how derivatives could allow information about market conditions to shape prices, and the ways that corruption could cause such trading to benefit speculators rather than its real market functions. Recognizing corruption, however, was only a first step on the path to using regulation to make the market work better. Without actual laws outlining which practices were allowed and which were not, people with interests in particular outcomes could still use whatever means their private institutions allowed to create the outcomes they desired.

The corruption of the NYCE and its revision committee—its population of bears with interests in keeping prices lower than supply and demand justified—meant that manipulation had too powerful a hand in shaping the price of cotton. Nonetheless, because the price was a product of manipulation rather than real market conditions and good information about those conditions, the underhanded practices of the bears left them vulnerable. Undaunted by the failure of Sully, away down in New Orleans the bulls were still active. When market conditions were right, the crooked bears and the dishonesty enabled by the New York Cotton Exchange provided the bulls with a new opportunity to corner the market.

CHAPTER 7

The Revenge of the Bears

LEGISLATORS HAD DEMANDED REPORTS ON the cotton exchanges, and regulators created them. The Bureau of Corporations published its first reports in May 1908. These investigations had denounced the practices of the New York Cotton Exchange, especially its pricing of different grades, which had damaged the market so severely in 1906. The sunshine approach to regulation quickly became inadequate, however. Without actual regulation—laws to forbid specific behaviors and institutions to enforce those laws—profitable practices, however disreputable, would continue. New York bears had learned how to make money by shorting the market to keep prices low. But because those low cotton prices had developed from market manipulation and the corruption of market information rather than real changes in supply and demand, the bears were left vulnerable to corners and bull campaigns that raised the price when conditions were right. As in 1903, these conditions included not only supply and demand shocks, but also hubris by bears who had for so long controlled prices through bravado and banknotes. In addition to hubris, the New York bears had connections. When William P. Brown put together a new bull campaign from New Orleans and threatened again to corner the market in 1910, the bears made use of their own networks to beat the bulls back.

According to some accounts, Sully's failure in 1904 had allowed the bears to resume the practices of short selling that depressed cotton's base price.[1] The 1905 and 1906 scandals and

Herbert Knox Smith's 1908 report showed that ample room for price manipulation still existed—whether the corruption reached into the government bureaus intended as providers of disinterested information, as in the case of the USDA's 1905 window-shade scandal, or only as far as the cozy confines of the New York Cotton Exchange and its revision committee in 1906. Without regulation, the market mechanism was not working accurately to allow supply and demand to establish the price. Nonetheless, despite the efforts of bear operators, the price of cotton slowly and fitfully rose after the successful bear attack on Sully in the spring of 1904. Supply was often short of demand, which is why bear operators, so practiced in shorting the market and profiting from the resulting depressed price, needed to resort to manipulations to continue their successes.

The Panic of 1907, however, punctured the rising prices in the cotton trade. In 1906–1907, the cotton crop had broken records at 13.5 million bales, but the 1907–1908 crop presented poorer prospects. High prices prevailed for the first nine months of 1907, for both raw cotton and finished goods. Mills signed contracts many months ahead to deliver high priced goods, riding "an extraordinary world-wide demand" for goods manufactured of cotton. Although manufacturing capacity was rising "in all industrial countries beyond anything ever known before," demand for cotton goods was keeping up while the boll weevil still threatened supply. The high prices of mills' futures contracts led "most sane observers" to view the cotton market as "highly inflated and overextended." Cotton was not the only market in this condition. In October the bubble burst. The 1907 Panic, "with its paralysis of credits and utter uncertainty as to the future," lowered all prices. In New York, middling cotton dropped from 13.5 cents a pound to 10 cents in seven months, while print cloths fell from 5.75 to 3 cents per yard. The cotton trade spent 1908 adjusting its contracts to meet the new conditions and, despite heavy losses "in many directions," the thirty-five Fall River mills in Massachusetts paid an average 6.9% dividend, and a hundred Lancashire mills averaged profits of 16% for the year ending November 30, 1908. Profits had been higher in 1906 and 1907, of course, but these figures indicate that cotton mills had weathered the 1907 Panic safely.[2]

The mills were ravenous. Despite the developing panic, world consumption of cotton reached 18.86 million bales in the year beginning September 1, 1907. The next year spindles consumed 19.5 million bales, and in 1909–1910 they would require between

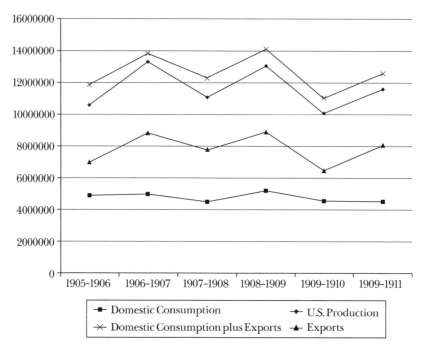

Figure 7.1 Supply and Demand, 1905–1911

If overproduction had ever really been a problem for the United States in the cotton trade, that was no longer true by the latter half of the 1900s. In every season, the amount of cotton produced in the United States was less than the combined total of bales consumed and bales exported, conditions that made another bull campaign all but inevitable.
Source: Department of Commerce, Bureau of the Census, *Bulletin 125: Cotton Production, 1913*. Washington, D.C.: GPO, 1914, p. 29, Table 15.

20 and 21 million bales. If "all the world's spindles were kept busy throughout the year," they would actually need about 22.5 million bales of raw cotton, but there would not be 22.5 million bales available. In 1907–1908 the United States produced only 11.5 million bales; "spinners and merchants" had held in reserve a million bales more from the previous US crop, and the remainder came from Egypt and India, both of which had produced larger than usual quantities. The next year (1908–1909) proved the largest crop on record, at 13.8 million bales, but "purchases by spinners kept pace." By early 1909 "it became apparent that spinners were going to take more American cotton for the year than they had ever taken before." Prices deflated in the aftermath of the 1907 Panic did not stay low for long. That fall and winter the New York price of middling cotton never dropped below nine cents, which had seemed "exceedingly high" just ten years earlier.[3]

The 1909–1910 Corner

These conditions combined to make the cotton market ripe for another corner by bull operators. First among these circumstances was the environment of the market: mills needed ever-increasing quantities of cotton from the fields of the US South, but that supply was volatile and varied year by year. Second, information available to all tended to help the bulls, especially because bear operators did not operate in response to accurate information. They believed themselves impervious to market conditions and manipulated prices to suit themselves—and that was the third condition for running a successful corner. Taken together, bear hubris, market conditions, and good information provided bulls wiser than Dan Sully their next opportunity. The huge crop that reached the market beginning in fall 1908 may have persuaded the bears that their short positions would last, but the long-term trend was in the opposite direction. So were the bull operators.

On November 16, 1908, the first contracts for delivery of the 1909–1910 crop were made in New York at 8.35 cents per pound. By January 4, the first business day of 1909, the price was 8.75 cents and by January 23 had reached 9.5 cents per pound, where the price stayed until April.[4] By then, the planting season had begun. The eastern crop was fine, but across the central and western growing regions, heavy rains in April, May, and June prevented growers from planting as usual in the first half of 1909. What was planted stood uncultivated, and what was cultivated "had been so nearly drowned out that it was badly stunted." The wet spring likely explained the flourishing of the pink boll rot, a fungal disease.[5] This meant that an "unfavorable planting season" led into "a still more unfavorable period for cultivation."[6] Then came a hot, dry summer which, according to some reports, "played havoc with the small bolls." The crop was very light, even without taking into account the boll weevil, advancing in 1908 and 1909 from Louisiana into Mississippi.[7] With the weather and the weevil at work, some calculations indicated that fall 1909 would be a "crop disaster."[8]

Nonetheless, the textile mills of New England were "selling ahead on goods and yarns without hedging."[9] This was extraordinary behavior. Cotton was typically hedged from the time it was harvested (sometimes from the time it was planted) until someone finished sewing the clothing it eventually became; there was no other reliable way of guarding against price fluctuations. Yet the northern manufacturers were promising future deliveries of their finished products at lower prices than the cost of their raw materials. Perhaps they were misled by the assessment offered at the end of April 1909 by the president of the National Association of Cotton Manufacturers. He thought that the "spinnable superiority" of the large 1908 crop would result in "greater goods production" and an excess the next year—even though he recognized that the 1909 crop would need to be at least as large as the one harvested in 1908 in order to meet the "augmented requirements" of the mills.[10] Despite the rainy weather through the spring and summer, cotton manufacturing trade publications indicated in July 1909 that the new crop might be large: 3.3 million bales had already moved into sight, compared to 2.7 the year before—a figure more in line with the usual movement of the crop to market.[11]

Lancashire also was, according to a report in the *Textile World Record*, "talking short time because of high priced cotton and large stocks of unsold yarn. Under these conditions the advance in prices has somewhat the appearance of manipulation."[12] If manipulation were the cause of high agricultural prices, then perhaps spinners were making sensible predictions. Then again, perhaps the New York bears had led the US textile manufacturers to a fatal miscalculation. Some observers of the market claimed that "the clique of bear gamblers here [in New York] assured them that they would drive cotton back down ... and hold it there until they could stock up" on raw cotton.[13] Short sellers did not hesitate to incorporate manufacturers into their networks when they bet on lower prices and believed they could make the bear market a reality, as they had done so many times before. Regardless of the reason, the spinners and bear brokers of New York and New England were betting on lower prices and playing a dangerous game.

Brown and Hayne once again prepared excellent bait for the bears. Their method was much the same in 1909–1910 as it had been seven years earlier. They would buy cheap contracts for future delivery far in advance, at lower than spot prices, which bears were offering in their usual attempt to force prices lower. Then, when delivery came due the next summer, the bulls would happily pay for the promised cotton—at the lower price. The bulls calculated that cotton prices would rise, however, because less cotton existed than the bears had gambled. To make deliveries, bearish short sellers would have to buy at the ever-rising prices, and then deliver it for the lower figures their contracts had promised.[14] If not enough cotton existed—if the summer shortage reached the extreme point it had done in late summer 1903—they would have to settle their contracts at whatever price the bulls who had bought those promises would accept. The summer shortage was the hinge on which a successful corner—or even just a simple rise in price—would turn.

Brown and Hayne were not the only people taking advantage of the bears' short sales by using a summer shortfall. Lots of people had made that calculation and would therefore buy those contracts from the bears. Brown and Hayne enlisted cotton spinners and manufacturers from Alabama, Georgia, and the Carolinas into their plans, and their promises to purchase cotton in the future gave the New Orleans bull pool a cushion of financing—a guaranteed demand for the deliveries the bears might make on their contracts.[15] Some of the people trading the long side of the market were also hooked into different networks, such as Morris H. Rothschild, a German Jewish immigrant who ran a dry goods store and a cotton warehouse and owned 20,000 acres of plantation land in a cotton processing and marketing town in southwest Mississippi known as "Little Jerusalem."[16]

There were also more bulls trading outside the New Orleans clique. Eugene G. Scales, for example, was a veteran of the 1903 campaign, but this time it seems that he struck out on his own. Born in Texas during the Civil War, by 1900, he was managing an oil mill near Killeen. Legend had it that he pawned his watch for $200 (some sources said $800) to get into trading in New Orleans. After his participation in Brown's 1903 bull pool he became "one of the biggest cotton operators in the South."[17] By late 1909, Scales was trading in New York, buying considerable quantities of cotton for future delivery. Some thought that he was associated with the most famous bull trader of the day, the Chicago Wheat King James A. Patten. Patten had made a name for himself over the previous decade by cornering a variety of grains—oats in 1902, corn in 1908, and wheat in 1909. He saw similar opportunities in cotton.[18] In addition to celebrities like Patten, there were other powerful traders outside the South who thought the bears were wrong and took the bulls' position, going long in the market. Robert Means Thompson was a Boston attorney and Navy veteran before getting involved in mining in the 1870s. He made a fortune as the first chairman of the International Nickel Company in 1902, and he used some of that money to become a silent partner in S.H.P. Pell and Company, his son-in-law's cotton brokerage.[19]

These men went long in the cotton market, but whether or not they did so in association with William P. Brown would never be proven. Brown spent the fall of 1909 in New York City, buying at low prices the promise of future deliveries, taking the first steps toward huge profits in the summer when supply grew tight and prices rose. Visible cotton had already begun to vanish by October, very early in the crop calendar.[20] Prices touched fifteen cents from time to time that fall. High quotations stimulated "immense profit-taking," but still the rates remained relatively calm—an "ominous calm"—through the first week of December, as the harvest wound down and the trade awaited the new government reports.[21] On December 8, 1909 the Census Bureau revised downward an estimate provided by the National Ginners' Association, from 9.43 to 9.36 million bales already ginned.[22] Two days later, the USDA released a "sensationally low estimate" that the 1909–1910 crop would total no more than 10.08 million bales. By Christmas Day, reports indicated that "ginning is practically over" and confirmed the USDA prediction of little more than ten million bales. "Despite the aggressive retaliatory tactics resorted to by the spinning element of the trade," future prices reached sixteen cents by Christmas Day—nearly double the price of the first contracts made more than a year earlier.[23] It was Christmas indeed in New Orleans.

For the bears, the bad news kept coming. In January 1910 the government reported that only 9.8 million bales had reached the gins, which "practically confirmed the agricultural bureau's estimate" of 10 million bales total.[24] The "admitted demand by spinners" stood at 13.5 million bales, and this figure seemed conservative.[25] The previous year the world's spindles had together consumed between 13.3 and 13.4 million bales, while new mills had since opened in England.[26] It was very early in the season for such a threat to bear dreams. Usually a crop shortage would come in the summer, in the gap between one crop reaching market and the next being harvested. With a shortage emerging in January, the summer threatened catastrophe. The vice president of the NYCE publicly recognized, in the pages of the *New York Times,* that "insatiable was the demand from spinners."[27] The bears, as ever, were selling low-priced contracts for future delivery, but it was not just the bulls who were buying. Spinners were also buying with the expectation of actually taking delivery at the discount prices. Since they had not hedged, the only way they could get their cotton was to let the contracts mature and demand delivery. If the price did not actually fall as the bears expected, the bears would be faced with both bulls and mills demanding cotton they could not produce. Brown openly predicted an eventual twenty-cent price.[28] Yet the low-priced contracts made back in the fall of 1908 still stood and threatened to come due when the price was peaking and real cotton could not be found.

By January 1910, the New York and New England interests "realized into what a hole they had sold themselves for May, July and August delivery."[29] At first they worked to lower the price, as the brokers had promised the manufacturers they could do. Two bear raids drove down the price a cent each time, but in the face of the continuing grim government reports, the downward impulse lacked momentum.[30] It took considerable volume to effect a price slump in January. In New York, "the group of operators and brokers who gather in Delmonico's afternoons" believed that one day's business (January 14) "had never been exceeded on the floor." Though no one yet recorded the number of individual transactions, the crowd at upscale restaurant Delmonico's believed that contracts for a million bales had traded hands in a single afternoon, and trading did not conclude until after 5:00 p.m.[31] The next day, the price of futures lay "below the parity of spots" (futures for the current month were always a bit cheaper than spots since it cost money to actually handle the cotton if it were delivered—but in this case, that gap was greater than these costs), despite government information reporting an impending scarcity in the summer crop gap.[32] The bears' strategy was risky, almost desperate. To break prices down, they had to sell large volumes of contracts. If they sold large volumes and drove prices back down, they were in the clear. But if the prices did not fall and instead continued to rise in response to the limited supply and insatiable demand, they had just dug themselves in deeper, so deep they could not hope to climb out.

Even momentary success by the bears could destroy the fortunes of an overextended bull, however. The bears employed tactics that had worked, even if only briefly, in 1903 and 1904. They called margins "with great exactness." They were aided in driving prices down a hundred points in a single day by a storm that cut telegraph contact between New York brokers and "their connections west and south." This "prevented buying orders coming in by bargain-hunters in the outlying districts" and delayed the arrival of such purchases from Liverpool. Commission firms who wanted "additional margin" from their clients but could not reach them via wire instead sold their contracts, further lowering the price. Those with limited resources could get caught on a "tobaggan" of prices coasting downward at increasing speed. Eugene Scales began to sell in the middle of January, according to some accounts, and rapidly lost six million dollars on his contracts, adding another two millions to the debit side of his accounts before the month was through. Despite his losses, he was not driven entirely from the market and would reappear in the summer, shuttling between the Oriental Hotel in Dallas and the Waldorf Astoria in New York, as the war between bears and bulls heated up.[33]

Brown and Hayne spent most of that January in New York, fighting the battle against the shorts. "Calm and serene in the midst of all the speculative carnage . . . backed up by a daily strengthening statistical position," the bull leaders sent signals to both "frightened shorts" and "weak longs" of their confidence that prices would soon begin to rise. They took quick profits on the price spurts their appearance in the pits could stimulate.[34] At the end of that month, once the bears had pushed futures lower than spots, Brown headed back to New Orleans to celebrate Mardi Gras. For a New Orleans businessman, not even a cotton corner could stand in the way of celebrating with his krewe. He stopped to visit with an old friend for a few minutes on the station platform in Atlanta, and a newspaperman asked for a word. Brown spoke plainly: "The crop is, as has been published, 10,300,000 and . . . consumption is at the rate of 13,000,000." He refused to say that the price slump was due to speculation, but instead ascribed it to the unloading of longs, perhaps including Scales's difficulties in his calculations. "Remember I am a member of both exchanges," he explained, "and want to be very careful how I am quoted."[35] Little cotton from the crop remained, he pointed out. Even if the "entire visible supply" of the world reached the mills, supply in the summer would fall far short of demand. As long as spot cotton held firm, the bears were in trouble. Nonetheless, Fuller Callaway, accompanying Brown on the train, came out to report news of a 14 to 29 point slump, and Brown climbed back aboard.[36]

At this point, however, the bulls had stumbled. Bringing the Wheat King Patten into the pool was probably a strategic error, however useful his trading skills and cash might have been. Patten was a known villain. He had cornered the market in wheat the year before, making at least $2 million for himself and another $2 million for his backers in April 1909. His photograph on the cover of *Harper's Magazine* in May 1909 was captioned "The Man Who Raised the Price of Bread." His corner was also the subject of an early film by D. W. Griffith, *A Corner in Wheat*, which ended with the speculator slipping into a grain elevator and smothering in the wheat.[37] Public feeling was likewise rising against those who cornered commodities markets in order to raise the prices of raw materials. After all, higher agricultural prices damaged not only the plans of manufacturers but also the budgets of consumers who needed clothes as much as bread. Unlike cotton, much of which was shipped overseas directly or made into cloth that was traded to foreign countries, grain was consumed at home. Patten's corners pushed up the price of bread for the masses, making him a target of hatred for those who opposed futures trading in general.

The "wholesale condemnation from every part of the world" that Patten received from his wheat speculation carried over from one commodity to the next.[38] When he went to England and visited the Manchester Cotton Exchange in March 1910, he was "jostled and driven out" into the street by "hustling and hooting" mobs of brokers.[39] He took refuge in an office on Exchange Street. Though the booing and hooting crowd pursued him there, Patten eventually found an exit down a fire escape, into a cab waiting to take him the station. The gathering corner in cotton, the one run by the "Wheat King," was apparently well known to cotton brokers who had long made their profits by keeping prices low—and not just in Manchester.[40]

The Bears Deploy Their Networks

As the New York bears stared down their summer shorts watching spring prices marching upward, "they saw no honorable, legitimate way out."[41] So they turned to their friends in high places to attack the bulls on battlefields other than the rings of trade. The New York Cotton Exchange did not lack for powerful connections. Its own counsel was Henry W. Taft, who was at that moment also serving as a special assistant in the office of the New York District Attorney.[42] Back in 1882 he had served a kind of unpaid apprenticeship—an arrangement that gave "desk room" and experience to recent law graduates—with the valedictorians of two classes at Yale Law School, one of whom later became Solicitor General of the United States. Another man at the desk would later become president of the New York City Bar Association, while another became Chief Justice of the US Supreme Court. Yet another was George W. Wickersham. Wickersham entered the prestigious law firm Strong & Cadwalader in 1883, and Taft joined him there in 1889, while the firm was moving from skyscraper to taller skyscraper on Wall Street, and "built his reputation defending corporate interests, especially railroads and banks."[43] When the government hired a trustbuster, Taft's "intimate knowledge of corporate practices" made him an excellent match.[44] In 1909, Wickersham was appointed US Attorney General—by Henry

Taft's brother, William Howard Taft, the president of the United States.[45] With Taft as its lawyer, the network of the NYCE had direct links to both the highest office in the land and the nation's most powerful prosecutor.

On Tuesday afternoon, April 19, 1910 seven members of the New York Cotton Exchange filed in to a federal grand jury courtroom in New York City "to aid in an inquiry into an alleged pool to corner the crop of cotton" in May and June.[46] Ernest E. Baldwin represented at least three of them. He had been Taft's predecessor, the lawyer for the New York Cotton Exchange in the first years of the twentieth century, at the same time serving as assistant US attorney. Baldwin also represented a man named David H. Miller, who somehow possessed "exact knowledge" of a secret agreement among the bulls dated February 26, 1910. This was the very piece of evidence that prosecutors would use in their case that the bulls had acted in restraint of trade, in violation of the Sherman Antitrust Act of 1890.[47] Miller was a trader on the New York Cotton Exchange and intricately bound into its network. Together with Henry W. Taft, Miller had been the receiver for the failed firm of Daniel J. Sully & Co. in 1904.[48] Soon after Taft recommended Miller for a postmaster's job, describing

Figure 7.2 Henry W. Taft (second from right, back row) was the attorney for the New York Cotton Exchange, and his connections linked the institution into networks of power. He was also the law partner of George Wickersham, who served as Attorney General in the administration of President William H. Taft, Henry's brother (center, front row). Library of Congress.

him as "much respected by the members of the [New York] Cotton Exchange."[49] As the grand jury heard the testimony of the New York brokers, Miller had a copy of the bull pool's contract "in his pocket." He also demonstrated "inside knowledge ... of the facts in possession of the Federal authorities."[50]

The contract that Miller shared with the grand jury alleged that the New Orleans bulls had agreed with a host of unindicted coconspirators—mostly southern textile manufacturers, recruited by J. W. Cannon, Lewis W. Parker, and Fuller E. Callaway—to purchase futures in 300,000 increments (half for the spinners, half for the brokers), hold it for a rise in price, and then sell at a profit. The restraint of trade took place, according to the indictment, when the parties to the contract agreed not to sell until a certain date or until a certain price were reached (November 1, 1910, or fifteen cents, respectively). Likewise damaging, according to the prosecution, was the agreement to take any cotton tendered on contracts out of the market—to have it "shipped out of New York City" and to forbid its retender on the New York, New Orleans, or Liverpool market before November 1.[51] In their defense, the bulls argued that this would "return [cotton] to the legitimate channels of trade," to the mills rather than the speculators on the exchanges. The spinners must have agreed, since they had contracted (according to the prosecution) to receive the cotton at the higher price bull brokers could produce. Wickersham, however, was happy to learn of that explanation, as "it gives a suggestion of their line of defense."[52]

Evidence against the men included their telegrams, which indicated more casual, friendly understandings. Callaway, Parker, and Cannon found southern spinners ready to buy cotton at the higher price to which the bulls would push the market. Their promises probably provided a cushion of capital for the bulls in their battles against the bears. The money needed to pull off a corner likely came—as did the crop information on which the bulls had been betting back in 1902—from a wide array of sources. For example, Brown heard from a correspondent working a section for transactors who wired a report that he "had none signed up but ... 60 agreed to." Brown replied that he wanted him to "get the different parties as you get them in line to sign up the agreement. In that way we will clinch the matter and get through with it much quicker."[53] Those manufacturers who signed the contract with the bulls agreed not to sell their cotton contracts or any spot cotton they happened to acquire.[54] These agreements, the basis for the grand jury's indictment, dated from the end of February, but Callaway at least had been working by Brown's side a month earlier, when the two men stopped on the platform in Atlanta on their way from New York to New Orleans for Mardi Gras.[55] Brown had taken a long view, as well as a long position, when constructing his network.

Callaway, Parker, and Cannon—the spinners in the bull pool—represented major manufacturing interests across the South. Lewis Parker had been a South Carolina lawyer before entering the textile business near the start of the twentieth century. He bought firms until, before the First World War, he was president or treasurer of sixteen mills comprising 525,000 spindles. James W. Cannon had made towels the basis of a cotton empire centered on Kannapolis, North Carolina, and had been responsible for advertising and branding carried out by his son as those business strategies had first developed in the home goods markets in the 1920s. No men were better respected or bigger players among southern spinners. Fuller Callaway, too, was a textile manufacturer from Georgia. He had invested in his first mill in 1895, at the age of twenty-five.[56] These New South industrialists found their interests aligned with those of the bull brokers. They had joined the network first formed among the brokers, banks, and buildings that Brown linked together back in 1902, then parlayed into the spectacular corner of 1903. The most powerful spinners in the region were on Brown's side. They stood ready to buy cotton at the price they knew he could produce on the exchanges.

Why would spinners and their representatives ally themselves with the bulls who were raising the price of the raw material that went into their products? Economically one might think that cheaper raw materials are always better for those who use them, but in fact the volatility in prices made planning and pricing difficult for spinners and manufacturers, which is why they usually hedged their purchases. Regular and predictable prices for ginned cotton allowed mills more certainty in pricing their own goods, the finished textiles they produced. Manufacturers sold goods for delivery in the future, as far as a year ahead of time. Such firms viewed futures trading on the exchanges and the hedging that futures trading permitted as crucial protections "against violent fluctuations in prices" of both raw materials and finished goods.[57] It is possible, too, that the high-handed attitude of the New York brokers inspired some sectional feeling on the part of southern manufacturers, physically surrounded as they were by southern cotton farmers.[58] The bears' condescending behavior won them few friends among the southern textile manufacturers. The story of how the contract between bull brokers and southern spinners eventually came into the hands of the New York district attorney demonstrates both the attitude of the New England interests and its results.

The Smoking Gun

W. B. Tanner, treasurer of the Montgomery Cotton Mills in Alabama, had been approached around March 1, 1910, about "acting in cooperation with other spinners in the South and purchasing cotton on the New York Cotton Exchange," with the purpose of "preventing manipulation of the market and to steady the market at a price which seemed legitimate, based upon the law of supply and demand." It seemed like a good plan to Tanner. He thought the price would soon rise, that low prices were the product of "manipulation of cotton prices on the New York Cotton Exchange," specifically the bear raid of January, which then had created "a consequent decline in cotton-goods prices," including those made by his own mill. This "demoralization" of prices in both raw materials and finished goods seemed to him unnatural and bound to change. Yet Tanner also wanted to know more about the men behind the offer. He had long "reposed confidence" in the New York cotton merchants Craig & Jenks, his "confidential advisers in cotton matters" with whom he regularly traded information about the cotton market.[59] Tanner informed them of the offer and asked their advice. Could Craig & Jenks vouch for Brown and Hayne? Were they perhaps in business together on the New York Exchange?[60]

Approached by the bulls (probably by Fuller Callaway), Tanner had asked his friends in New York what they knew of the plan. He thus inadvertently revealed the bull campaign to the bears. In response, Craig & Jenks accused the bulls of "scouring the earth" for help raising prices to relieve their long positions—to raise the price so they could sell their contracts without a loss. This they characterized as an "utterly footless, uncommercial, and highly speculative" strategy—not remarking that this was exactly what the bears would need to do to meet their obligations, although in reverse—to lower the price of cotton as contracts came due, so they could buy bales to deliver on their contracts. Craig & Jenks spoke rather cruelly to Tanner. "The very idea of a spinner entering into cahoots with a lot of professional speculators is abhorrent to a conservative business man," they told him. They threatened that "the treasurer of the mill that entered into any such deal" should be "promptly fired from the corporation." Though Tanner had asked that his inquiry be kept confidential, they asked his permission to share it "without even naming the point from which it comes."[61] The treasurer requested a meeting; at first the New York firm dismissed the idea, then summoned him to their offices.[62] There, on April 29, Tanner learned that the document he had sent for approval would be submitted by its recipients to the US District Court as part of a case against Brown and Hayne.[63]

Craig & Jenks was one of the firms that Ernest Baldwin represented, and he joined the meeting between Tanner and the New York cotton brokers. According to Tanner's account of the meeting, Baldwin indicated that he had been the assistant district attorney for seven years. This was the position now occupied by the man prosecuting the case. Both Baldwin and the prosecutor were also on intimate terms with the attorney general, George Wickersham. When Baldwin joined the meeting at Craig & Jenks's offices, he reported to the Alabama cotton-mill treasurer that "Wickersham felt disposed to be lenient" toward Tanner, although the proceedings "were very serious" and could lead to "imprisonment and fine" for those associated with the contract. Moreover, "Baldwin pictured in very strong terms all the degradation and humiliation that would fall upon" Tanner and his family too in the course of prosecuting the bulls.[64] The intimidation backfired, however. Tanner "let them bluff him" but then went back south and told Fuller Callaway, his contact in the bull pool, "I will fight to the last ditch, and I am going to find Frank Hayne and tell him I have done wrong. I am not going to keep on doing wrong. I am through with these people." According to Callaway, "The man had 'come back.' "[65] Despite the threats against him, and the bluffing of New York bears who blamed the bull pool for the very sort of dirty tricks they were using, Tanner returned to the bulls with his story.

Craig & Jenks had already testified before the grand jury. Baldwin knew that Craig & Jenks, along with several other of his clients testifying against the bulls, were short the market.[66] It seemed obvious to many observers that the case taking shape against the New Orleans bulls was largely got up by those who opposed them in the market, by bears with an interest in keeping prices low. Even the *New York Times* swirled with rumors that the case against the bulls then taking shape in the grand jury was the result of business strategy employing political machinations and connections, though the paper usually defended the city's cotton exchange against charges that it served gamblers rather than actual trade in the commodity.[67] The Chicago broker James

A. Patten, who had just cornered wheat and seemed to many the head of the bull operation, speculated publicly that the prosecution was in league with the bears, who had promised "sensational developments and a big break in prices" when the indictments were handed down: "This indicated that the step was known in advance by the bear clique."[68] The bulls blamed the bears. Frank Hayne received a telegram from Rome, Georgia, and quoted it to the *New York Times*: "Are all the bears so scared that they have to call for the policeman?"[69]

Apparently the bears were scared, and did call for a policeman. Their arrogance led them to believe they could control the market as they had done for decades, using the agricultural calendar and the farmer's need to sell out and pay his bills to keep the price of cotton artificially low, even as demand rose around the world. The bears found themselves caught by the market as prices surfed upward. The bulls, however, who had once again laid an ingenious trap for the bears, now found themselves ensnared in a federal case.

CHAPTER 8

A Perpetual Squeeze

THE PROSECUTION OF THE BULL network rode a wave of popular distrust for business sweeping the country. When James Patten had cornered the wheat market the year before America had been reminded of the lesson that corners were bad, the product of manipulation and the cause of higher prices for goods consumers needed. Other cases of monopoly, such as Carnegie's US Steel and Rockefeller's Standard Oil, have been better remembered historically as examples of the dangers of consolidation and Big Business's corruption of the political system during the Gilded Age. Farmers likewise fought the power of middlemen and monopolies in the marketing of the products of their fields and turned to political activism to advocate for government control of the markets, the railroads, and the telegraph on which so much of their potential profits relied. On all sides, the power of business seemed to corrupt the nation's democratic ideals and to damage the ordinary American worker and farmer, the producers of the goods that other men had turned into the source of their power. As the federal case took shape in the secret rooms of prosecution and indictment, the cotton trade continued. As spring became summer in 1910, the usual gap between the crops threatened to squeeze the shorts.

At the end of April, May contracts were coming due. According to the news, the "bear shortage reaches extraordinary figures." The bears did all they could, "scouring the country for cotton," trying to persuade both New England and southern mills "to secure shipments" of cotton for May delivery in New York. They were having little success, however. The mills were "loth to let their cotton go." They would need the fiber for their spindles. While fifty thousand bales had been sent from England in an effort to make the bulls "quit their position," there were rumors that English brokers had sailed for New York City to try to get their bales back.[1] Still, on April 29, "a flood of cotton delivery notices" promising the fulfillment of May contracts reached the bulls, who "stood up" to the "shock of deliveries" of 202,000 bales, contracts they had bought at prices between 8 and 9 cents a pound. The bulls had to pay out something close to $9 million. Since May cotton had reached 14.5 cents a pound the day before, the bales they received were worth $14.6 million.[2] Bull pool profits were around $5.5 million for the single day's business—if they could dispose of all the cotton they had received without lowering its price.[3]

The prosecution used the deliveries to identify the men who received the cotton, subpoena them, and demand their business records to see where the cotton would go. The exchange was "fairly flooded with subpoenas." Receivers of cotton were ordered to produce for the court all of their account books and trade documents "minutely" since November the year before. The prosecutors intended their "drag net" to entangle any buyers who had been acting in league with the bull pool. The records of transactions led the way to the ultimate recipients of the cotton, firms and brokers who had bought contracts for future deliveries, bulls who had by their purchases demonstrated their belief that the price would rise. The news focused on the investigation of James Patten, a convenient target as the villainous Wheat King.[4] From Chicago, he spoke to the newspapers in the same rational terms that Brown had always used. Hedging gone mad, was his view of the cotton market that summer, in which firms that had bought 100 bales had sold 200 and now had little ability to meet such a contract. Patten denied holding out for an exorbitant price, according to reports. He "roasted the bears," arguing that enough cotton was for sale in southern cities for those who held contracts to meet their obligations—if they would pay the price to get it. He suggested that "instead of appealing to the United States government for help," they meet their contracts.[5]

On the other side of the market, firms on the short side, bears and their allies, were failing by the end of April. The Tefft-Weller Company, an old and established firm, "one of the oldest wholesale dry goods houses in New York and one of the last survivals of the old-time New York merchant firms," was one victim of rising prices. Tefft-Weller stood among the "founders of the wholesale district," but had miscalculated when it stocked up on goods the fall before. It was reported to be reorganizing, with "friends supervising," on April 22.[6] The destruction of such a substantial member of the New York merchant community must have demonstrated vividly just how much the world was changing. The next report of a cotton house's failure came the following day. News broke in New York that the Knight-Yancey firm, a cotton brokerage of Decatur, Alabama, had deposited all its property and account books with the courts "for adjudication." In New York, this seemed like a pretty small failure, one that would not entangle too many city firms. The president of the New York Cotton Exchange declared that the firm's bankruptcy would cause no big losses in New York, and "$20,000 would cover the damage."[7] It seemed that most of the New York bears were managing to make their deliveries and ride out the storm.

The failure of Knight-Yancey, however, alerted the firm's creditors—mostly in Liverpool—to a certain sloppiness in the relationship between actual cotton and financial instruments that had emerged in the operations of the cotton trade. At the root of the problem lay the simple bill of lading, which Knight-Yancey (and others) had apparently regularly forged.[8] This was a problem: the bill of lading was fundamental to modern commercial life. The word "lading" is an antiquated version of "loading," and as a noun the term means cargo or freight—a bill of lading is a legal document that refers to specific articles of freight that the shipper uses to identify the ownership of the goods. When Knight-Yancey would contract to sell cotton to an English firm, it would "then draw a draft upon the foreign buyer, or his banker" for the purchase price of the cotton. As proof of the transaction, the seller would attach to the draft a bill of lading "purporting to show that the cotton had been shipped." The seller would then send the draft to a New York "note broker" who would discount the note (pay the draft to Knight-Yancey, having discounted a fee from the amount of the draft) and send the draft on to the bank account of the cotton buyer—with the bill of lading attached, indicating what the draft had purchased.[9]

The bill of lading promised that the specified goods were on the way. Yet Knight-Yancey had not actually bought the cotton named in the bill of lading when the payment was drawn against it. The bill of lading was a forgery, but one that could be corrected in the ordinary course of trade so long as prices did not rise too rapidly. When things went smoothly for Knight-Yancey, it could use the draft on the bill of lading to then buy cotton and forward it. If it saw prices were going up it could buy cotton immediately, but if prices were heading lower, then every day of delay meant a bit of extra profit for Knight-Yancey. This bill of lading trick was one more way traders could make money on a bear market.[10] When the firm failed this forgery came to light, as no cotton was yet on its way as the documents promised, and money had been paid out on the nonexistent cotton. Banks overseas, the banks of the cotton's purchasers, lost between $3 million and $4.5 million when Knight-Yancey and fellow forgers went into bankruptcy. The railroads, or perhaps just a few of their agents, had played a role in facilitating the falsification of documents, and the problem occupied bankers on both sides of the Atlantic for the remainder of the year.[11] Frauds, failures, federal cases: the cotton trade must have seemed thoroughly corrupt that year.

An Unsettled Season

The controversies concerning forged bills of lading, old merchant firms failing, and the federal case against the bull pool all stood silhouetted against the storm clouds of the market that spring of 1910. At the end of April, as bear firms were making their deliveries and testifying to the federal government against the bulls, the clouds grew darker around them. "The May squeeze may prove only preliminary to a second corner to be tried in the July option," reported the *Atlanta Constitution*, and "arrangements have been made by all bull leaders to secure and pay for all the cotton that will be delivered."[12] When the bulls withstood "the shock of delivery" of more than two hundred thousand bales in the last days of April, confidence in their finances received a boost.[13] Then, on the first of May, as if to leave no doubt as to their resources, the bulls turned their attention to buying July deliveries. This "gave the shorts a shiver."[14] The bulls were taking all the cotton they could deliver and buying new contracts for delivery later in the season. Could they create a perpetual squeeze and boost the price month after month, however high they pleased?

As the summer began, however, the price floundered. Six months after the bears had stuffed down the cost of cotton in January, no real upward spikes emerged. The plentiful deliveries of April had been repeated in May, which ended "without any signs of a squeeze." By the first of June, May deliveries totaled nearly as many bales as the entire year before.[15] Such a large quantity of cotton would fulfill the bears' contracts and require payment from the bulls, expenditures that might exhaust bulls' resources and make it hard to meet margins should prices rise. Hefty deliveries worked to keep prices down as well. They congested the spot markets. The bulls had to distribute and sell the cotton they received—first in April and then more in May—even as "curtailment continue[d]" at the Fall River mills.[16] By the end of May, favorable crop reports "gave the bears an inning" as the price dropped between $2.10 and $3.25 per bale.[17] On June 2, a "decidedly bearish" report on the crop's acreage and condition appeared, predicting between 13 and 14 million bales with an average condition of 82.[18] With large quantities delivered and good condition reports on the crop in the ground, perhaps the bears would win this year, again.

Information affected the price as thoroughly as did supply and demand, however, and some sources related to conditions beyond the cotton economy. By June 5, gossip around the exchange was that "indictments had been handed down in the bull cotton pool case." Market actors recognized that this "may have had some effect on the selling." At the end of the day "denial was made of such report" for the time being, as "the evidence was still being considered by the Grand Jury."[19] Everyone knew what was coming. The market stayed dull and the price of July deliveries hovered around fifteen cents, with August and September lower than that. Certainly some of this price stability had to do with market conditions, as the bulls awaited the summer shortage after a disappointing spring. "Advices" from Manchester and Liverpool were generally reported as "disappointing" and "discouraging" through the middle of the month, and "favorable weather prevailing" likewise obliged the bears.[20]

Then, on June 17, 1910, after months of rumors and speculation, the New York grand jury finally submitted its indictments to Judge Charles M. Hough of the United States Circuit Court. The bench issued warrants for James A. Patten, Eugene Scales, Robert Means Thompson, Morris Rothschild, and others, along with the New Orleans bulls Frank Hayne and William P. Brown, for "unlawful conspiracy to monopolize" the cotton trade. The men appeared personally in court to plead not guilty and were released on bail at $5,000 apiece.[21] Many of the bulls hired the New York attorneys Spooner & Cotton to represent them in court and thus brought political firepower onto their own side as former Senator John C. Spooner was a partner in the New York firm.[22] However, Patten—as a Chicagoan and outsider to the bull pool—hired his own attorney.[23] This was no surprise. Patten had never really been part of the New Orleans bull pool and had only met Brown and Hayne and Scales when "we came together incidentally by virtue of our taking a similar view of the market."[24] He had his own supporters, out of Chicago, "his associates in grain speculation."[25] Nonetheless, the indictments claimed that all bulls had conspired together to buy more cotton than existed, to refrain from selling, and to buy at a higher price in the future.

The Bear Network Further Revealed

James Patten declared publicly—early and often—that the indictments were motivated by malice, not justice. "The bear crowd in New York undoubtedly instigated the investigation," he told anyone who asked.[26] Many observers agreed with him. It seemed obvious that the case was propelled by bear operators. For example, Craig & Jenks, who had delivered the correspondence of Tanner, the Alabama mill treasurer, into the hands of the grand jury, delivered 100,500 bales on May contracts. That put them among the largest of the shorts. But the bear brokers were themselves part of a wider network, one that encompassed the prosecutors. The district attorney's office often employed lawyers who were at the same time representing the New York Cotton Exchange. For example, a few years earlier, as he had indicated to Tanner, Ernest Baldwin had been an assistant district attorney at the same time as he was the lawyer for the New York Cotton Exchange.[27] Apparently it was perfectly legal—the district attorney had every right to "prosecute business for himself as an attorney."[28] In the summer of 1910, however, the district attorney and the Exchange's lawyer were different men. Serving the Exchange was Henry W. Taft, and it was hard to sneak anything past Henry W. Taft. He may not have been a district attorney, but his brother was still the president of the United States, and the attorney general was his law firm partner George Wickersham. The attorney general's office had sent the New York prosecutors the information about the bulls.[29] And the prosecutor himself also had solid social connections on the New York scene.

The prosecutor was Henry A. Wise, US District Attorney for the southern district of New York, which included New York City. The grandson of a Virginia governor, Wise "comes of good stock," the New York legal community knew, "connected with many prominent Virginia, Kentucky, and Pennsylvania families."[30] Wise first worked for his father, "a well-known lawyer, orator, and author" in New York City, before serving in the New York office of the US Attorney General. There he made a name for himself in commercial and antitrust litigations.[31] Wise saw a clear connection between acquiring monopoly power, cornering the market for a commodity, and sowing destruction in the financial world. It was in his power to see that such behavior was punished. After being named the youngest New York district attorney, in March 1909, Henry A. Wise turned his enthusiasm and talent for antitrust litigation to pursuing the bulls.[32]

Did this web of interconnections between the government and the New York Cotton Exchange mean that the prosecution was corrupt? Congress did later investigate the Department of Justice, especially its expenses, and uncovered at least modestly unscrupulous activities throughout the justice system. For example, Attorney General George Wickersham had no problem with investigators in his office spending government money on alcohol to obtain information from witnesses: "Sometimes a glass of beer will cause a man to talk."[33] But the networks in which the bear brokers of the New York Cotton Exchange were enmeshed were not necessarily deliberate. Men who knew each other and trusted one another would work together. Taft, for instance, had recommended David H. Miller for a postmaster job after sharing with him the experience of handling Sully's bankruptcy. Actors might become parts of networks that then structured their behavior, but without choosing to do so and without any particular goal. In other words, the links among Taft and Wickersham and Wise, between the New York Cotton Exchange and the attorney general and the district attorney's office, may have developed by chance, without any intention of linking the NYCE to the power of federal and local prosecutors.

Yet this case did seem fishy. Even the *New York Times* felt that the prosecution had overreached: "Hitherto those who have raised prices too high ... have paid the penalty in the market." If the price rose above those justified by the conditions of supply and demand, the market would correct the situation. The "attempt to punish by court procedure methods of trade which hitherto have been tested economically" would demand the determination of an "ideal price for cotton, based on an official inquiry," which the *Times* thought was ridiculous. "There is no suggestion of fraud, or of gambling in options, or of reckless plunging," it argued. Let the market judge the bulls.[34] Even Henry Wise later said as much: "They can speculate all they want. They can only get up to a certain point when it bursts."[35] Of course, this was true for any speculator pushing prices beyond the point that supply and demand would dictate. In the case of the bulls, however, sober calculations of market conditions had combined with nerve and timing and financial resources to push the price so high. They played off bear hubris that the price could be kept low and used market conditions to threaten once again to corner the market. Even the prosecutor knew that if they were wrong, the bubble would eventually burst. Nonetheless, the bulls had been indicted, and prosecutors, not the market, would try to decide if they had behaved illegally when they pushed the price so high.

Evoking market justice raises another question: did the prosecution affect the price of cotton, deliberately or not? The *Journal of Commerce,* a New York publication, indicated that the June 17 indictment was intended "to break the markets $1 per bale." For Wickersham, this was not a problem. It affected only "speculators," occurring as it did after farmers had "practically sold their cotton" for the year.[36] While Wickersham did recognize that the prosecution might deter "combinations in the future which tend to enhance the price of their products," instead of those combinations that were short selling and lowering the price to ensure their profits, that did not seem to him reason to refrain from acting.[37] Moreover, when faced with the accusation that he had dropped the price of cotton by 15 points, Wickersham joked, "I did not know I was so potent," before soberly declaring that "I try to be very cautious in what I do say."[38] Wise, too, contested the notion that the indictments had lowered the price of cotton just by threatening with criminal prosecution those who would raise it.[39] Yet the numbers speak for themselves. On the Friday of the indictment, distant months (October through January) did experience a significant dip in price—around 8 to 10 points a pound, which meant 40 or 50 cents per bale. However, this was noticeable only because of how quickly the figure regained its previous level. By June 30, the cost of delivery in the fall months had recovered all the value lost as the indictment became public.

In fact, however, there was a technical flaw in the complaint; the grand jury was a special one, "sworn ... to consider this special case" even though "another Federal grand jury was sitting at the time."[40] Knowing that the indictment might not stand, the prosecution drew up a second "amplified" indictment, but kept it a secret through the summer. The existence of the second indictment was not made public until about December 1910. The second indictment had been drawn up by a young attorney named Felix Frankfurter and was amplified from the beginning because, according to Wise, "the allegations in the first indictment were not broad enough; that the first indictment was too limited, and that it ought to be broadened. [We] framed it according to ... what we saw would be the defense."[41] The bulls had demurred on several points of the indictment. Felonies and misdemeanors should be charged separately, and here they had appeared in a single indictment. Some counts alleged conspiracy, while others "allege[d] substantive crimes which

Table 8.1 Cotton Futures Prices, 1910

1910	May	June	July	August	Sept.	Oct.	Nov.	Dec.	Jan.	Feb.	March	Apr.	May	June	July	Aug.	Oct.
May 20	14.96	14.97	15.02	14.82	13.66	12.82	12.72	12.66	12.62		12.68						
May 27	14.96	14.90	14.93	14.59	13.48	12.76	12.65	12.56	12.54		12.58						
June 3		14.73	14.78	14.37	13.17	12.37	12.27	12.20	12.16		12.20						
June 10		15.26	15.36	14.78	13.34	12.56	12.45	12.28	12.38		12.26						
June 17		14.86	14.92	14.49	13.02	12.37	12.26	12.17	12.13		12.14						
June 24		15.06	15.08	14.74	13.23	12.48	12.34	12.28	12.23	12.22	12.24						
June 30			15.34	14.72	13.16	12.54	12.39	12.34	12.30	12.29	12.21						
July 9			15.47	14.79	13.40	12.80	12.66	12.63	12.63	12.64	12.67		12.70				
July 14			15.93	14.86	13.40	12.76	12.62	12.58	12.56	12.56	12.58		12.61				
July 22			15.93	15.26	13.72	13.10	12.94	12.92	12.87	12.88	12.92		12.97				
July 29				15.24	14.15	13.66	13.53	13.53	13.45	13.46	13.50		13.55				
Aug. 5				15.61	14.28	13.50	13.41	13.39	13.35	13.37	13.40		13.42	13.45	13.46		
Aug. 12				15.69	14.44	13.68	13.59	13.59	13.56	13.57	13.61		13.63	13.63	13.64		
Aug. 19				15.95	14.20	13.49	13.40	13.40	13.38	13.39	13.44		13.48	13.47	13.45		
Aug. 25				16.32	14.15	13.49	13.38	13.38	13.36	13.43	13.38		13.46	13.44	13.43		
Sept. 1					13.98	13.47	13.38	13.38	13.37	13.38	13.45		13.51	13.50	13.48		
Sept. 8					13.54	12.92	12.92	12.94	12.92	12.95	13.01		13.03	13.01	13.01		
Sept. 15					13.61	13.14	13.07	13.06	13.01	13.04	13.09		13.12	13.10	13.09		
Sept. 23					13.53	13.26	13.20	13.22	13.20	13.24	13.29	13.31	13.35	13.32	13.31		
Sept. 30						13.55	13.58	13.73	13.74	13.80	13.87	13.91	13.96	13.94	13.95		
Oct. 7						14.32	14.36	14.46	14.49	14.55	14.69	14.73	14.79	14.74	14.79		
Oct. 13						14.73	14.74	14.79	14.84	14.90	14.97	15.01	15.00	15.02	15.05		
Oct. 21						14.30	14.19	14.29	14.33	14.36	14.42	14.47	14.52	14.52	14.52		
Oct. 28						14.45	14.38	14.48	14.43	14.47	14.45	14.47	14.52	14.50	14.47		

Date											
Nov. 4	14.38	14.53	14.40	14.45	14.53	14.56	14.62	14.58	14.55		
Nov. 11	14.45	14.60	14.55	14.64	14.73	14.78	14.89	14.85	14.84	14.54	
Nov. 18	14.26	14.32	14.27	14.34	14.42	14.48	14.57	14.54	14.54	14.23	
Nov. 25	14.90	14.91	14.89	15.00	15.16	15.22	15.30	15.26	15.25	14.89	
Dec. 2		14.80	14.80	14.91	15.04	15.10	15.21	15.17	15.17	14.81	13.31
Dec. 9		14.84	14.87	14.98	15.14	15.17	15.30	15.28	15.28	14.98	
Dec. 13		14.69	14.76	14.87	15.05	15.12	15.25	15.23	15.23	14.87	13.56
Dec. 16											
Dec. 22		14.86	14.87	15.02	15.18	15.28	15.37	15.40	15.40	15.06	13.69
Dec. 23											
Dec. 29		14.59	14.61	14.80	14.91	15.00	15.11	15.13	15.13	14.83	13.44

Source: *New York Times*, assorted dates.

Did the prosecution of the cotton bulls affect the price of the fiber? The June 17 indictment of the men who would raise the price of cotton did indeed drop the figures, but only momentarily. The bulls' goals reflected real-world conditions of supply and demand, so the price went rapidly back up. From the *New York Times*, Fridays and Saturdays, May 20-Dec. 29, 1910.

are not conspiracies."[42] In addition, Patten's lawyer claimed that prec-
edent had established that transactions made in New York were not
interstate trade and thus could not be subject to the Sherman Act.[43]
Having learned from the response to the first indictment the way the
bulls would defend themselves, the second indictment against them
was drawn to curtail that prospect.

The Summer Shortage Becomes a Perpetual Squeeze

As the prosecution proceeded, the market that summer illustrated
a drama of bull triumph against bear hubris, a story that had begun
well before the summer, and one that threatened never to end.
Indeed, the price dip that accompanied the June 17 indictment was
the bulls' worst moment in the market that year. July began with a
bang when a government report predicted acreage that would produce only 12.7 to 13.0 million bales of about average condition.[44]
Weather reports the same day menaced the crop, as "the rains were
unfavorable in the centre and East, and the drought unfavorable in
the West."[45] Such weather reports had a tendency to raise the price,
but other news counteracted them. Many mills had curtailed production, and the smaller number of looms and spindles operating would
reduce demand.[46] Nonetheless, in July, week after week, the price
rose for deliveries in every future month through December. Yet
with the prosecution looming, the bulls did not push it as far as they
could. In the middle of July "one of the bull leaders" offered 100,000
bales of July cotton at 17 cents. He would not aim any higher; this was
the price he would accept to settle his contracts with sellers.[47] That
was the week that the newspapers reported that the federal grand
jury had taken up "a second investigation" that would rewrite the
flawed indictment with a new one at the end of the year.[48]

   The day-to-day drama of the market in July likewise stressed
the bulls, who were facing prosecution at the time. Sometimes battles in the marketplace carried over outside the trading ring: "The
atmosphere ... had been getting electric while July cotton went to
new records and as suddenly sagged on Tuesday," July 19—a day of
"excited trading." When July prices broke, Hayne bought 25,000
bales in an attempt to "stop the decline"—common practice in the
midst of a bull campaign.[49] Lamar Fleming Jr., whose father had
transplanted his family and cotton merchant firm to New York City
from Augusta, Georgia,[50] was sending telegrams to his clients, telling them that "the bulls were routed." One of these wires had come
into Hayne's hands. To tell his side of the story, the proud South

Carolinian promptly wired the recipient "some vivid language about the source of the rumors affecting the bulls." This vivid description came to Fleming's attention, and he sought out Frank Hayne "in Delmonico's opposite the exchange" and "hostilities quickly began." The men "drew down the lightning" in "a good old-fashioned fist-fight" before "the cotton men who frequent the Delmonico café" pulled them apart.[51]

The New York waterfront and warehouse district were just as chaotic, as cotton arrived from all directions to satisfy the July contracts. Vessels coming up the coast from Savannah and Charleston filled the warehouses with unfamiliar bales. Those that could not get their usual berths unloaded the cotton onto lighters, small boats used for moving cargo around the harbor. Ships arrived from Liverpool and Bremen bringing cotton back to rescue short-sellers, just as had happened in 1903. "Special cotton trains have been put on the same schedule as the fruit trains," one newspaper wrote, "treating cotton for urgent delivery like perishable produce." Inspectors and weighers worked all week, even Sunday, trying to keep up with the flow of cotton bales coming into the city.[52]

Figure 8.1 While not much actual cotton traded through New York in the twentieth century (see Figure 3.2), an emergency such as Brown and Hayne's second corner in 1910 could crowd the New York waterfront with ships, unloading cotton bales onto a lighter like this one for delivery to the warehouse to satisfy contracts. New York Public Library.

By the end of July, the bears were still in a bad position. The government indicated that the condition of the crop had dropped further, from 80.7% of "normal" on June 25 to 75.5% a month later. The National Ginners' Association's condition estimate of 73 was even worse. The heat in Texas threatened the season's quantity as well as the quality, and hopes of a 13 million-bale crop were dashed—a 12 million total seemed more likely at the start of August.[53] That was the month that the shortage really finally began to squeeze. By late August, the price leapt up. August futures on the New York Cotton Exchange closed at 16.82 on Saturday, August 27, but by the time the trading floor opened on Monday, realizations of just how little cotton was available had increased the opening price to 16.95. It quickly hit 20.00, yet only fifteen thousand bales changed hands. Brown offered to sell 100,000 bales at that price, and the New York traders viewed that as the new "level fixed in the open market" for settling August contracts. The market was, once again, well and truly cornered. The new crop as yet offered no relief, and already the bulls were predicting shorter crops and higher prices in 1911.[54]

September 1 was the start of the new crop year. Traditionally the summer shortage would have begun to ease off by then, as the new harvest would relieve short sellers and the flood of fiber would push down prices. From September it was easier to predict what January would bring. In the new calendar year, the agricultural credit accounts would come to an end and farmers' bills would come due, forcing them to sell, and forced sales would push prices down. The bears had spent years counting on this seasonal cycle of credit to lower the value of the crop, and they likely expected it to happen again in 1911. This time, however, the price did not drop very far. Throughout September, the price of January, February, and March deliveries was at most only a little lower than the price of October, November, and December contracts. Then, on October 3 the Census Bureau reported that so far in 1910, the quantity of cotton ginned was falling short of both 1908 and 1909 figures.[55] This stimulated a rapid price rise in the middle of the month that could not be sustained for long, but still future contracts sold in October never fell below 14 cents. As the autumn progressed, even higher prices in distant months kept contracts for spring delivery near 15 cents, and often above it.[56] As 1910 drew to a close, this did not change. What had been a corner seemed to become a perpetual squeeze.

That fall, too, the bills of lading controversy contributed to increasing prices. While the fraudulent activities of the Knight-Yancey firm and other cotton brokers resulted in criminal prosecution of the principal individuals, distrust remained, and buyers demanded new arrangements.[57] As cotton brokers learned the new and still-evolving requirements of the export trade, cotton shipments slowed down. In a September 1 report from New Orleans, the *New York Times* found that "southern cotton men" were suggesting that marketing and moving the new crop could become "a serious problem." They claimed that the British bankers who financed their countrymen's purchases were demanding "radically different" shipping practices, including guarantees of shipments made only from "concentrating points," where only a limited number of railroad agents would have the power to sign a through bill of lading for the cotton.[58] This put the burden on the railroads to guarantee that cotton had really shipped. In fact, however, "foreign bankers" did not understand "the bill of lading as a distinctly railroad document," and they wanted American banks to be the ones to guarantee the validity of a bill of lading.[59] Since "the National banking laws countenance no such procedure" and banks could not feasibly station their employees everywhere a bale of cotton was shipped and a bill of lading required, the New York banks refused, and state banks in the South followed suit.[60] Slowing shipments and deliveries could create shortages that helped bulls raise prices.

Bankers on both sides of the Atlantic would need to approve any new plans for buying cotton and paying for it before delivery. The American Bankers' Association created a Bills of Lading Committee, and its members met with "the accredited representative of the foreign bankers" to discuss an idea that emerged in October: a private guaranty company that would "guarantee signatures on export bills for a fixed price." There were objections to this plan. "Southern interests" argued that the proposal was "a direct reflection upon their business honor" and also "placed a tax" on cotton shipments that applied to "no other commodity exported."[61] The bankers' groups pointed out that a trusted cotton merchant could ship without paying for such a guarantee "if he found any European banks willing to accept his bills," but this seemed an unlikely situation if most brokers paid for their guarantees. Nonetheless, bankers knew they could ignore these protests. The trade could bluster and complain, but buyers' demands would need to be met.[62]

On the other hand, some disagreements were more serious. By the end of October, the Liverpool Cotton Association had expressed its refusal to accept such guarantees. This threat could have "indefinitely prolonged ... the settlement of the controversy," since the Association represented the largest market for cotton in the world.[63]

Yet by the end of the year, the problem seemed solved. Bankers withdrew most of their demands. Apparently the government prosecution of the miscreants—for "fraudulent use of the mails"—indicated to buyers that the forgery was extraordinary and did not represent ordinary business practice. Arresting the forgers and putting them "behind bars" demonstrated that "there is no objection to inculcating commercial morality by the usual processes of government."[64] Yet the long drama and the autumn negotiations had favored the bulls. All the suggested solutions had involved shifting some of the risk across the Atlantic, so that British bankers would be less exposed to potential losses. As long as the bankers paying out drafts for cotton in transit were based in Britain, where there were no producers of cotton, only consumers, they would tend to align with the bearish interests of their clients.[65] The new arrangements, the *New York Times* assessed, with American interests guaranteeing the crop during its passage, would shift the market in favor of the bulls. The controversy was just one more element in the bull network, pushing the market to their side. Throughout the fall, the prices kept rising.

The Status of the Prosecution

At the same time, however, government scrutiny was bringing the bull pool to the breaking point. Eugene Scales sued Morris Rothschild for "selling out on the pool" during the high prices created during the August 1910 corner. It was unclear, with the prosecution still menacing, whether Rothschild's contractual agreement not to sell cotton was even legal—or was it a restraint of trade? Could a man breach an illegal contract?[66] The Sherman Anti-Trust prosecution moved slowly through the courts. In spring 1911, the defendants moved to quash the indictment and demur on several of its counts; the New York Circuit Court upheld some of the counts and sustained the defendants on the others. The questions the defendants had posed about the case finally went to the Supreme Court of the United States in October 1912.[67] Its decision in *United States v. James A. Patten, et al.*, handed down in the first week of 1913, ruled for the government. The Supreme Court decided that a corner did in fact restrain trade, since its participants bought in excess of available supply—though of course this practice was inherent to futures trading.[68] There were also those who sold what they did not have, what they never expected to have—bears. Their practices, however, were outside the scope of the indictment.

With the Supreme Court decision early in 1913, the prosecutors could move forward against the bull pool. Shortly thereafter, Patten pled guilty. For a moment, the New Orleans men held fast, but they were reindicted once again (in order to leave Patten out of the counts of conspiracy) on July 2, 1913. By the end of the year, they stopped fighting. They pled no contest to charges they bitterly resented and did not believe.[69] As Frank Hayne later testified, his nolo contendere plea "acknowledged in no shape or form any guilt whatsoever." He would "rather have gone to jail or gone to h—l than to have [pled] guilty."[70] The punishment was negligible: the bull pool members were fined four thousand dollars each. They could easily earn that much trading a single contract any summer's day.[71]

Was the case against the bulls "the first step toward ending deals in all futures"? Some had predicted as much when the bears first testified against the bulls in the spring of 1910.[72] Farmers, too, had sought such an outcome for decades. From the Bureau of Corporations' report to the prosecution of the bull pool for its members' cotton corner, the path seemed clear to abolish the derivatives entirely. Futures trading served a purpose, however, which most participants in the trade understood. It created conditions in which information about crop size and manufacturers' future needs could influence the price of the good and make it better reflect conditions of supply and demand than did immediate trades in spot cotton. It allowed for hedging, so that people who used cotton in their businesses could better weather price volatility. Those market functions only actually worked when similar conditions and information flowed rapidly and efficiently throughout the market. That happened all too rarely in the real world of business networks, financial power, and competing member-regulated exchanges, each with its own pools of men on opposite sides of the market. The bulls gave up their contest against the insinuations that they had behaved illegally by demanding delivery. If that stifled the operation of the futures market, the whole cotton trade trembled in the balance.

CHAPTER 9

The Cotton Futures Act of 1914

TEN YEARS OF CONFLICT BETWEEN New York bears and New Orleans bulls had resulted again in a return to the *status quo ante*. For the cotton world to change, a new battle was needed—one that incorporated new actors and took place in the houses of Congress rather than the rings of trade. Laws were needed to break the impasse, which had resulted from the private, self-regulating nature of the cotton exchanges. Competition between the exchanges had prevented agreements between NYCE and NOCE, the two exchanges that sanctioned futures trading and regulated the trades of their members. Because each exchange set the rules for its members, and because bears held power on one exchange while bulls usually called the other their home, the exchanges' practices had resulted in different market outcomes. In New York, the rules of the exchange—especially the fixed differences that priced the grades of cotton delivered on futures contracts—had been used by brokers to push prices down. In New Orleans, the Crescent City's place in the delivery of spot cotton, real cotton arriving from the fields and the gins, and the commercial differences system of pricing grades that reflected real conditions of supply and demand had been used by brokers to corner the market twice and raise cotton prices dramatically.

In the war between the two market positions represented by the two cotton exchanges, neither bulls nor bears had resisted using public resources to try to gain private advantage. The federal government had already begun to throw sunshine on the markets—the form of regulation favored by Theodore Roosevelt and his trust-busting administration. In the mid-1910s, transparency gave way to laws regulating the practices of exchange. While farmers had long objected to futures trading and advocated simply outlawing the practice entirely, the market regulation that eventually emerged in 1914 was more nuanced and cautious. The legislators listened to the market operators and crafted laws that standardized practices across the exchanges. At the same time, the final form of the regulation validated the bulls' practices by forcing the New York Cotton Exchange to do business more like the New Orleans Cotton Exchange. The bulls had cornered the world market in cotton twice and raised the price of cotton, enriching themselves and relieving for a moment the poverty of millions of cotton farmers across the South. But their real accomplishment was even more significant. Their usual practices became the standards for market behavior, as the federal Cotton Futures Act of 1914 required that even the New York Cotton Exchange operate under the rules of New Orleans, the rules of the bull brokers on their home field.

This larger task of regulating the cotton trade required a new network. Brown had built his bull network in 1903, and the bears in 1910 countered with their own network that included elements of the federal government. But the humble and hungry boll weevil had built its own network in the years around 1905, including southern farmers' organizations, the Congressmen and Senators who represented them, and the bull pool of mostly southern spinners and New Orleans brokers. After lying dormant for a few years, that weevil-instigated network began to stir into action. As southern legislators gained political power in Congress, some shifted their focus from the old Populist dream of destroying futures trading to the more modern goal of regulating it. Instead of haughtily telling hayseed political hacks not to meddle with what they did not understand, figures from the cotton trade would assist them by patiently explaining just which parts of the trade were causing the problems. When the legislators listened, the witnesses effectively wrote the legislation to fix the market and make price reflect real-world conditions of supply and demand.

Congress Goes After Futures Trading

As the federal prosecution of the bulls limped toward a dénouement, public opinion and party politics were mobilizing against the bears. The fourth and fifth parts of Herbert Knox Smith's report on the cotton exchanges were published on December 6, 1909, and they demonstrated in detail how the NYCE system of fixed differences depressed the price paid to the producer.[1] The report showed how the depression of future prices in New York depressed spot prices in the multitude of interior markets where most cotton first entered the trade, even if it had less noticeable effect on spot prices in the larger markets.[2] "When the future contract ceases faithfully to represent cotton, an exchange becomes little better than a bucket shop," wrote Smith, echoing the populist critique of all futures trading for the previous twenty years. "In some respects it becomes worse than a bucket shop. No one claims that a bucket shop influences the price of cotton."[3] With the conclusion of Smith's report, it was finally clear that the operations of the New York Cotton Exchange directly hurt not just well-dressed brokers but all the farmers in dusty overalls as well.

As the Bureau of Corporations' explanations sank in, they sparked outrage. Southern cotton producers who had grown up with an instinctive hate of the shysters who bought and sold cotton but would not know which end of a hoe was which finally had an authoritative voice condemning the exchanges. Unsurprisingly, perhaps, the press responses took a regional tone. The *Atlanta Constitution* noted that Smith's report criticized the NYCE while suggesting that the NOCE's practices were much superior.[4] The editor of the *Atlanta Constitution* compared gamblers on the NYCE to "dishonest croupier[s] at the roulette table" and demanded, "if laws on the statute books are not sufficient to reach the flagrant and outrageous practices of the New York exchange, laws that will do so should speedily be enacted."[5] The *New York Times*, on the other hand, defended "Our Cotton Exchanges" on the editorial page, asserting that "Whatever the defects of the New York system, it approves itself to those who do business under it, or they would alter it."[6] Smith himself issued a clarification ten days after his report, hoping to convince the public to read his nuanced conclusions carefully: futures trading was beneficial, necessary even, but there was urgent need to reform some of the ways it was handled, especially on the NYCE.[7]

Those farmer activists who wanted to abolish futures trading altogether read Smith's report more simply. It provided them, and their supporters in Congress, with ammunition to support a large-scale push for strong legislation against futures. Charles S. Barrett, president of the Farmers' Union, declared war on January 2, 1910 in a message to all members announcing a "determined and organized fight against the New York Cotton Exchange and other institutions which exist solely for the purpose of gambling in cotton and other products of the soil." Officers and leading members of the organization would go to Washington, D.C. to demand effective legislation and would "stay there and camp on the trail of congress until something definite is done."[8] "We have at last learned how to go about the enforcement of the rights of American farmers," Barrett thundered, "and that is by using the ballot as a bullet."[9] Southern Democrats in Congress took note. By the third week of January, three bills had been introduced to prevent gambling in futures and the House Committee on Agriculture had scheduled hearings.[10]

The hearings in the first half of February provided more heat than light. The main feature was misguided questions from deeply confused Congressmen looking for black and white answers, which elicited cryptic answers from cotton traders. Some of the witnesses, however, agreed that something should be done. Lewis Parker, the South Carolina mill owner and president of the American Cotton Manufacturers' Association who was part of the 1910 bull pool, said that the cotton exchanges as they presently operated at the mercy of the NYCE were "a positive menace and a curse to both the manufacturer and the producer" because they made it impossible for manufacturers to know the price they would have to pay for cotton.[11] W. B. Thompson, president of the New Orleans Cotton Exchange, testified as well. He asked the Committee on Agriculture to resist the calls of the Farmers' Union to abolish all futures trading, though he readily acknowledged that the problems with the existing system needed correcting. Bucket shops, where wagers were made on the price of cotton but no enforceable contracts were entered into, were no different than gambling halls and should be abolished. Thompson's more substantive point, and the one on which he diverged from the president of the New York Exchange, was his objection to "uncommercial contracts." "The remedy for the evil of the unfair contract," Thompson argued, with an eye turned toward New York,

is very plain and of easy accomplishment. A law establishing a national standard of classification of the marketable grades of cotton, upon which all arbitrations on contract deliveries must be made, prohibiting any contract on which can be delivered unmarketable cotton or useless stuff, or cotton of a value uncertain and not readily ascertainable, and providing that all cotton delivered on contract shall be

paid for on the basis of actual differences in the spot value
of the grades delivered on the market and at the time of
delivery, would effectively and immediately eradicate this
evil influence.[12]

Keep unspinnable trash cotton from being used to fulfill contracts
and abolish the "fixed differences" system that allowed NYCE members to manipulate the price of cotton, and then the evil would dis-
appear. The Committee on Agriculture, however, was not yet ready
for the subtlety of this suggestion about classification and the impact
of grades on prices.

At the beginning of April 1910, the Committee reported a new
bill combining the several it had been considering, and it was a blunt
instrument indeed. Grain exchanges were excluded from its operation. The new proposed law made it a crime "for any person to send
a message over the telegraph or telephone lines, by wireless or cable,
or through the mails, offering to make or enter into a contract for
the purchase or sale of cotton for future delivery, without intending that such cotton shall actually be delivered or received."[13] W. B.
Thompson was dismayed, calling the proposed legislation "illogical
in conception, unjust and discriminatory in design, of more than
doubtful constitutionality, and exemplifying not the beneficial, but
the pernicious phase of legislative interference with business."[14]
Not even all the cotton farmers thought it was a good idea. One
from Alabama worried that it would be "disastrous" for cotton farmers like himself. Without the protection of hedging on the cotton
exchanges, cotton buyers would simply pay farmers less for the staple. Despite these shortcomings, the Farmers' Union supported the
bill. Its members had been sending bags of mail for weeks to their
congressmen urging them to pass the law. The House passed the bill
in late June, but it died in committee in the Senate, where only 25 of
92 senators were southern Democrats.[15]

A very similar story played out the next year, in the Sixty-
Second Congress. Starting in December 1911, congressmen introduced bills very much like those considered in 1910. "Cotton
Tom" Heflin of Alabama alone introduced six different bills all
aimed at "gambling in futures" or trying to distinguish between
"cotton futures or actual cotton."[16] Meanwhile in the Senate,
"Cotton Ed" Smith of South Carolina was introducing a bill to
create standard grades for cotton and to regulate contracts for
future delivery, much more in line with the suggestions made two
years earlier by W. B. Thompson and others who sought reform

of cotton futures marketing rather than an outright ban.[17] Arthur Marsh of the NYCE had published an erudite defense of cotton exchanges, arguing that they were "indispensible in the economy of modern commerce."[18] Thompson himself again testified before the House Committee on Agriculture, urging government control of cotton exchange practices and grading.[19]

As in 1910, however, nothing would stop the House of Representatives from passing a bill to effectively abolish futures trading in cotton. House Resolution 56 would make it illegal to send a message offering to make a contract for purchase or sale of cotton "without intending that such cotton shall be actually delivered and received"; "proof of failure to deliver or receive the cotton called for in any contract for future delivery shall be prima facie evidence that there was no intention to deliver or receive said cotton when said contract was made." That made hedging impossible, since any futures contract would have to result in delivery.[20] Besides, as the legislators should have known, the Supreme Court in 1905 had held that "clearing methods constitute delivery in symbolic form, being thus merely a convenient and inexpensive way of accomplishing what would otherwise be a very burdensome and useless process."[21] The Senate noted that H.R. 56 had been passed, but let it die a quiet death, just like Cotton Ed Smith's less cataclysmic bill to get the federal government involved in grading cotton and regulating the cotton exchanges.[22]

What doomed these congressional attempts to control the cotton futures trade was not necessarily the merits or flaws of particular bills, but the basic political structure of Congress during these years. In the House of Representatives, Republicans had a majority but the party was divided between conservatives allied with Speaker Joseph G. Cannon and the progressive "Insurgents."[23] Southerners were an important constituency of the Democratic Party, but the Democrats lacked the numbers to do what they wanted, even if they could bring themselves to risk the approbation of their voters by cooperating with Republicans. There were, however, a few southern Democrats less shackled to the dominant race-baiting themes of southern politics and more willing to engage with Republicans on reform. Most important among them was Frank Lever of South Carolina, elected in 1900 and appointed to the Committee on Agriculture in 1902. Lever was willing to cooperate with Insurgent Republicans, and by 1913, he was chair of the Committee on Agriculture in a House of Representatives controlled by the Democrats.[24]

Figure 9.1 Senator Ellison D. "Cotton Ed" Smith of South Carolina started his career in public life working for the Southern Cotton Association and in 1914 worked with Frank Lever in the House of Representatives to get the Cotton Futures Act of 1914 passed. Library of Congress.

The Cotton Futures Act of 1914

Things changed decisively with the 1912 election. Suddenly both houses of Congress had Democratic majorities, and a cotton bill would almost certainly be passed at last in the Sixty-Third Congress. The attorney to the New York Cotton Exchange no longer had a brother in the White House. Independent of potential federal regulation, elements of the cotton trade had long been trying to coordinate their practices and improve many aspects of the trade, not just the problems introduced by the NYCE. These activities got a boost in the new political climate, and their supporters found the NYCE much more cooperative. The president of the NYCE called for a meeting of all the nation's cotton exchanges. The conference held in Memphis in January 1913 had representatives from numerous cotton exchanges and chambers of commerce in cotton centers. They created a network of state organizations and, most importantly, the National Association of Cotton Exchanges.

Figure 9.2 A. Frank Lever, a Congressman from South Carolina, was the principal author of the Cotton Futures Act of 1914 that finally regulated cotton futures trading in the United States. Library of Congress.

This was a framework for creating standard practices for the cotton trade, especially in relations between American cotton producers and European spinners. The chair and leader of the new organization represented the Texas Association of Cotton Exchanges, a sign of New York's slipping grip on power.[25]

Each reform added to the momentum for further reform, a common pattern in the Progressive Era. A conference of representatives from American and European cotton exchanges met in Liverpool at the beginning of June 1913. It wanted "all cotton interests [to] work towards the adoption of a standard classification for American cotton of all growths, which shall be worldwide."[26] Some argued that the Liverpool standard be adopted, but American representatives pointed out that that standard did not work so well for grades below middling, and delegates from the South pointed out that the NOCE "was committed to State Government classification."[27] Another meeting of American cotton exchanges in Washington in October 1913 confirmed plans to form a permanent association and to adopt standard grades, either the Liverpool standards or those promoted by USDA.[28] Finally, in March 1914, the Augusta Cotton Exchange, in conjunction with NOCE, called for a world conference on cotton to be held in Augusta, Georgia as early as May. At stake was the way the New York Cotton Exchange was damaging the trade. The conference focused on the "objection to the present form of New York Cotton Exchange contracts."[29] As a great deal of the trade recognized, "there will never be fair dealing until the New York exchange adopts the New Orleans exchange contract."[30] By the time the Augusta conference met, however, the Cotton Futures Act of 1914 would be making its way through Congress, relieving the exchanges of the burdens of self-regulation.

The Cotton Futures Act of 1914 was different than the failed bills of 1910 and 1912. Those bills were just the latest versions of the Butterworth Bill of 1890, a reflexive attack on the futures market as a whole, determined to kill off a whole way of doing business, to throw out baby with bathwater. The Cotton Futures Act of 1914 had much more in common with Cotton Ed Smith's bill of 1912 and the suggestions made by W. B. Thompson of NOCE. It sought to cure the two main ills of the NYCE: the use of fixed differences and the wide range of low grades of cotton that were deliverable. The day the Congress convened, Smith introduced a bill (S.110) to the Senate that sought to regulate the business of cotton exchanges by setting standard practices. It was enforced through the post office, denying the use of the mails and other modes of communication to any contracts that failed to meet those standards. More moderate than the various proposals that had come before the House, it did not attempt to ban futures altogether. It did, however, require contracts to specify the exact grade being sold, the price of that grade, and the date of delivery. This would have avoided the problems of inaccurate differences, but it would make a contract so rigid as to be unmarketable. Hedging would become impossible with such contracts. Despite its defects, S.110 passed the Senate on March 28, 1914 and went to the House Committee on Agriculture.[31]

Frank Lever, the South Carolina congressman who had worked with the Republican Insurgents before the House shifted to a Democratic majority in 1912, was now the chair of the House Committee on Agriculture. He was committed to getting a bill passed that would regulate, but not destroy, the cotton exchanges.[32] With the clock ticking on the Congressional calendar, Lever knew that just waiting for Smith's bill to pass the Senate might leave too little time for the House to give it meaningful consideration before the last term of Congress before the 1914 elections, when the political calculation that favored a cotton bill might change. Better to get a House bill through and iron out the differences in a conference committee. He introduced a bill of his own and scheduled three days of hearings in April 1914 that featured prominent voices from the cotton industry who had previously called for similar legislation, including Lewis Parker.[33] Also testifying were two of the cotton traders who had been prosecuted by the Department of Justice in 1910, Frank B. Hayne and Robert Means Thompson—it was in these hearings that Hayne spoke about his role in the 1910 bull pool, in which he so dramatically denied any wrongdoing. Most of the witnesses agreed with him that the Lever bill was preferable to the Smith bill.

Lever's bill accepted the need for a certain amount of flexibility and ambiguity in futures contracts—that a futures contract conveyed information about the market even when it did not result in actual delivery. Smith's bill intended to force traders to commit to a specific grade for each contract, but that would effectively create separate markets on the Exchange for each of the grades, since contracts would no longer be interchangeable between grades. Lever's bill kept the basis contract intact. Smith's bill tried to satisfy some cotton growers who wanted a distinction made between the lush "gulf" cotton from the states around the Gulf of Mexico and the slightly scruffier "upland" cotton grown elsewhere, but this again would have created separate markets. Lever argued that the law should rely on the USDA for grading, and the federal Department of Agriculture made no such geographical distinctions. Enforcement of Smith's bill would have been handled by keeping offending contracts from being communicated via the mail, the telephone, or the telegraph. But Lever knew the SCA had tried and failed to get the Postmaster General to use his existing powers against NYCE practices—and that those denied communication by telephone could use window-shades. Lever's bill used a more powerful instrument—the unavoidable demands of Congress's taxing power—instead.[34]

Men like Hayne and Thompson understood the market. Their essential demands of regulation were: first, government grades should be adopted without modification; second, the Secretary of Agriculture should be the one to establish commercial differences for the exchanges, using spot prices in a handful of spot markets for his evaluation; third, deliveries should be even-running, that is, all one hundred bales in a contract should be the same grade, or else a penalty of $1 per bale would be assessed; fourth, "each bale should be separately marked and tagged, and identifiable as to weight, grade, and number, and date of its classification, and no recertification will be necessary for such lots as may be retendered"; fifth, no more **pro forma deliveries** would be permitted; sixth, no cotton certificated longer than a year could be tendered or recertificated, which had been a way of clearing out the trash cotton sitting in New York warehouses; seventh, minimum standards for the quality of cotton deliverable on contracts should be set; and eighth, a notional tax should be assessed on contracts following these rules (5¢ per bale) and a crippling tax should be assessed on those not following the rules ($5 per bale).[35] When Lever finally reported out a modified version of S.110, these were the basic stipulations of the bill.[36]

After a conference committee, the bill was signed on August 18, 1914.[37] The Cotton Futures Act became law. After nearly a quarter of a century of effort, the federal government had taken control of cotton futures trading but had done so in a way that would not extinguish it. At first the federal government had tried to make the cotton trade work better by the sunshine version of regulation, by spreading crop information, first through the Department of Agriculture, and later through the newly-permanent Census Bureau as well. Shining light onto the market had not worked, however. The price of cotton had still depended on information provided by unscrupulous operators who used their expertise to benefit themselves and kept prices low, impoverishing the farmers. Even when the information went to all—even when the corruption that created the 1905 window-shade scandal had been rooted out—disinterested information was not enough to break the market power of the bear operators centered around the ring of the Cotton Exchange in New York. That took money and willpower and the actions of individuals as they formed networks for their own profits: William Perry Brown and Frank B. Hayne, who cornered the market twice, bore the pain of federal investigation and the insults of the Secretary of Agriculture, and even suffered indictment at the hands of an attorney general who was tied to their opponents in trade, the New York networks. They persevered. In the end, their actions were validated by the law. The regulation that eventually emerged from the federal government made the practices of their Exchange the law of the land. The bulls had won the battle in the market, and their representatives used laws to remake the market in their image.

Conclusion

THE NEW YORK COTTON EXCHANGE OPENED right on schedule at 10:00 a.m. on Friday, July 31, 1914, after two days of falling prices as traders dealing with the usual end-of-month rush struggled as well to keep up with the situation in Europe. Soon after trading began, though, news from the continent found its way to the floor: Germany had mobilized its massive military machine. War was about to envelop Europe, and the effect on the cotton trade would be cataclysmic. "The bottom fell out of the market," as one journalist explained simply. In less than an hour, August cotton dropped from 11.05 to 9.60. December fell further. At 11:16 a.m., the president of the Exchange closed the floor and announced that trading was over until the following Tuesday.[1] That same day, in an unprecedented move, the New Orleans Cotton Exchange suspended trading indefinitely.[2] The First World War was about to change the world of cotton and the trading relationships that had taken shape over centuries. Closing the exchanges was only the first dislocation the war would cause, but it was a dramatic break with the past.

The plunging prices and short trading day in New York caused at least three firms to fail, including S.H.P. Pell and Company. When the prices began to collapse, Pell and Company were long of the market by nearly a quarter million bales, and they simply could not recover. Pell had "been known as the premier bull house in the cotton world" and was generally understood to be controlled by its "special partner," Robert Means Thompson, a member of the 1909–1910 bull pool. The next Monday, the attorney for some of

Pell's creditors filed for an involuntary petition of bankruptcy in US District Court. That attorney, representing Pell's creditors, was none other than David H. Miller, who had been involved in winding up Sully's business in 1904, had provided the document that led to the prosecution of the bull pool in 1910, and who had just seen the bulls, including Thompson, walk away from the case with *nolo contendere* pleas and nominal fines. Now Thompson pledged his own millions to make good Pell's losses since "the firm was generally recognized as his, and as hundreds of its creditors felt more secure because of his connection with it, he should see to it that their faith in him and the firm did not cost them money." That same Monday, the NYCE bowed to the inevitable and announced the indefinite closure of the Exchange.[3] Farmers had wanted to stop all cotton futures trading for twenty-five years. Now they got their wish, just two weeks before the Cotton Futures Act finally became law.

With the exchanges closed, the price of cotton tumbled. Cotton that brought 12.50 in July was selling for as low as 6.00 by October, just as the bulk of the crop began to come to market.[4] Southerners scrambled for solutions. The "buy-a-bale" movement in early September encouraged patriotic Americans to each invest fifty dollars to buy a bale of cotton at 10.00 and then hold it until the price stabilized, somewhere above 10.00.[5] Southern farmers' organizations and politicians, led by Frank Lever, demanded stronger federal action. The Farmers Union wanted the federal government to buy about a third of the crop at 12.00 and then legislate a crop reduction for the following year, but President Woodrow Wilson refused. He still believed in limited government activity and opposed federal intervention on behalf of any specific group. He did, however, support Lever's bill to set up federally supervised warehouses so farmers could borrow money against warehouse receipts.[6]

As the implications of the war became clear, the obstacles to reopening the exchanges began to seem less daunting. They key issue would be to adjust outstanding contracts to a lower basis price after several weeks without trading. A syndicate of financial institutions in New York subscribed $1.5 million to loan to brokers, to be recovered by a transaction surcharge.[7] The New York Cotton Exchange and the New Orleans Cotton Exchange both reopened for business on Monday morning, November 16, 1914, and trading proceeded relatively smoothly.[8] By the autumn of 1915, the "cotton crisis" had passed, and prices climbed steadily from October 1915 until 1920.[9]

The Cotton Futures Act of 1914 was the beginning of the federal government's long effort to provide direct oversight of markets where complex financial instruments were traded, markets that had important effects on producers, traders, and consumers. At first, however, things did not look good. Frank Lever, anxious to get legislation passed, modified the bill sent over from the Senate by essentially gutting it and putting entirely new provisions in the empty shell. The problem was that the Cotton Futures Act of 1914 was, in its enforcement mechanism, a taxation bill, so it fell foul of the first clause in Article One, Section Seven of the Constitution, which stipulates that taxation bills must originate in the House of Representatives. A New York cotton brokerage challenged the law, and it was deemed unconstitutional in US District Court in October 1915.[10] Rather than fight the ruling up to the Supreme Court, the federal government decided to pass a new law.[11] The political calculus that led to the bill's passage in the first place had not changed, and despite the New York Cotton Exchange's protests, cotton futures trading had not ground to a halt. A replacement bill, much the same as the first, was passed on August 11, 1916.[12] A few years after the war, in 1922, the Grain Futures Act regulated that trade, and the Commodity Exchange Act of 1936 combined federal oversight of most major commodities into one law, eventually leading to the formation of the Commodity Futures Trading Commission in 1974.[13]

Other outcomes of this crisis emerged from the prosecution of the bulls. While Supreme Court decisions in other antitrust cases, including those against Standard Oil and American Tobacco, had qualified the Sherman Act to apply to businesses that "unduly" restricted competition or that "injuriously" restrained trade, nonetheless *United States v. Patten* 226 US 525 (1913) outlawed corners on commodities markets.[14] The justices who made the ruling had no better understanding of those markets than the Populists and the Democratic representatives of southern farmers who had attacked futures trading for years. The ruling made a certain outcome on the market illegal but said nothing about the market practices that made that outcome possible. The Supreme Court could not very well attack futures trading itself since *Chicago Board of Trade v. Christie Grain*, 198 US 236 (1905) had explicitly declared futures trading to be legal, precisely because of the possibility that contracts would mature and money would be exchanged for goods. However, the Supreme Court supported the government's charge: short selling was fine even when more cotton was sold than actually existed, but buying from short sellers and then demanding the cotton was not.

In other words, futures trading was justified by the possibility of delivery, but actually insisting on delivery was a restraint of trade. This seems contradictory. Knowing just how much cotton would be available had long been at the heart of futures trading, and the number of bales of cotton traded on futures contracts had usually exceeded the number of bales actually produced each year because most futures contracts never matured. Nonetheless, *Patten* was now the law of the land, and it meant that the federal government could use the Sherman Anti-Trust Act of 1890 against corners on commodities markets in the future.

The dance between the bulls and bears significantly impacted the structures within which both groups had operated. They formed the institutions that structured their actions and allowed the bulls to corner the market twice and raise the price of cotton, despite insults and criminal prosecutions. The bears' institutions put the power of the federal government behind their goals. Finally, a hungry insect helped the bulls join farmers into networks. When Congress finally saw a shift from Republican to Democrat majorities, their organizations and representatives passed the laws that made the market act as the bulls had long desired. World War I would change all this, but for the moment, in 1914, the bulls were triumphant—in the market and in the institutions of government that enforced their rules on even their opponents.

But what of the actors who played such an important role in changing the world of cotton in the first decade of the twentieth century? Frank B. Hayne remained an important businessman in New Orleans. He served on the Board of Directors of the New Orleans Cotton Exchange and for a time as its president.[15] He left his mark on the physical city, too, as one of the organizers of the New Orleans Lakeshore Land Company in 1910, which developed Hayne Boulevard on the east side of the Inner Harbor Navigation Canal.[16] His stature increased even further during World War I when he was the first chairman of the New Orleans chapter of the American Red Cross.[17] A local encyclopedia remembers him as a promoter of Mardi Gras who helped make New Orleans "famous all over the world."[18]

Unlike Hayne, Daniel Sully was not destined for such glory. Over the decade discussed here, he had lost both his shirt and his reputation. The young cotton king of the first corner who called original margins on Brown in the spring of 1903 failed miserably and dramatically in just the same way when others called his margins in 1904. He survived his failure, but would never again ascend to such commanding heights. It is not easy to trace his career after his resounding crash. One of his obituaries would later claim that in 1910, he had launched a new venture in Britain, introducing a new type of cotton gin.[19] The result was, in his own words, "more business troubles." The *New York Times* found him in 1912 running a boarding house in his grandiose one-time summer home on Watch Hill, in Rhode Island.[20] His wife, so tightly bound into his business before his collapse, had died ten months earlier.[21] He still had a gift for market timing, however, and the real estate savvy that led him, at the height of his glory, to buy a house in the newly-developed neighborhood of New York City's Upper East Side. In 1920 he moved west, to Beverly Hills, which was just being developed. Ten years later, he died there at age 69, of heart failure.[22]

William P. Brown, the cotton bull, surprisingly failed to appear when the New Orleans Cotton Exchange reopened in November 1914. He made no public comment when the Supreme Court invalidated the Cotton Futures Act of 1914, nor when Congress passed its replacement in 1916. While the law remade the market according to his own practices, he played no public role. Where was he? Brown had spent the late summer of 1914 in Atlantic City, suffering from congestion of the lungs at the Marlborough-Blenheim Hotel. While the trading floors stood silent, on October 5, 1914, he died in New Orleans at the age of fifty-three.[23]

The cotton bull was dead, but the new laws meant that Brown's actions would live on. Yet his story was forgotten. The marvelous corner of 1903 was pinned on Daniel Sully, who failed the following spring; the intertwined drama of rising prices and federal prosecution of 1910 was associated more with Patten than with the country boy from Caledonia, who had moved to New Orleans and parlayed his poker-playing cool into several fortunes, including the grandest house on St. Charles Avenue. Brown was dead, but the Cotton Futures Act validated his life and work, his networks and connections that stretched from the Crescent City to the rings of trade in New York.

Why is the story of the cotton kings significant, and why has it not been told before? Although it had been mostly lost to history, the contest between the cotton kings on opposite sides of the market, the dance of the bulls and the bears, was well known to their contemporaries—albeit not always entirely understood. William Garrott Brown mentioned it as he remarked on New Orleans's bright future in 1904.[24] W.E.B. Du Bois had a chapter about the cotton corner in his 1911 novel about postbellum cotton brokering, *The Quest of the Silver Fleece;* he certainly understood the way

bull brokers did good work for farmers, and that the two sometimes worked together.[25] Yet after the Progressive era the story of
the 1903 corner was swallowed up by Sully's failure in 1904, and
the bull campaigns of 1909–1910 have generally been ascribed
to James Patten, the Wheat King. Taken seriously, this forgotten
history has the potential to illuminate both the regional power
dynamics at the beginning of the twentieth century and the nature
of government regulation of markets. The events described here
do not figure in the standard accounts of the Progressive era, but
the very reasons for their absence are precisely what make them
important.

This struggle between New Orleans and New York over cotton
futures trading does not fit the usual accounts of the antitrust movement because the actors are unfamiliar. The story of the Gilded Age
and the rise of large-scale business organizations has traditionally
been told a bit like a Shakespearian tragedy. John D. Rockefeller
starts out a poor boy and eventually Standard Oil gets too powerful and abuses other companies and the public. The villains of the
antitrust story are men and their corporations acting in the market. In *The Cotton Kings*, though, it is not so much particular corporations that are using monopoly power to prevent markets from
working properly so much as the markets themselves. Individual
bear traders could come and go, but it was the market in which
they traded—the New York Cotton Exchange—that was the problem. This very transience of the individual traders and firms gave
the market the impression of naturalness. The idealization of "the
market" in recent decades has made it that much harder to realize
that sometimes it was the market itself that was restraining trade. If
the market behaved in ways people thought was natural, then there
would be no reason to explore its history.

When antitrust regulation took shape, the problem it sought
to control was powerful corporations or unscrupulous traders using
their market position to push prices up. Standard Oil wanted to control the whole supply of oil so it could raise prices and get more
profit. The earliest laws about commodities were meant to prevent
traders from forestalling or engrossing grain supplies and pushing
the price of bread beyond the reach of the poor. When the New
Orleans bulls pushed up the price of cotton, the assumption was that
they were doing something wrong. Keeping the prices low by manipulating the market, as the NYCE had been doing, did not raise the
same alarms because it was not part of the larger pattern by which
monopolistic corporations raised prices and hurt consumers.

The Cotton Kings tells an unusual story. Most historians of this period depict white men in the South, especially rich and powerful ones, working against progressive reform rather than for it. Since at least C. Vann Woodward's 1951 *The Origins of the New South*, with its chapter on "Progressivism—For Whites Only," southern whites were painted as opposing every progressive reform from compulsory education to cattle tick eradication. Arguing that Yankees were malevolently and systematically damaging the South went out of fashion in the 1950s, but when it comes to cotton prices, it is hard to understand the conflict between New York and New Orleans in anything but sectional terms, and equally hard to see the corrupt practices of the NYCE as anything but the profiteering of Yankee money interests at the expense of southern farmers, white and black.[26]

Notably, the practices and values that governed the cotton trade after the Cotton Futures Act of 1914 came from within the trade itself, the honest part of the trade that wanted to use futures trading to decrease price volatility, to allow the best information to shape prices, and to hedge risk. The capacity for the honest parts of a financial market to drive out the dishonest parts, with the help of assertive federal regulation, should give us all hope. The power of government and regulation to establish practices that benefited all market participants, and helped make the price of cotton more accurately reflect the actual real-world conditions of supply and demand, is a power worth preserving, remembering, and celebrating.

> I do not know whether I have made that clear to you or
> not. It is clear to me, but sometimes I get a thing so clear
> to myself that I can not explain it to anybody else.[27]
> —Fuller Callaway, 1914

ESSAY ON SOURCES

I T IS ALWAYS A bit daring for a historian to claim that no one has ever written about a topic, but the cotton corner of 1903 comes close to that status. Jonathan Robins's dissertation makes use of the episode in his examination of the global cotton trade and the Atlantic Empire in the first two decades of the twentieth century.[1] When other historians have noticed the cotton corner of 1903, they have attributed it to Daniel J. Sully and bundled it into his failure in 1904. His spectacular failure has proven more memorable than the earlier success of more modest men. The relatively consistent rise in prices between William P. Brown's and Frank B. Hayne's corner in summer 1903 and Sully's failure in 1904 makes sense of this interpretation, although this book contradicts it, emphasizing instead the corner over the failure. Likewise with the corner of 1909–1910: because James A. Patten was already well known for cornering wheat in Chicago in spring 1909, he is often given credit for being in charge of the 1910 cotton corner as well. The Supreme Court case that ruled that corners could be prosecuted under the Sherman Anti-Trust Act bore his name.[2]

To trace this story, this book draws upon several distinct bodies of literature. Its principal contribution consists in following these actors as they formed networks, and in linking together some previously disconnected themes. The historical interaction between futures trading, private regulation that used membership in an exchange as its enforcement instrument, and eventually the standardization of such rules by government is the larger narrative these men created. Therefore the book has made use of scholarship on futures trading and the role of information in setting commodity prices, private regulation and the networks it required, and finally the Progressive era regulation of new financial derivatives in order to standardize practices across the exchanges, and grades of cotton along the way. That regulation made cotton prices better reflect supply and demand. Without them, privately enforced rules and biased information prevailed, leaving the cotton farmers of the South trapped within a structure where their crops did not pay the cost of producing them.

This history straddles many categories—business history, southern history, social history, political history, environmental history—but it is not economic history as such. No theories or formulae backed up by data are used. The incidents speak for themselves, and perhaps this history—and the data collected to support our understanding of more narrative sources—will prove useful to economic historians. *The Cotton Kings* is in part a social history of New Orleans, but—controversially perhaps—the reader will find no people of color, no poor people, and few women. When women do appear in this story, it is as wives and daughters of powerful white men. They were only supporting actors to our principal characters. A brief anecdote from William P. Brown's life illustrates the reasons for these absences. When New Orleans segregated its streetcars in 1902, Brown became the second person to be fined for defying the Jim Crow ordinance "by taking a seat in the negro compartment."[3] Of course, this is not to say that Brown was some sort of civil rights hero. Rather, he was just a man for whom time was money. Being on the exchange in time for the opening bell was well worth the twenty-five dollar fine he had to pay. These omissions are regrettable but hopefully understandable. This story focuses on cotton futures trading, and, in the period and contexts covered, it was, in fact, simply powerful white men who traded cotton futures.

While the scholarship on cotton is vast, the literature on cotton marketing, cotton exchanges, and futures trading is less so. It begins with primary sources: as changes took place in the early twentieth century, some authors wrote books to explain the marketing of cotton with reference to both contemporary practices and their origins. These texts have served as primary sources and secondary sources, analysis of what was present-day to its authors, but from today's vantage point is an interpretation of the past. The most important of these was M. B. Hammond's 1897 *The Cotton Industry*.[4] The report on the cotton exchanges by Herbert Knox Smith was also a significant source for the history of the development of cotton marketing in the late nineteenth century, as were certain publications that emerged from the statistical work of the agricultural census.[5] When the marketing of the American cotton crop began to change in the 1930s with the advent of greater federal government involvement at a number of levels, there was another brief flurry of writing. These histories, like those a generation earlier, provided a wealth of knowledge and a series of practical interpretations that proved invaluable.[6]

Cotton marketing rose in importance to historians when a University of Chicago graduate student, Harold Woodman, attempted "to learn more about the movement of the cotton from the plantations and farms in the South to the consuming mills in the North and abroad."[7] Starting with the rise of cotton production after the adoption of Eli Whitney's cotton gin and continuing to the eve of the Great Depression, Woodman's 1968 book, *King Cotton and His Retainers: Financing and Marketing the Cotton Crop of the South, 1800–1925*, fell squarely within the broad body of scholarship about the South led by C. Vann Woodward, a central concern of which was the question of change versus continuity in the institutions and personnel of the South across the Civil War. *King Cotton and His Retainers* provided an important foundation about the practical business of cotton that underlay a generation or more of scholarship about the problems of land tenure, cotton production, and poverty in the American South.[8] Around the same time, L. Tuffly Ellis was also writing about the postbellum cotton trade, particularly in Texas.[9] Other scholars refined Woodman's ideas and pursued leads from his work, mostly in the antebellum and immediate postbellum period, though John R. Killick carried the story further into the nineteenth century, while at the same time pursuing the transatlantic aspects of the trade.[10]

Killick's work prefigured more recent interpretive shifts in which historians of the United States have begun to pay much more attention to global processes and world history. One part of this movement has been the study of particular commodities, each of which reveals important things about how global trade and the transfer of information, materials, and labor occurred: salt, cod, chewing gum, and so on.[11] As part of this trend, Harvard historian Sven Beckert has cornered the market on the global history of cotton, producing two influential articles and *The Empire of Cotton: A Global History*, though—like our bulls—he has company in the globalization of cotton history. Giorgio Riello's prize-winning *Cotton: The Fabric That Made the Modern World* traces its path to a global commodity in the mid-eighteenth century, while Andrew Zimmerman explores the connections between cotton production in the American South and Africa in *Alabama in Africa: Booker T. Washington, the German Empire, and the Globalization of the New South*.[12] These histories, more worldly than national, link agriculture to world trade in welcome ways and provide the backbone for understanding the relationship between the cotton exchanges of New York and New Orleans and the world-wide demand for cotton, as well as its supply.

Relatively little has been written on the cotton exchanges themselves, at least by historians. L. Tuffly Ellis wrote about the first decade of the New Orleans Cotton Exchange in 1973, and Kenneth J. Lipartito published an article in 1983 about the New York Cotton Exchange, but Robert Bouilly's 1975 dissertation remains the best historical overview.[13] On the other hand, both economists and economic historians have done considerable work on the histories of the commodity exchanges and the various types of trades that took place there. In particular, Jeffrey Williams's study of commodity exchanges and the periodization of their development emphasizes the importance of futures trading in their development. The early sophistication of the market in future deliveries provides insights about the development of agricultural marketing in general before federal involvement in the twentieth century. Since intricate and refined futures trading emerged early enough to be noticed by 1847—the same year the Oxford English Dictionary supplies for the first usage of the terms "bulls" and "bears"—it is a signpost to understanding the development and importance of private regulation, applicable only to members in commodity exchanges.[14] For that reason the history of private commercial law, a subject principally addressed by legal scholars, has often used case studies of cotton exchanges and other commodity exchanges in its examination of private regulation.[15]

As for cotton futures trading, it is a derivative of traditional cotton marketing and spot sales that rose to prominence after the Civil War. The historical discipline has not devoted much attention to financial derivatives, their appearance and development in modern economic life. For a long time, most of those who really understood futures trading were the ones in the pits. Some, like Brown, were too busy making fortunes to bother writing much about it, while others, like Sully, obviously did not understand the market as well as they thought they did. Proper economists began writing about futures trading in the early twentieth century, as did some political scientists who wrote as the regulations discussed here began to be put in place.[16] Economists, of course, have continued to study futures trading, sometimes including brief accounts of its history. An entire journal devoted to the subject has been published for more than a quarter century, and the theories developed in its pages relate to many of the themes our historical analysis uncovers: the influence of information on the behavior of prices, the importance of hedging in smoothing volatility, the role of seasonality and an agricultural credit calendar in the pricing of commodities.[17] Yet the models and data presented there seem disconnected from the history, especially the role of human effort in affecting the movement of prices and the importance of regulation in making those prices reflect market conditions.

The importance of information and its influence on prices is one of the principal defenses of futures trading offered by market participants, economic theorists, and economic historians alike. This book emphasizes the imperfection and manipulation of the information contained within futures prices, and claims that people needed to act—to corner the market—in order to make information (and the prices that reflected that information) work as it should. Both economic theory and traders in financial derivatives, including futures, demonstrate how futures trading plays a role in reducing price volatility. Though sympathetic with this defense of both futures markets and fictitious dealing (selling what one does not own), it is worth noticing that the literature's conclusions about the way that price equilibria emerge from futures markets often rely on the trans-actors' "absence of asymmetric information." The battle over prices is a battle over information. In the real world, crop predictions dic-tated prices, and inflated estimates of supply kept prices low. This history uncovers the difficulties of providing accurate information and distributing it to all market participants. Even with disinterested suppliers of market information, getting the price to reflect increas-ing demand and limited supply took work—financial resources, market corners, and eventually federal regulation. Historical stud-ies like *The Cotton Kings* may eventually offer new understanding of economic theories and models of prices.[18]

In fact, economists have used information theory as a correc-tive to neoclassical views that naturalize price and have contrib-uted significant and useful theories of imperfect information, and asymmetrically known information, in the development of eco-nomic equilibria.[19] Historians' treatment of information is, unsur-prisingly, different than that used by economists. In an age when computing and communication technology have improved at an unprecedented rate, scholars have begun to pay attention to how information circulated in the past and what effects that had.[20] Early work tended to focus on the eighteenth and early nineteenth centuries, when advances in transportation and communication allowed messages to be carried more quickly. Recent studies have begun to complicate the subject by venturing into the era of the telegraph, later in the nineteenth century, when for the first time information was not "limited by the speed with which messengers could travel and the distance at which eyes could see signals," as Daniel Walker Howe explained it.[21] The field of communication and information history is now advancing deeper into the century, examining the California Gold Rush and the Civil War, as well as the postbellum shifts accompanying telephony and near-instantaneous transatlantic communication.[22] Historians of technology have provided their unique perspectives on the origins of the information age—in the context of European economic expansion, imperialism, and the development of the nation-state.[23]

The history of information has developed separately from the history of government regulation of business and markets, although the first regulatory movements in both state and federal government consisted of "sunshine commissions": efforts to shed light on business practices and thus bring best practices to light. As business grew in the late nineteenth century, regulation more often took the path of working against market tendencies, especially when regulators viewed big as bad in the merger movement and monopoly period of business history. Yet traditional historians have long grasped that twentieth-century business and government have developed hand-in-glove, rather than opposed to one another. After all, business interests are hardly uniform or monolithic. Different sectors have different goals—compare, for example, merchants and bankers, manufacturers and utility companies. Likewise, competition between firms can create different practices that skew market mechanisms. The actions of the New Orleans and New York Cotton Exchanges related in this book illustrate that exact point. Indeed, the history of regulation indicates the importance of government in mediating the relationships among competing interest groups, and very often relies on expertise provided by industry and business itself.[24] While some scholars have seen Populism and political action as an attack on business practices, scholars including Charles Postel and Elizabeth Sanders have emphasized the interactions between the two.[25]

The new "history of capitalism" also has begun to turn historians' attention to the topics of futures trading and commodity exchanges. Perhaps the interest has been inspired by the computer-ization of futures trading (and many other financial markets), which makes the world of open outcry trading and blackboards seem more distant.[26] Cotton exchanges are now hotels and shopping centers. Or perhaps this recent history of new forms of exchange, new deriva-tives, and faster-flowing information has provided signals to histori-ans about the origins and importance of the older version of trade. Jonathan Ira Levy wrote the best overview of the key issues in the history of futures trading for this period, and his 2012 book puts commodity futures trading in the context of a range of financial instruments and practices designed to mitigate risk as American capitalism grew rapidly in scale and complexity.[27] *The Cotton Kings* probably takes a more jaundiced view of the role of futures trad-ing in mitigating risk: in a well-regulated market, perhaps, but the market did not regulate itself very well and getting effective federal regulation was a slow process. Commodities trading is inherently global, so this account of cotton futures trading should be read in the context of studies of futures trading of other commodities in various countries and international overviews.[28]

There is an older history of capitalism that studied how the eco-nomic system developed in concert with the nation-state, although it relied on the profit-seeking of private investors. It has been a subject of interest more for European and world historians than scholars of US history, though that is beginning to change. There has been a longstanding interest in political economy among US historians, who have relied principally on the interactions between institutions and market mechanisms—which is to say, between businessmen and laws. In this they have been joined by political scientists, sociologists, anthropologists, geographers, and scholars from an array of other disciplines who use historical cases to examine the development of capitalism.[29]

The newer history of capitalism is more closely tied to intellec-tual history: the frameworks that explain Adam Smith, for example, or the relentless revolution of Joyce Appleby that relies so heavily on changes in mentalité to explain industrialization and the rise of the capitalist system. Moreover, recent work in the history of capitalism tends to rely on abstract notions—market laws and market forces, imperialism and capitalism, space and time—whereas this book seeks to avoid abstractions.[30] While Jonathan Ira Levy's 2006 article "Contemplating Delivery" paid attention to conflicting ideas about futures trading and how those affected behavior in the market and the relationship between commerce and government regulation,

The Cotton Kings is much more interested in the actual mechanics of trading, rather than ideas about it. The delivery of physical cotton on futures contracts is the crux of the 1903 corner, not ideas about delivery. For a similar reason we have little to say about bucket shops, where information about prices was used to place bets on the market but without the possibility of delivery. David Hochfelder has made a compelling argument that these bucket shops expanded the involvement of everyday people with commodity and stock exchanges and thus changed attitudes toward the development of these markets, but this work focuses on the markets themselves and the things that changed prices there.[31]

In these pages, the history of capitalism is returned to its grubby reality rather than its grand theories—to small individual actions performed by people seeking profits, without presupposing the economic system within which they operated. The actions they performed and the institutions and networks they built or deployed for their individual gain can illuminate as much about the history of capitalism as do examinations of the theories of economic structures. This approach assumes humans were the agents of change, and their actions are more important than their mindsets in understanding how they created the modern capitalist system and the modern regulatory state.

"Agency" is a fraught word in historical studies in the last half-century or so. Once upon a time, historians thought that only powerful white men in the West had agency to make things happen rather than just have things happen to them.[32] In tandem with the social upheavals of the 1960s came the new social history and the realization that many more kinds of people had exercised agency than previously admitted. "History from the bottom up" was the rallying cry, which required that people on the bottom have the will and the power to effect historical change. Whole new subdisciplines took shape around this change.[33] Eventually the steam went out of the 1960s social movements. The political left, which had championed these new subaltern histories, faltered with the end of the Cold War and, some claimed, the end of history itself. The shine of agency began to dim. If people have agency, why do their actions often have such little effect? One labor historian described agency as nothing more than a "patina of volition."[34] The pendulum swung back, emphasizing the constraints, the failures people had faced, pointing out the difference between people trying to change the world and those succeeding.[35]

Of course, some historians toiling in other fields had long since necessarily taken a different view of agency and what might count as an agent. Historians of medicine knew the power of the tiniest organisms to lay low the mighty. If part of agency is the ability to make others do things, then the mosquito, for instance, has plenty. Joyce E. Chaplin explained how the mosquito's need to reproduce and, in the process bite humans and transmit malaria, shaped ideas about colonial South Carolina and guided how people interacted with their environment.[36] Timothy Mitchell made an even more intricate argument about the role a 1942 malaria epidemic played in the war over Egypt being fought at the same time. As Mitchell points out, earlier studies limit themselves by "having already decided who counts as an agent." "No explanation grounded in the universalizing force of human projects and intentions," he argues, "can explore whether the very possibility of the human, of intentionality, of abstraction depends on, at the same time as it overlooks, nonhuman elements."[37] Larger animals matter, too. As Pekka Hämäläinen argues, "Horses did bring new possibilities, prosperity, and power to Plains Indians, but they also brought destabilization, dispossession, and destruction."[38]

The Cotton Kings' discussion of the boll weevil fits within this tradition. Agency is not the same thing as intentionality. Critics of agency may point out that intentions do not always have an effect, but many things have effects other than their intentions. Historians of science and technology have enlarged this insight and applied concepts of nonhuman agency to objects and artifacts. If mosquitoes, horses, and boll weevils have agency, it is because they function as agents in human stories. When human stories are told with these agents added back in, they shed light on how humans have used the actions of these organisms to their own ends. Humans use the whole corpus of elements as agents, not all of which are animate. The institutions of the cotton exchanges embodied the goals and behavior of their members and at the same time shaped the actions of those participants with their rules and customs and physical devices such as the rings of trade and the chalkboards on which workers recorded changing prices. A chalkboard might be an agent, as much as a weevil or a hurricane or a poker-playing cotton broker. This is not new. Scholars in science and technology studies have long noted the importance of nonhuman, sometimes inanimate agents in the laboratory and in the field. This interpretation of the cotton trade at the turn of the last century borrows from these insights.[39]

These insights, that nonhumans can be agents, are applied from other fields to business history, which by its very nature began as a chronicle of great men. William P. Brown is indeed powerful, but he could not have done what he did without the boll weevil nor the elegant building that stood on the corner of Gravier and Carondelet. A basic tool for analysis comes from actor-network theory (ANT), especially as articulated by Bruno Latour in his *Reassembling the Social: An Introduction to Actor-Network Theory*.[40] As Latour explains, ANT comes out of the study of science, where the interplay between ideas, people, and objects and the way these three kinds of things form networks that bring about change is perhaps most readily apparent. Business history has long given much attention to understanding how networks shape firms, industries, and practices, and in recent years some business history has begun to use the more capacious understandings of how networks might be assembled and operate provided by ANT.[41]

Understanding how people formed networks was built upon an examination of links between New Orleans businessmen at the beginning of the twentieth century. Historians' interest in the New Orleans business community and its banks focuses primarily on the antebellum period. There is surprisingly little after that watershed.[42] In the 1960s, Joy J. Jackson wrote about New Orleans business and political history in the Gilded Age, up to 1896.[43] Burton I. Kaufman wrote a couple of articles in the early 1970s about New Orleans and foreign trade in the early twentieth century.[44] At present, Scott P. Marler is the leading scholar in an otherwise almost empty field, with an overview article and a book.[45] A few scattered works give portraits of individual business leaders.[46] Studies of banking in New Orleans, and even the South as a whole, in this period are even more scarce. Larry Schweikart carries the story of banking in the South up to Reconstruction, and a 1972 book by George D. Green covers Louisiana more specifically from the time of the Louisiana Purchase to the Civil War, but only a 1999 dissertation and an article in a festschrift cover the period between the Civil War and World War I in the South.[47] With so little written, this book does not really challenge an existing historiographical consensus as much as illuminate one part of New Orleans's postbellum business history. Hopefully it will inspire further work in a rich field.

NOTES

INTRODUCTION

1. As Jonathan Robins points out, "Industry and agriculture were able to organize without state intervention, but all ultimately lacked the power to reform existing state institutions or create new and effective ones." Robins, "The Cotton Crisis: Globalization and Empire in the Atlantic World, 1902–1920" (PhD diss., University of Rochester, 2010), 28.
2. "Cotton Soars Again," *New York Tribune*, May 20, 1903.
3. Harold D. Woodman, *King Cotton and His Retainers: Financing and Marketing the Cotton Crop of the South, 1800–1925* (Columbia: University of South Carolina Press, 1990 [1968]), ix–xiv, 5–71.
4. Woodman, *King Cotton and His Retainers*, 269–294.
5. M. B. Hammond, *The Cotton Industry: An Essay in American Economic History* (New York: Macmillan, 1897), 301.
6. A.W.B. Simpson, "The Origins of Futures Trading in the Liverpool Cotton Market," in Peter Cane and Jane Stapleton, *Essays for Patrick Atiyah* (Oxford: Clarendon Press, 1991), 179–208.
7. Jonathan Ira Levy, "Contemplating Delivery: Futures Trading and the Problem of Commodity Exchange in the United States, 1875–1905," *American Historical Review* 111, no. 2 (April 2006): 307–335, studies the development of the 1905 Supreme Court case *Board of Trade v. Christie*, which drew the distinction between fictitious produce traded in bucket shops, where delivery was not expected but transactors merely bet on price movements, and the legitimate futures trade, which rested upon this promise of eventual delivery of goods.
8. The volume of trade made London the largest stock exchange as well, and our emphasis on the battle between New York and New Orleans should not obscure the importance of English markets in setting prices. Leslie Hannah, "J. P. Morgan in London and New York before 1914," *Business History Review* 85, no. 1 (Spring 2011): 113–150.
9. Hans Hirschstein, "Commodity Exchanges in Germany," *Annals of the American Academy of Political and Social Science* 155 (May 1931), 208–217; Julia Laura Rischbieter, *Mikro-Ökonomie der Globalisierung: Kaffee, Kaufleute und Konsumenten im Kaiserreich 1870–1914* (Köln: Böhlau Verlag, 2011), 132–182.
10. Chicago *Daily Tribune*, January 21, 1890; *House Journal*, 51st Cong., 1st Sess., January 20, 1890, p. 137. For a discussion of the Butterworth Bill and related initiatives, see Jonathan Lurie, "Commodities Exchanges, Agrarian 'Political Power,' and the Antioption Battle, 1890–1894," *Agricultural History* 48, no. 1 (January 1974): 115–125.

11. Levy, "Contemplating Delivery," 307–309; David Hochfelder, "'Where the Common People Could Speculate': The Ticker, Bucket Shops, and the Origins of Popular Participation in Financial Markets, 1880–1920," *Journal of American History* 93, no. 2 (Sept. 2006), 335–358.

12. "The Butterworth Bill," *Atlanta Constitution*, April 16, 1890, p. 4.

13. "For And Against Futures," *Chicago Daily Tribune*, April 12, 1890, p. 5.

14. "Board Of Trade Men Don't Like It," *Chicago Daily Tribune*, January 21, 1890, p. 3.

15. "The Butterworth Bill," *Atlanta Constitution*, April 30, 1890, p. 4; "The Question of 'Futures,'" *Atlanta Constitution*, May 9, 1890, p. 6.

16. "Cotton and the Butterworth Bill," New Orleans *Daily Picayune*, April 30, 1890, p. 4.

CHAPTER 1

1. See Paul M. Gaston, *The New South Creed: A Study in Southern Myth-Making* (Montgomery, Ala.: NewSouth Books, 2002) for the best overview of this idea.

2. "William Perry Brown," in *The National Cyclopedia of American Biography*, vol. 15 (New York: James T. White & Co., 1916), 258; US Federal Census of Population, 1860, Mississippi, Lowndes County, Caledonia, p. 42; W. L. Lipscomb, *A History of Columbus, Mississippi, During the 19th Century* (Birmingham, Ala.: Dispatch Printing Co. 1909), 122–126; Paul Hays, "John Cherry Brown (1833–1877)" www.findagrave.com/cgi-bin/fg.cgi?page=gr&GRid=34262215 (accessed May 29, 2012); Mack Egger, Dale Darnell, and Earlene Egger, *In the Beginning—"Up Home": A History of Caledonia, Lowndes County, Mississippi* (Caldeonia, Miss.: n.p., 2004), Billups-Garth Archives, Columbus-Lowndes Public Library, Columbus, Miss.; *Report of the Joint Select Committee to Inquire into the Condition of Affairs in the Late Insurrectionary States*, Vol. 12, Mississippi, vol. II (Washington, D.C.: GPO, 1872), 673, 770; US Federal Census of Population,1880, Mississippi, Lowndes County, Caledonia, p. 154A; Vernon (Alabama), *Pioneer*, May 26, 1876; "'Poker' Brown's Rise To Cotton King From Clerk," Chicago *Tribune*, May 23, 1903, Brown Scrapbook; US Federal Census of Population,1880, Mississippi, Lowndes County, Columbus, p. 206A; "Mississippi Proud Of Brown The New King Of Cotton," New Orleans *Daily States*, May 25, 1903; Advertisement, Vernon (Ala.) *Courier*, September 12, 1889, p. 4; G. L. Goldsmith, *Columbus in One Hundred Verses: Including a Directory of its Mercantile and Industrial Institutions* Columbus, Miss.: G. L. Goldsmith, 1889), 32.

3. Advertisement, Alexandria *Louisiana Democrat*, December 6, 1882, p. 4.

4. Thomas D. Clark, *Pills, Petticoats and Plows: The Southern Country Store* (Indianapolis: Bobbs-Merrill, 1944), 317–318; Gerald Carson, "Cracker Barrel Store: Southern Style," *Georgia Review* 9, no. 1 (Spring 1955), 29; Alfred B. Shepperson, *The Standard Telegraphic Cipher Code for the Cotton Trade* (New York: Alfred B. Shepperson, 1881).

5. James McManus, *Cowboys Full: The Story of Poker* (London: Souvenir Press, 2010), 49–66. Recent writers, building on the popularity of poker since the advent of the Internet, have emphasized the similarities and connections between poker and capitalism, especially finance and futures trading. As Ole Bjerg has argued, "Poker is a game that requires a very particular set of skills related to the art of navigating in an environment that is ultimately governed by chance." Ole Bjerg, *Poker: The Parody of Capitalism* (Ann Arbor: University of Michigan Press, 2011), 10. See also Aaron Brown, *The Poker Face of Wall Street* (Hoboken, N.J.: Wiley, 2006), 157–170, for the argument that gambling and futures trading have fundamental similarities (unlike contemporary observers in the late nineteenth century, Brown does not see this as a bad thing).

6. "'Poker' Brown's Rise To Cotton King From Clerk," Chicago *Tribune*, May 23, 1903, Brown Scrapbook, Folder 1, Box 1, William Perry Brown Papers, Historic New Orleans Collection, New Orleans.

7. Untitled clipping, *New York Press,* May 24, 1903, Brown Scrapbook.

8. "Mississippi Proud Of Brown The New King Of Cotton," New Orleans *Daily States*, May 25, 1903, Brown Scrapbook.

9. "William Perry Brown," in *The National Cyclopedia of American Biography*, vol. 15 (New York: James T. White & Co., 1916), 258; Hubert Humphreys, "Photographic Views of Red River Raft, 1873," *Louisiana History* 12, no. 2 (Spring 1971): 101–108; M. B. Hammond, *The Cotton Industry: An Essay in American Economic History* (New York: Macmillan, 1897), 174–177; "Society," *New Orleans Daily Picayune*, Dec. 30, 1894, p. 12; *Soards' New Orleans City Directory* (New Orleans: Soards' Directory Co., 1893), 390; *Soards' New Orleans City Directory* (New Orleans: Soards' Directory Co., 1895), 164; *Soards' New Orleans City Directory* (New Orleans: Soards' Directory Co., 1897), 157; Paul Hays, "John Cherry Brown (1833–1877)," http://www.findagrave.com/cgi-bin/fg.cgi?page=gr&GRid=34262215, (accessed 29 May 2012); United States Federal Census of Population,1900, Louisiana, Webster Parish, Police Jury Ward 4, District 111, p. 4.

10. "Modern New Orleans in the New Century," New Orleans *Daily Picayune*, September 1, 1901, p. 12; "To Attract Foreign Ships," *New York Times*, October 27, 1896; John Kendall, *The History of New Orleans* (Chicago: Lewis Pub. Co., 1922), Ch. 38.

11. *New York Cotton Exchange, 1871–1923* (New York: New York Cotton Exchange, 1923), 21; Hammond, *The Cotton Industry: An Essay in American Economic History* (New York: Macmillan, 1897), 301; Meigs O. Frost, *"Hester Says-" An Intimate Personal Sketch of the World's Greatest Cotton Authority* (New Orleans: Theo. H. Harvey Press, 1926), n.p.; United States, Bureau of Corporations, *Report of the Commissioner of Corporations on Cotton Exchanges*, Part 1 (Washington, D.C.: GPO, 1908), 55–56.

12. James E. Boyle, *Cotton and the New Orleans Cotton Exchange: A Century of Commercial Evolution* (Garden City, N.J.: Country Life Press, 1934), 110.

13. United States, Bureau of Corporations, *Report of the Commissioner of Corporations on Cotton Exchanges*, Part 1 (Washington, D.C.: GPO, 1908), 54–55; Hammond, *The Cotton Industry: An Essay in American Economic History* (New York: Macmillan, 1897), 302.

14. *Rules Governing Business in Contracts for the Future Delivery of Cotton in the New Orleans Cotton Exchange, Adopted January 1880* (New Orleans: Clark & Hofeline Steam Power Book Printers, 1880); *Charter, Constitution, By-Laws and Rules of the New Orleans Cotton Exchange* (New Orleans: L. Graham & Son, 1894), 7.

15. See Lisa Bernstein, "Private Commercial Law in the Cotton Industry: Creating Cooperation through Rules, Norms, and Institutions," *Michigan Law Review* 99, no. 7 (June 2001): 1724–1790.

16. *By-Laws and Rules of the New Orleans Cotton Exchange, Embracing All Rules Governing the Spot and Future Contract Cotton Business in the New Orleans Market. Including Revisions Up To November 29ᵗʰ, 1894* (New Orleans: L. Graham & Son, 1894), 45–46.

17. One of the best explanations of hedging is found in G. Wright Hoffman, *Future Trading upon Organized Commodity Markets in the United States* (Philadelphia: University of Pennsylvania Press, 1932), 4, 142–143. See also the entry for **hedging** in the glossary in this book.

18. For a good account of how information could be used to manipulate markets at this time, see Richard White, "Information, Markets, and Corruption: Transcontinental Railroads in the Gilded Age," *Journal of American History* 90:1 (2003): 19–43.

19. "Cotton," New Orleans *Daily Picayune*, January 15, 1890, p. 7; "Cotton," New Orleans *Daily Picayune*, March 1, 1890, p. 10; "Cotton," New Orleans *Daily Picayune*, March 15, 1890, p. 10; Lee Davis, *Natural Disasters*, new ed. (New York: Facts on File, 2008), 188; "Cotton," New Orleans *Daily Picayune*, April 12, 1890, p. 10; "Cotton," New Orleans *Daily Picayune*, April 17, 1890, p. 7; "Rising Rapidly," New Orleans *Daily Picayune*, April 15, 1890, p. 1; "Back Water," New Orleans *Daily Picayune*, April 22, 1890, p. 1; "The Inundation," New Orleans *Daily Picayune*, April 23, 1890, p. 1.

20. "Cotton," New Orleans *Daily Picayune*, April 19, 1890, p. 10.

21. "The Outlook for Cotton," New Orleans *Daily Picayune*, April 24, 1890, p. 4.

22. "Cotton," New Orleans *Daily Picayune*, April 26, 1890, p. 10.

23. "Cotton," New Orleans *Daily Picayune*, April 29, 1890, p. 7.

24. Glenn Porter and Harold C. Livesay, *Merchants and Manufacturers: Studies in the Changing Structure of Nineteenth-Century Marketing* (Baltimore: Johns Hopkins University Press, 1971); Scott P. Marler, "Merchants and the Political Economy of Nineteenth-Century Louisiana: New Orleans and Its Hinterlands," (PhD diss., Rice University, 2007), xv, 4; John Churchill Chase, *Frenchmen, Desire Good Children, and Other Streets of New Orleans* (Gretna, La.: Pelican Publishing, 2007; orig. pub. 1949), 252.
25. "Society," *New Orleans Daily Picayune*, December 30, 1894, p. 12.
26. Howard J. Jones, "Biographical Sketches of Members of the 1868 Louisiana State Senate," *Louisiana History* 19, no. 1 (Winter 1978), 100–102.
27. Thomas O'Connor, *History of the Fire Department of New Orleans* (New Orleans: n.p., 1895), 306.
28. Justin A. Nystrom, *New Orleans After the Civil War: Race, Politics, and a New Birth of Freedom* (Baltimore: Johns Hopkins University Press, 2010), 116–118; Henri Schindler, *Mardi Gras Treasures: Costume Designs of the Golden Age* (Gretna, La.: Pelican Publishing Co., 2002), 72.
29. Alcée Fortier, *Louisiana: Comprising Sketches of Parishes, Towns, Events, Institutions, and Persons, Arranged in Cyclopedic Form* (Madison, Wisc.: Century Historical Association, 1914), 3:759–762.; Theodore D. Jervey, "The Hayne Family," *South Carolina Historical and Genealogical Magazine* 5, no. 3 (July 1904): 168–188; Andrew Morrison, *New Orleans and the New South* (New Orleans: Metropolitan Pub. Co., 1888), 119; *Biographical and Historical Memoirs of Mississippi, Vol. II, Part II* (Chicago: Goodspeed Publishing Co, 1891), 600–601.

CHAPTER 2

1. *Regulation of Cotton Exchanges: Hearings before the Committee on Agriculture, House of Representatives, Sixty-Third Congress, Second Session, Regarding Various Bills Relative to the Regulation of Cotton Exchanges, April 22 to 25, 1914* (Washington, D.C.: GPO, 1914), 130. For more on the role of information in the cotton market, see Jonathan Robins, "The Cotton Crisis: Globalization and Empire in the Atlantic World, 1902–1920" (PhD diss., University of Rochester, 2010), 33–36, and Jamie L. Pietruska, "'Cotton Guessers': Crop Forecasters and the Rationalizing of Uncertainty in American Cotton Markets, 1890–1905," in Hartmut Berghoff, Philip Scranton, and Uwe Spiekermann, eds. *The Rise of Marketing and Market Research* (New York: Palgrave MacMillan, 2012): 49–72. Criticism of this argument about the performative role of information can be found in Emmanuel Didier, "Do Statistics 'Perform' the Economy?" in Donald MacKenzie, Fabian Muniesa, and Lucia Siu, eds., *Do Economists Make Markets? On the Performativity of Economics*, ed. (Princeton, N.J.: Princeton University Press, 2007): 276–310.
2. Meigs O. Frost, *Hester Says. ∴ An Intimate Personal Sketch of the World's Greatest Cotton Authority*, pamphlet, (New Orleans Sunday States, n.d. [1926]), no page numbers.
3. Those who believe in the natural efficiency of markets assume that everyone participating in a market has equal access to information. We do not believe such markets exist in the real world. As Joseph Stiglitz and others established in the 1980s, markets more often operate on the basis of "information asymmetry": some people know more than others. The seminal article is Joseph E. Stiglitz and Andrew Weiss, "Credit Rationing in Markets with Imperfect Information," *American Economic Review* 71, no. 3 (June 1981): 393–410.
4. "Effect on Cotton Exports," *New York Times*, July 12, 1900; James L. Watkins, *The Cotton Crop of 1899–1900*, US Department of Agriculture, Division of Statistics, Miscellaneous Series—Bulletin No. 19 (Washington, D.C.: GPO, 1901), 5.
5. United States. Bureau of the Census, *Cotton Production and Distribution, Season of 1914–15* (Washington, D.C.: GPO, 1915), 54.
6. United States. Bureau of the Census, *Cotton Production and Distribution, Season of 1914–15* (Washington, D.C.: GPO, 1915), 56; John A. Todd, *The World's Cotton Crops* (London: A. & C. Black, 1923), 20; Jonathan Robins, "The Cotton Crisis: Globalization and Empire in the Atlantic World, 1902–1920" (Ph.D. diss, University of Rochester, 2010), 11.
7. United States. Bureau of the Census, *Cotton Production and Distribution, Season of 1914–15* (Washington, D.C.: GPO, 1915), 57.
8. John A. Todd, *The World's Cotton Crops* (London: A. & C. Black, 1923), 200.

9. John A. Todd, *The Marketing of Cotton: From the Grower to the Spinner* (London: Sir Isaac Pitman & Sons, 1934), 189.

10. Department of Commerce, Bureau of the Census, *Bulletin 125: Cotton Production, 1913* (Washington, D.C.: GPO, 1914), 27, Table 14.

11. John A. Todd, *The Marketing of Cotton: From the Grower to the Spinner* (London: Sir Isaac Pitman & Sons, 1934), 30.

12. Jonathan Robins, "The Cotton Crisis: Globalization and Empire in the Atlantic World, 1902–1920" (PhD diss., University of Rochester, 2010), 40–41.

13. Barbara Hahn, *Making Tobacco Bright: Creating an American Commodity, 1617–1937* (Baltimore: Johns Hopkins University Press, 2011), 106; Robins, "The Cotton Crisis," 37–38.

14. The Chief Statistician of the Department of Agriculture was well aware of this problem. See "Enumeration of Cotton Gins," *Crop Reporter* 1, no. 9 (January 1900), 2.

15. D. A. Farnie, "Ellison, Thomas (1833–1904)," *Oxford Dictionary of National Biography*, Oxford University Press, 2004 www.oxforddnb.com.catalogue.ulrls.lon.ac.uk/view/article/58116 (accessed April 4, 2011).

16. Thomas Ellison, *The Cotton Trade of Great Britain* (London: Effingham Wilson, Royal Exchange, 1886), 250; "Heavy Demand For Cotton," *Boston Evening Transcript*, November 2, 1903, p. 4. Both the examples here were brokers based in Liverpool; for decades, southern cotton farmers and traders had considered Liverpool as dominated by bears as New York. An early example of a dispute over crop estimates can be found in 1886, when Julius Runge, a Galveston cotton merchant who had attempted to corner cotton two years earlier, argued "that if the New York and Liverpool bears are bolstering up their big crop estimates by anticipating a yield of a million and a half bales from Texas, they are going to find themselves sadly mistaken later on in the season." "Dispute About Cotton Yield," Fort Worth *Daily Gazette*, November 30, 1886, p. 5. On Runge, see Henry Hauschild, "RUNGE, JULIUS," *Handbook of Texas Online* www.tshaonline.org/handbook/online/articles/fru26 (accessed September 9, 2012). Published by the Texas State Historical Association. For a recent history of economic forecasting in this vein, see Walter Friedman, *Fortune Tellers: The Story of America's First Economic Forecasters* (Princeton, N.J.: Princeton University Press, 2013).

17. Letter from James Wilson, Secretary of Agriculture, to Sen. W. B. Allison, reprinted in *Congressional Record*, 57th Cong., 1st Sess., Senate, 1807–1808; "Report of the Statistician for the Fiscal Year 1900," *Crop Reporter* 2, no. 10 (February 1901), 1–2; Willard Lee Hoing, "James Wilson as Secretary of Agriculture, 1897–1913 (PhD Diss., University of Wisconsin, 1964), 165. H. Parker Willis, "The Adjustment of Crop Statistics," *Journal of Political Economy* 11, no. 1 (December 1902), 5–9. See the whole series of articles by H. Parker Willis in the *Journal of Political Economy*: "The Adjustment of Crop Statistics," 11, no. 1 (December 1902): 1–54; "The Adjustment of Crop Statistics: II," 11, no. 3 (June 1903): 363–398; "The Adjustment of Crop Statistics: III," 11, no. 4 (Sept. 1903): 540–567. Henry C. Taylor and Anne Dewees Taylor, *The Story of Agricultural Economics in the United States, 1840–1932: Men, Services, Ideas* (Ames: Iowa State College Press, 1952).

18. *Congressional Record*, 57th Cong., 1st Sess., Senate, 1804. The Senator in question was Ben Tillman.

19. Letter from James Wilson, Secretary of Agriculture, to Sen. W. B. Allison, reprinted in *Congressional Record*, 57th Cong., 1st Sess., Senate, 1807–1808; "Report of the Statistician for the Fiscal Year 1900," *Crop Reporter* 2:10 (February 1901), 1–2.

20. Pietruska, "'Cotton Guessers,'" 52.

21. "The Department of Agriculture and the Census," *Crop Reporter* 2, no. 1 (May 1900), 2. For a thorough critique of the problems of this method, see a series of articles by H. Parker Willis in the *Journal of Political Economy*: "The Adjustment of Crop Statistics," 11, no. 1 (December 1902): 1–54; "The Adjustment of Crop Statistics: II," 11, no. 3 (June 1903): 363–398; and "The Adjustment of Crop Statistics: III," 11, no. 4 (Sept. 1903): 540–567. See also Robert E. Snyder, "Federal Crop Forecasts and the Cotton Market, 1866–1929," *Journal of Southwest Georgia History* 7: (1989–1992), 43–44.

22. "The Crop Reporting Service of the Division of Statistics of the Department of Agriculture," *Crop Reporter* 3, no. 3 (July 1901), 4.

23. "The Crop Reporting Service of the Division of Statistics of the Department of Agriculture," *Crop Reporter* 3, no. 3 (July 1901), 4; "Cotton Acreage and Condition," *Crop Reporter* 3, no. 2 (June 1901), 4.

24. "Posting of Crop Reports in Post-Offices," *Crop Reporter* 3, no. 4 (August 1901), 8.

25. Thomas D. Clark, *Pills, Petticoats and Plows: The Southern Country Store* (Indianapolis: Bobbs-Merrill, 1944), 96–98; Mark V. Wetherington, *The New South Comes to Wiregrass Georgia, 1860–1910* (Knoxville: University of Tennessee Press, 1994), 22–23; Gerald Carson, "Cracker Barrel Store: Southern Style," *Georgia Review* 9, no. 1 (Spring 1955), 34; John A. Todd, *The Marketing of Cotton: From the Grower to the Spinner* (London: Sir Isaac Pitman & Sons, 1934), 34.

26. Henry M. Neill, born in Belfast in 1838, immigrated to American before the Civil War and was one of the founders of the New York Cotton Exchange. He later settled in New Orleans and was in the cotton business with his brother, the firm being based in Liverpool. Victims of his bear estimates probably took a certain pleasure in learning that a New Orleans streetcar had run him down and killed him in September 1906. "Henry M. Neill Killed," *New York Times*, September 13, 1906.

27. Watkins, *Cotton Crop of 1899–1900*, 29.

28. "Table 15.—Production, Consumption, Exports, and Net Imports of Raw Cotton, For the United States, 1790 to 1913," Department of Commerce, Bureau of the Census, *Cotton Production: 1913* (Washington, D.C.: GPO, 1914), 29.

29. James L. Watkins, *The Cotton Crop of 1899–1900*, U.S. Department of Agriculture, Division of Statistics, Miscellaneous Series—Bulletin No. 19 (Washington, D.C.: GPO, 1901), 5.

30. Watkins, *Cotton Crop of 1899–1900*, 29.

31. "Bogus Cotton Estimates," *Atlanta Constitution*, August 17, 1899, p. 4.

32. Watkins, *Cotton Crop of 1899–1900*, 29; "W. H. Bacheller & Co.'s Cotton Letter," *Atlanta Constitution*, September 16, 1899, p. 8; "Neill Makes His First Reduction," *Atlanta Constitution*, October 12, 1899, p. 10; "The Feeling About Neill Is Mixed," *Atlanta Constitution*, November 14, 1899, p. 2; "This Year's Cotton Production," *New York Times*, October 25, 1899, p. 10.

33. Watkins, *Cotton Crop of 1899–1900*, 31.

34. Watkins, *Cotton Crop of 1899–1900*, 5, 23, 29; "Cotton Report of Mr. H. G. Hester," *Crop Reporter* 2, no. 5 (Sept. 1900), 6.

35. Advertisements, *Atlanta Constitution*, October 10, 1900.

36. Hoing, "James Wilson as Secretary of Agriculture," 163, 166.

37. Richmond Mayo-Smith, "A Permanent Census Bureau," *Political Science Quarterly* 11, no. 4 (December 1896): 589–600; John Cummings, "The Permanent Census Bureau: A Decade of Work," *Publications of the American Statistical Association* 13, no. 104 (December 1913): 605–638.

38. "Work Of The Census Bureau," Charleston *News and Courier*, November 18, 1901, p,1.

39. Hoing, "James Wilson as Secretary of Agriculture," 164; *Congressional Record*, 57th Cong., 1st Sess., Senate, 1821.

40. *Congressional Record*, 57th Cong., 1st Sess., Senate, 1821.

41. *Act of March 6, 1902 Providing for the Establishment of a Permanent Census Office* (Washington, D.C.: GPO, 1902), 5.

42. Thomas K. McCraw, *Prophets of Regulation: Charles Francis Adams, Louis D. Brandeis, James M. Landis, Alfred E. Kahn* (Cambridge, Mass.: Belknap Press of Harvard University Press, 1986).

CHAPTER 3

1. "Labouisse," *New Orleans Times-Picayune*, June 6, 1902, p. 3.

2. "9,901,000 Bales," *Atlanta Constitution*, September 3, 1895, p. 6; "Cotton Situation," *Atlanta Constitution*, August 4, 1895, p. 14; "Bad For the Cotton," *Atlanta Constitution*, August 28, 1895, p. 3; "Worms Eating the Cotton," *Atlanta Constitution*, September 4, 1895, p. 1; "Cotton and Prices," *Atlanta Constitution*, September 27, 1895, p. 4; "Cotton Breaks 56 Points," *New York Times*, October 22, 1895, p. 1; "Two Million Short," *Atlanta Constitution*, September 28, 1895, p. 9.

3. "Cotton," New York *Evening Post*, October 10, 1895, p. 11; "Fifty Per Cent Shorter," *Atlanta Constitution*, October 14, 1895, p. 1; "Shrinkage of the Crop," *Atlanta Constitution*, October 15, 1895, p. 5; "One Man's Success," *Atlanta Constitution*, October 16, 1895, p. 3; "Decline of Cotton," *Atlanta Constitution*, October 11, 1895, p. 3; "Cotton," New York *Evening Post*, October 14, 1895, p. 11.

4. "Cotton," New York *Evening Post*, October 15, 1895, p. 11.

5. "They Lose But Smile: Pelicans take the Adverse Turn in the Tide Without a Murmur," *Atlanta Constitution*, October 22, 1895, p. 1.

6. "Editorial," New York *Evening Post*, October 17, 1895, p. 6.

7. "Cotton Holds Chief Place," *New York Times*, October 18, 1895, p. 9.

8. "They Lose But Smile: Pelicans take the Adverse Turn in the Tide Without a Murmur," *Atlanta Constitution*, October 22, 1895, p. 1.

9. "Cotton Breaks 56 Points," *New York Times*, October 22, 1895, p. 1; "They Lose But Smile: Pelicans take the Adverse Turn in the Tide Without a Murmur," *Atlanta Constitution*, October 22, 1895, p. 1; "Big Fortunes Lost," *Atlanta Constitution*, October 22, 1895, p. 1; "Sharp Break In Cotton," *New York Times*, October 20, 1895, p. 3.

10. "Cotton Breaks 56 Points," *New York Times*, October 22, 1895, p. 1.

11. "Cotton Breaks 56 Points," *New York Times*, October 22, 1895, p. 1. Another excellent example of this system of financing and how it affected individual traders can be found in *Johnson v. Miller*, Supreme Court of Arkansas, Nov. 18, 1895, as recorded in *Southwestern Reporter*, vol. 53 (St. Paul: West Publishing Co., 1900), pp. 1053–1056.

12. "The Activity in Cotton," New York *Evening Post*, October 17, 1895, p. 2; "Big Fortunes Lost," *Atlanta Constitution*, October 22, 1895, p. 1; "A Shout Went Up," *Atlanta Constitution*, October 23, 1895, p. 3; "Cotton Market Quiet," *Atlanta Constitution*, October 24, 1895, p. 7.

13. "The Reaction Commences in American Cotton," *London Daily Mail*, May 22, 1903, p. 2.

14. "Entirely Too High," *Atlanta Constitution*, October 23, 1895, p. 10.

15. "Made Millions," *New Orleans Daily States*, July 4, 1900, Brown Scrapbook.

16. Jamie L. Pietruska, " 'Cotton Guessers': Crop Forecasters and the Rationalizing of Uncertainty in American Cotton Markets, 1890–1905," in Hartmut Berghoff, Philip Scranton, and Uwe Spiekermann, eds. *The Rise of Marketing and Market Research* (New York: Palgrave MacMillan, 2012), 58–61, has an excellent account of Neill's estimates and their effect on prices during this season.

17. "Made Good Sized Fortunes," *Boston Transcript*, July 30, 1900, Brown Scrapbook; "Hester Puts Cotton Crop for Year at 9,436,416 Bales," *Atlanta Constitution*, September 4, 1900, p. 3; "What Caused the Rise in the Price of Cotton," *Atlanta Constitution*, September 7, 1900, p. 2; "S. Munn, Son & Co's Cotton Letter," *Atlanta Constitution*, September 9, 1900, p. A6.

18. Erik Larson, *Isaac's Storm: A Man, a Time, and the Deadliest Hurricane in History* (New York: Crown, 1999).

19. "Fell in with the Liverpool and New York Markets," *Atlanta Constitution*, September 11, 1900, p. 10; Lake Providence (La.) *Banner-Democrat*, September 15, 1890, p. 2.

20. George A. Hero, receipt on W. P. Brown's letterhead, October 8, 1901, Folder 8, Box 2, Brown Papers; Audrey Sherman, "The History of the New Orleans Cotton Exchange, 1871–1914," (MA thesis, Tulane University, 1934), 84; *Charter, Constitution, By-Laws and Rules of the New Orleans Cotton Exchange* (New Orleans: L. Graham & Son, 1885), 24.

21. Horace Gumbel, receipt on W. P. Brown's letterhead, August 13, 1901, Folder 8, Box 2, Brown Papers.

22. Bruno Latour, *Reassembling the Social: An Introduction to Actor-Network Theory* (New York: Oxford University Press, 2005), 39, 214–216.

23. Jonathan Robins, "The Cotton Crisis: Globalization and Empire in the Atlantic World, 1902–1920" (PhD diss., University of Rochester, 2010), 32.

24. Sven Beckert, *The Monied Metropolis: New York City and the Consolidation of the American Bourgeoisie, 1850–1896* (New York: Cambridge University Press, 2001).

25. Sherman, "History of the New Orleans Cotton Exchange," 82–83.

26. *New Orleans City Directory* (New Orleans: Soards, 1895), 164; *New Orleans City Directory* (New Orleans: Soards, 1896), 152; *New Orleans City Directory* (New Orleans: Soards, 1897), 157; *New Orleans City Directory* (New Orleans: Soards, 1898), 153, 154; *New Orleans City Directory* (New Orleans: Soards, 1899), 154; *New Orleans City Directory* (New Orleans: Soards, 1900), 161.

27. *New Orleans City Directory* (New Orleans: Soards, 1901) 300, s.v. Equitable Building.

28. "Two Skyscrapers," T.D.? [Times Democrat] June 21, 1901, Brown Scrapbook.

29. Scott P. Marler, *The Merchants' Capital: New Orleans and the Political Economy of the Nineteenth-Century South* (Cambridge: Cambridge University Press, 2013), chapter 6; on the pre-1840 expansion of New Orleans banking and commercial institutions see Robert Earl Roeder, "New Orleans Merchants, 1800–1837" (PhD diss., Harvard University, 1959), 118–119, 295.

30. Rixford J. Lincoln, "The City of New Orleans: A Review of the City's Banking and Commercial Interests," *Banker's Magazine* 65, no. 4 (October 1902): 471–480 (quotation 475).

31. "A National Bank Closes," *New York Times*, September 9, 1896; "Panicky in New Orleans," *New York Times*, September 12, 1896; "Southern Bank Reorganized," *New York Times*, July 7, 1901; "Union National Bank," pamphlet, [1890s–1901?], Brown Scrapbook.

32. "A Third Trust Company for Greater New Orleans," New Orleans *Daily Picayune*, February 21, 1902, Brown Scrapbook; Union National Bank Board of Directors, "Resolutions," typescript, n.d. [March 9, 1902], Folder 10, Box 2, Brown Papers; "A Third Trust Company for Greater New Orleans," New Orleans *Daily Picayune*, February 21, 1902; "Southern Trust Company," New Orleans *Daily Picayune*, March 25, 1902, Brown Scrapbook; "To Handle Millions," *New Orleans Daily States*, May 20, 1902; Brown already was "a large stockholder and director" of the Hibernia; see "W. P. Brown & Co.," *New Orleans Daily States* Industrial Edition, Jan. 15, 1903; both, Brown Scrapbook; "Paying Teller Touches Bank," *New York Times*, May 12, 1901.

33. "Another Big Banking Deal," *New Orleans Daily States*, May 19, 1902, Brown Scrapbook. Also, compare the listings in *New Orleans City Directory* (New Orleans: Soards, 1901), 424; and *New Orleans City Directory* (New Orleans: Soards, 1902), 412; with *New Orleans City Directory* (New Orleans: Soards, 1903), 436; William A. Colledge, Nathan Haskell Dole, and George J. Hagar, eds., *The New Standard Encyclopedia*, 12 vols. (New York: University Society Inc., 1907): vol. 11, s.v. "trust."

34. "Report of the Committee on Banking and Currency," H.R. 12677, 60th Cong, 1st session, Report No. 1126 (Washington: US G.P.O., 1908), February 29, 1908, p. 22.

35. Rixford J. Lincoln, "The City of New Orleans: A Review of the City's Banking and Commercial Interests," *Banker's Magazine* 65, no. 4 (October 1902): 471–480, esp. 475–476, the total being $11,110 millions.

36. "Another Big Banking Deal," *New Orleans Daily States*, May 19, 1902, Brown Scrapbook; "A Trust Banking Co.," *New Orleans Daily States*, February 20, 1902; "Chicago Financier," New Orleans *Times Democrat*, April 20, 1902; "I. N. Perry Selected," *New Orleans Daily States*, April 20, 1902; all, Brown Scrapbook.

37. "The Hibernia Bank and Trust Company, of New Orleans," *Bankers' Magazine* 68, no. 5 (May 1904): 657–658; *The Picayune's Guide to New Orleans* (New Orleans: Picayune, 1903), 124. Also, compare *New Orleans City Directory* (New Orleans: Soards, 1902), 412 with *New Orleans City Directory* (New Orleans: Soards, 1903), 436; and *New Orleans City Directory* (New Orleans: Soards, 1904), 449.

38. "One Million Dollars of New Orleans Money," New Orleans *Times Democrat*, February 21, 1902, Brown Scrapbook.

39. "Deplore the Obstruction," *New Orleans Daily States*, October 18, 1901, Brown Scrapbook; Sherman, "History of the New Orleans Cotton Exchange," 80, 81; "Standing Committees, 1889–1890," in *Twentieth Annual Report of the New Orleans Cotton Exchange* (New Orleans: L. Graham & Son, Printers, 1890), n.p.; "Committee of Arbitration on Futures," in *Twenty-Third Annual Report of the New Orleans Cotton*

Exchange (New Orleans: L. Graham & Son, Printers, 1893), 6; "Annual Report of the Board of Directors," in *Thirty-Fourth Annual Report of the New Orleans Cotton Exchange* (New Orleans: L. Graham Co., 1904), 11; List of Directors in "Union National Bank," pamphlet, [1890s–1901?], Brown Scrapbook; "Deplore the Obstruction," *New Orleans Daily States,* October 18, 1901, Brown Scrapbook; George Kennan, *E. H. Harriman: A Biography in Two Volumes* (Boston: Houghton Mifflin Company, 1922), 93.

40. "One Million Dollars of New Orleans Money," New Orleans *Times Democrat,* February 21, 1902, Brown Scrapbook.

41. It actually worked out a bit higher than that, at 11.5 million bales, had that much been available. "The Cotton Situation," *Wall Street Journal,* August 29, 1903.

42. Untitled accounts, n.d., and October 15, 1902, Folder 8, Box 2, Brown Papers; "July & Aug. '03 Pool," Folder 9, Box 2, Brown Papers. For his strategy of selling to gain profits for future months, see the sources for his actions in May 1903.

43. "The New Cotton Famine: Remarkable History of the 'Corner,' " London *Daily Mail,* June 29, 1903, p. 5; "Brown Pulls Cotton Bears for Millions," *Atlanta Constitution,* September 30, 1903; "Three Great Battles Fought in Three Leading Cotton Exchanges," *New York Herald,* May 31, 1903, Brown Scrapbook; Latham, Alexander & Co., *Cotton Movement and Fluctuations,* vol. 30 (New York: Latham, Alexander & Co., 1903), 48.

44. Lee J. Langley, "City of New Orleans New Cotton Capital," *Atlanta Constitution,* March 27, 1904.

45. Alfred B. Shepperson, "Review of the Cotton Season of 1903–04," in *Cotton Facts* (New York: Alfred B. Shepperson, 1904), 2; "Three Great Battles Fought in Three Leading Cotton Exchanges," *New York Herald,* May 31, 1903, Brown Scrapbook.

46. For his Providence connection, see "From Buyer at $75 a Week / Sully Becomes a Money King," *New York Herald,* May 31, 1903, Brown Scrapbook. Further biographical information is available in "D. J. Sully Is Dead; Once 'Cotton King,' " *New York Times,* September 20, 1930, p. 11.

47. Daniel J. Sully, "Is the High Price of Cotton the Result of Manipulation?" *North American Review* 178, no. 567 (February 1904), 194–204.

48. "Daniel J. Sully Tells How He Became Cotton King," *New York Herald,* May 31, 1903, Brown Scrapbook; "Three Great Battles Fought in Three Leading Cotton Exchanges," *New York Herald,* May 31, 1903, Brown Scrapbook.

49. "Cotton King Sully Fails for Millions," *Philadelphia Record,* March 19, 1904, p. 12; "Sudden As Was His Rise," *San Francisco Call,* March 19, 1904; "Harris-Gates Cotton Deals," *New York Times,* May 18, 1904; "The Reaction Commences in American Cotton," London *Daily Mail,* May 22, 1903, p. 2. For further evidence of the tangle, see "Sully Corner Suits To Be Compromised," *New York Times,* June 26, 1907.

50. "The New Cotton Famine: Remarkable History of the 'Corner,' " London *Daily Mail,* June 29, 1903, p. 5; "Three Great Battles Fought in Three Leading Cotton Exchanges," *New York Herald,* May 31, 1903, Brown Scrapbook; "Sully Out of Cotton Market," Boston *Evening Transcript,* May 27, 1903; "Doesn't Hold a Bale," Nashville *American,* May 27, 1903.

51. Donald Pizer, *The Novels of Frank Norris* (Bloomington: Indiana University Press, 1966), 176.

52. "Fortunes in Cotton," *Wall Street Journal,* Aug 29, 1903; "W. P. Brown Tells Why He Is A 'Bull' On Cotton," New Orleans *Times-Democrat,* May 26, 1903, Brown Scrapbook.

53. "William P. Brown, Cotton Bull, and Plain Merchant," New York *World,* June 14, 1903, Brown Scrapbook.

54. "American Cotton Declines on Heavy Selling," London *Daily Mail,* May 16, 1903, p. 2; "Cotton Jumps and 'Change Riots at New 'King's' Visit," New York *Evening Telegram,* May 18, 1903; "Brown in Town; Cotton Up," New York *Sun,* May 19, 1903; both, Brown Scrapbook.

55. Some newspapers floated rumors that he had "allied with him interests in New Orleans, Liverpool and Egypt." Likely his squeeze in 1900 had helped him incorporate some

brokers and bankers to his side. See "Rise in New York Preceded by Advance in Liverpool," New Orleans *Times Democrat*, May 19, 1903, Brown Scrapbook; "A World-Wide Corner," New Orleans *Times Democrat*, May 20, 1903, Brown Scrapbook.

56. Lee J. Langley, "City of New Orleans New Cotton Capital," *Atlanta Constitution*, March 27, 1904.
57. "The Cotton Market Was Quiet," New Orleans *Daily States*, May 15, 1903; "Mr. Brown in New York," New Orleans *Times Democrat*, May 18, 1903; "New Cotton Bull is Coming Here," New York *Herald*, May 17, 1903; New York *Evening Post*, May 20, 1903; "Sharp Break in Cotton," Brooklyn *Citizen*, May 21, 1903; "Bears Depress Prices," Washington, D.C. *Star*, May 20, 1903; "Slump in Cotton," New York *Commercial Advertiser*, May 21, 1903; all, Brown Scrapbook.
58. "American Cotton Declines on Heavy Selling," London *Daily Mail*, May 16, 1903, p. 2; "Recent Bull Leader in Cotton Sails for Europe," Baltimore *Sun*, June 4, 1903, Brown Scrapbook.
59. "War Declared on Wild Cotton Bulls," *New York Herald*, May 21, 1903, Brown Scrapbook.
60. "'King' Brown To Lose Crown," *Atlanta Constitution*, May 24, 1903, p. 3.
61. "The Reaction Commences in American Cotton," London *Daily Mail*, May 22, 1903, p. 2.
62. "Under the rules of the NYCE all future contracts are 'rung in' at the market. That is, a broker who sells July at 11 cents puts up no margin so long as the price remains at 11 cents. For every point that it goes against him he is forced to pay 5 cents to the broker to whom he has sold. For every point the price moves in his favor he receives 5 cents from the other broker. No original margin is put up, the deal being carried along on the assumption that every broker will 'ring in,' that is, make his trades good, every day. But every broker has the right, under the rules, at his discretion, to call for original margin up to $5 a bale. This money is deposited with the secretary of the Exchange and for every dollar called the broker who calls must also put up a dollar. This money can never be drawn until the deal against which it is deposited is closed. The calling of original margin is a last resort." From "Sully tries to Wrest Crown from Brown," New York *American*, May 20, 1903. Also, "There would be a shaking out of the 'tailers if original margins are generally called, and there are those here who think it would ultimately result in a material strengthening of the situation, as the bulls are believed to have fully as much capital as any opponents," from item without headline, New York *Commercial*, May 21, 1903; both, Brown Scrapbook. Margins had originally been devised in Chicago as a means to allow transactions among members without valuing their reputations and regularly changing assets and liabilities—what today would happen in a credit check. See A.W.B. Simpson, "The Origins of Futures Trading in the Liverpool Cotton Market," in Peter Cane and Jane Stapleton, eds., *Essays for Patrick Atiyah* (Oxford: Clarendon Press, 1991), 205.
63. "Sully Tries to Wrest Crown from Brown," New York *American*, May 20, 1903, Brown Scrapbook; "'King' Brown To Lose Crown," *Atlanta Constitution*, May 24, 1903, p. 3; "War Declared on Wild Cotton Bulls," *New York Herald*, May 21, 1903, Brown Scrapbook.
64. Item without headline, beginning "There would be a shaking out ... ," New York *Commercial*, May 21, 1903, Brown Scrapbook.
65. "War Declared on Wild Cotton Bulls," New York *Herald*, May 21, 1903, Brown Scrapbook.
66. "Smash in Cotton Market," *New York Times*, May 22, 1903; "Cotton Prices Smashed," New Orleans *Times Democrat*, May 22, 1903; "Brown Routed by Crash in Cotton," *New York Herald*, May 22, 1903; both, Brown Scrapbook.
67. "$50,000,000 in Cotton Fight," *New York World*, May 22, 1903, night edition, p. 10.
68. Latham, Alexander & Co., *Cotton Movement and Fluctuations*, vol. 30 (New York: Latham, Alexander & Co., 1903), 49.
69. "Bull Leader Quits Campaign in Cotton," St. Louis *Republic*, May 25, 1903; "Brown Quits New York Cotton Pit," St. Louis *Globe Democrat*, May 24, 1903; "Short Was Brown's Reign," Cincinnati *Enquirer*, May 24, 1903; "King of Cotton Bulls Quits New York Arena," Atlanta *Journal*, May 24, 1903; "Bull Leader Quits Campaign in Cotton," St. Louis *Republic*, May 25, 1903; all Brown Scrapbook.

CHAPTER 4

1. "Smash in Cotton Market," *New York Times*, May 22, 1903.
2. "Cotton Soars Again," *New York Tribune*, May 20, 1903, p. 16; "Mills May Sell Cotton Supply," *New York Tribune*, May 20, 1903, p. 16.
3. "$50,000,000 in Cotton Fight," *New York World*, May 22, 1903, night edition, p. 10.
4. "$50,000,000 in Cotton Fight," *New York World*, May 22, 1903, night edition, p. 10.
5. "Cotton Bears Routed Brown," *New York World*, May 21, 1903, night edition, p. 10.
6. " 'King' Brown To Lose Crown," *Atlanta Constitution*, May 24, 1903.
7. Lee J. Langley, "City of New Orleans New Cotton Capital," *Atlanta Constitution*, March 27, 1904.
8. "Bull Brown in Form Again / Gives New Orleans Bears a Touch of the Horn," Memphis *Scimitar*, May 26, 1903.
9. "Brown Bids August to 12," New Orleans *Daily States*, May 26, 1903, Brown scrapbook.
10. Some newspapers floated rumors that he had "allied with him interests in New Orleans, Liverpool and Egypt." Likely his squeeze in 1900 had helped him incorporate some brokers and bankers to his side. "Rise in New York Preceded by Advance in Liverpool," *New Orleans Times Democrat*, May 19, 1903, Brown Scrapbook; "A World-Wide Corner," *New Orleans Times Democrat*, May 20, 1903, Brown Scrapbook.
11. "Cotton Goes Higher," *New York News*, June 4, 1903, Brown Scrapbook; "Cotton Acreage and Condition," *Crop Reporter* 5, no. 2 (June 1903), 10; "Calm Before the Storm," *Boston Evening Transcript*, June 2, 1903, Brown Scrapbook.
12. "Calm Before the Storm," *Boston Evening Transcript*, June 2, 1903, Brown Scrapbook.
13. "Cotton Goes Higher," New York *News*, June 4, 1903, Brown Scrapbook; "Cotton At Highest Price Since 1879," New York *Herald*, June 10, 1903, Brown Scrapbook; "The Cotton Situation," *Wall Street Journal*, August 29, 1903; "Cotton Again Goes Kiting," *New York Evening World*, June 8, 1903, night edition, 4.
14. "Cotton Crop in Texas," *New York Times*, July 11, 1903; "Cotton," *Atlanta Constitution*, June 14, 1904, p. 10; "The Cotton Market," *New York Tribune*, June 7, 1903, p. 14; "Calm Before the Storm," *Boston Evening Transcript*, June 2, 1903, Brown Scrapbook.
15. "Big Break in Cotton," Columbus *Press*, May 21, 1903, Brown Scrapbook.
16. "Liverpool needs 500,000 Bales of Cotton / As There Are Fewer Than 250,000 Available, the European Mills Will Be Compelled to Close Down," New York *American*, May 23, 1903; "Plan to Corner World's Cotton," Nashville *American*, June 14, 1903; "Sully Operating in Liverpool," Cincinnati *Enquirer*, June 14, 1903; "Sully," Cincinnati *Enquirer*, June 14, 1903; "Sully, Brown and M'Fadden," New Orleans *Daily States*, June 14, 1903; all, Brown Scrapbook.
17. "Rise in New York Preceded by Advance in Liverpool," New Orleans *Times Democrat*, May 19, 1903, Brown Scrapbook; "The Cotton Situation," *Wall Street Journal*, August 29, 1903.
18. "Rise in New York Preceded by Advance in Liverpool," New Orleans *Times Democrat*, May 19, 1903, Brown Scrapbook; "The Cotton Situation," *Wall Street Journal*, August 29, 1903.
19. " 'King' Brown To Lose Crown," *Atlanta Constitution*, May 24, 1903.
20. "The Cotton Situation," *Wall Street Journal*, August 29, 1903, p. 2.
21. "Wilson To Solve Cotton Problem," *Atlanta Constitution*, September 19, 1913, p. 5.
22. "Three Great Battles," New York *Herald*, May 31, 1903, Brown Scrapbook.
23. "$3 Jump in Cotton," New York *Mail and Express*, June 13, 1903; "Cotton Declined in Irregular Market," New York *Herald*, June 12, 1903; "Wild Close in Cotton," *New York Tribune*, June 11, 1903; "Slump in Cotton," New York *Mail and Express*, June 12, 1903; "Brown Has Not Settled with Bears," New Orleans *Stem*, June 11, 1903; "Plan to Corner World's Cotton / Sully, Brown and McFaddens Credited with It / New York Hears the Rumor," Nashville *American*, June 14, 1903, all Brown Scrapbook; Lee J. Langley, "City of New Orleans New Cotton Capital," *Atlanta Constitution*, March 27, 1904, p. 5.
24. "The Corner in Cotton," New Orleans *Daily Picayune*, June 24, 1903, Brown Scrapbook.
25. Lee J. Langley, "City of New Orleans New Cotton Capital," *Atlanta Constitution*, March 27, 1904, p. 5.

26. "The Corner in Cotton," New Orleans *Daily Picayune*, June 24, 1903, Brown Scrapbook; "The Cotton Situation," *Wall Street Journal*, August 29, 1903, p. 2.
27. "Have Made $10,000,000," New York *Tribune*, June 24, 1903, Brown Scrapbook; New York *Commercial*, May 21, 1903, Brown Scrapbook; "The Cotton Situation," *Wall Street Journal*, August 29, 1903, p. 2; "Bring Cotton from Liverpool," New York *Tribune*, July 1, 1903, Brown Scrapbook; "Called Out By the Corner," New York *Evening Post*, July 11, 1903, Brown Scrapbook.
28. "The Cotton Situation," *Wall Street Journal*, August 29, 1903, p. 2.
29. "Brown Pulls Cotton Bears For Millions," *Atlanta Constitution*, Sept. 30, 1903, p. 1.
30. Advertisement, *New Orleans Picayune*, September 1, 1903, p. 1:13.
31. Lee J. Langley, "City of New Orleans New Cotton Capital," *Atlanta Constitution*, March 27, 1904, p. 5.
32. C. P. Ellis, "The Greatest Market," *New Orleans Daily Picayune*, September 1, 1903, p. 4:5.
33. "W. P. Brown's New Avenue Home," *New Orleans Daily Picayune*, September 1, 1903, p. 9.
34. Judy Walker, "Romanesque Romance: The New Owner of a Landmark Uptown Mansion Opens It For the NOMA Tour," New Orleans *Times-Picayune*, April 9, 2011; "W. P. Brown's New Avenue Home," *New Orleans Daily Picayune*, September 1, 1903, p. 9; Dorothy G. Schlesinger, comp. and ed., *New Orleans Architecture: Vol. 7, Jefferson City* (Gretna, La.: Pelican Publishing, 1989), 75; Roulhac Toledano, *The National Trust Guide to New Orleans: The Definitive Guide to Architectural and Cultural Treasures* (New York: Wiley, 1996), 157; James F. O'Gorman, *H. H. Richardson: Architectural Forms for an American Society* (Chicago: University of Chicago Press, 1987), 65.
35. Judy Walker, "Romanesque Romance: The New Owner of a Landmark Uptown Mansion Opens It For the NOMA Tour," New Orleans *Times-Picayune*, April 9, 2011. In later life, Brown said, "I am what they call a hill-billy. I believe I would slowly die if I had to move away from the dear old South." *The Book of Louisiana, a Newspaper Reference Work* (New Orleans: Dameron Pierson, 1916), 113.
36. "Rex Reigns, Joy General," *New Orleans Daily Picayune*, February 16, 1904, p. 1.
37. Katherine Coman, "The Negro as a Peasant Farmer," *Publications of the American Statistical Association* 9, no. 66 (Jun. 1904), 48. For the same argument, see also H. Paul Douglass, *Christian Reconstruction in the South* (Boston: Pilgrim Press, 1909), 136.
38. *The Book of Louisiana, a Newspaper Reference Work* (New Orleans: Dameron Pierson, 1916), s.v. "William P. Brown." A newspaper article the spring after the 1903 corner suggested that as a result "the real wealth of the people of the cotton-producing states has increased more than a quarter of a billion dollars." "Fortunes In Cotton," *Wall Street Journal*, March 19, 1904, p. 6.
39. "Curtailment Planned," Boston *Daily Globe*, July 29, 1903, p. 4; "The Lowell and Other Strikes," *Literary Digest* 26:15 (April 11, 1903), 528.
40. "Ordered to Shut Down," Boston *Daily Globe*, August 1, 1903, p. 7; "High Price of Cotton," Boston *Daily Globe*, August 6, 1903, p. 4; "Stay Closed," Boston *Daily Globe*, August 9, 1903, p. 8; "Idle Spindles," Boston *Daily Globe*, August 15, 1903, p. 14; "Doors Reopen," Boston *Daily Globe*, August 31, 1903; "At Its Worst," Boston *Daily Globe*, September 5, 1903, p. 8; George Kennan, "The Strike in the Lowell Cotton-Mills," *The Outlook* (May 30, 1903): 269–273; Lewis E. MacBrayne, "New England's Great Rival," *National Magazine* 18, no. 5 (August 1903): 547–551.
41. Adelaide *Morning Advertiser*, June 26, 1903, p. 5; Adelaide *Morning Advertiser*, November 20, 1903, p. 5; Adelaide *Morning Advertiser*, September 11, 1903, p. 7; "The Cotton Trade," London *Times*, June 20, 1903, p. 9; Jonathan Robins, "The Cotton Crisis: Globalization and Empire in the Atlantic World, 1902–1920" (PhD diss., University of Rochester, 2010), 71–72, 74; Fred Baynes, "Bad Trade and Distress in Lancashire," London *Times*, October 13, 1903, p. 9.
42. Robins, "The Cotton Crisis," 74–79; W. H. Beveridge, *Unemployment: A Problem of Industry* (London: Longmans, Green, and Co., 1909), 221–223, esp. 221n.1.
43. British Parliamentary Debates, 124: 1026, July 1, 1903.

44. Alan Sykes, *Tariff Reform in British Politics, 1903–1913* (Oxford: Clarendon, 1979), 33.

45. "Mr. Morley in Manchester," London *Times*, October 20, 1903, p. 4.

46. "Mr. Chamberlain's Tariff," *Blackwood's Magazine* 174, no. 1057 (November 1903), 720.

47. "The American 'Cotton Corner' and Other Nations," *The Christian Advocate*, vol. 79, (September 22, 1904), 1532.

48. "French Fear Cotton Famine," *New York Times*, June 29, 1903; "Threatened Cotton Crisis in France," London *Times*, June 29, 1903, p. 6; "Germany Alarmed Over Threatened Cotton Famine," *New York Times*, July 19, 1903.

49. "The Cotton Trade," London *Times*, December 16, 1903, p. 12; W. Haslam Mills, *Sir Charles W. Macara, Bart: A Study of Modern Lancashire*, 2nd ed. (Manchester: Sherratt & Hughes, 1917), 142–149.

50. "Effects of the Cotton Corner," *The Standard [Chicago]*, 50, no. 52 (August 29, 1903), 1607; Robins, "The Cotton Crisis," 87–90.

51. "The American 'Cotton Corner' and Other Nations," *The Christian Advocate*, vol. 79, (September 22, 1904), 1532.

CHAPTER 5

1. "The American Cotton Crop," *Manchester Guardian*, December 23, 1903, p. 5.

2. Lee J. Langley, "Cotton Is Up to Stay Says Expert Brown," *Atlanta Constitution*, February 3, 1904, p. 6.

3. "Daniel J. Sully Tells How He Became Cotton King," *New York Herald*, May 31, 1903, Brown Scrapbook; "Three Great Battles Fought in Three Leading Cotton Exchanges," *New York Herald*, May 31, 1903, Brown Scrapbook, WPBP.

4. "Mrs. Sully's $300,000 Gift," *New York Times*, December 24, 1903.

5. "Sully Failure Affects Grains," *New York Times*, March 19, 1904; "Stock Exchange Notes: Daniel J. Sully Posted for Membership," *New York Times*, January 8, 1904; *Who's Who in America* (Chicago: A. N. Marquis & Company, 1906–1907), 1735; "D. J. Sully Trust Company Director," *New York Times*, December 18, 1903.

6. Daniel J. Sully, "Is the High Price of Cotton the Result of Manipulation?," *North American Review* 178 (February 1904): 194–204, esp. 201.

7. "Sully Forms Biggest Pool in History of Cotton Market," [Providence, RI] *Manufacturers and Farmers Journal*, February 8, 1904, p. 1.

8. "Cotton King Sully Fails for Millions," *Philadelphia Record*, March 19, 1904, p. 12.

9. "Panic in Cotton Pit," *New York Times*, February 3, 1904. This article claims that Sully has "the solid South behind him," while New England mill owners and Wall Street are united as one. It also sees him selling in order to drop the price, probably to buy more, when the market gets away from him. This is a market mechanism familiar from Norris's novel *The Pit*.

10. "Sully Stands Under Cotton," *Atlanta Constitution*, February 7, 1904.

11. "Sully Stands Under Cotton," *Atlanta Constitution*, February 7, 1904; Lee J. Langley, "Cotton Is Up to Stay Says Expert Brown," *Atlanta Constitution*, February 3, 1904, p. 6.

12. "Sully Stands Under Cotton," *Atlanta Constitution*, February 7, 1904; "The Sully Failure," *Literary Digest*, March 26, 1904, p. 438.

13. "Sully Forms Biggest Pool in History of Cotton Market," [Providence, RI] *Manufacturers and Farmers Journal*, February 8, 1904, p. 1.

14. "The Sully Failure," *Literary Digest*, March 26, 1904, p. 438.

15. "Sudden As Was His Rise," *San Francisco Call*, March 19, 1904.

16. "Bears Crush Daniel Sully, 'Cotton King,'" *St. Paul Globe*, March 19, 1904, p. 1.

17. "Sudden As Was His Rise," *San Francisco Call*, March 19, 1904; "Cablegrams: Cotton King's Collapse," Perth [Australia] *Sunday Times*, March 20, 1904, p. 1; "Sully Corner Suits To Be Compromised," *New York Times*, June 26, 1907.

18. "Sudden As Was His Rise," *San Francisco Call*, March 19, 1904. He claimed that sums owed him from Europe could not arrive in time to save him, but the lawsuits of later years indicated a more dire situation.

19. "Cotton King Sully Fails for Millions," *Philadelphia Record*, March 19, 1904, p. 12.
20. "Sudden As Was His Rise," *San Francisco Call*, March 19, 1904.
21. "Sudden As Was His Rise," *San Francisco Call*, March 19, 1904.
22. "The Cotton Market," *Sydney Morning Herald*, March 22, 1904, p. 5.
23. "The Cotton Market," *Sydney Morning Herald*, March 22, 1904, p. 5; "The Cotton Crisis/ Mr. Sully's Failure," *Adelaide Advertiser*, March 24, 1904, p. 4.
24. "The Sully Cotton Failure," *Fibre and Fabric: A Record of American Textile Industries in the Cotton and Woolen Trade* 39, no. 995 (March 26, 1904): 73–74.
25. "Effect of Sully Crash," *Philadelphia Record*, March 19, 1904, p. 12.
26. "Sully Corner Suits To Be Compromised," *New York Times*, June 26, 1907.
27. "Sully Failure Affects Grains," *New York Times*, March 19, 1904.
28. "Sully Corner Suits To Be Compromised," *New York Times*, June 26, 1907.
29. "The Man In the Street," *New York Times*, April 17, 1904.
30. "Harris-Gates Cotton Deals," *New York Times*, May 18, 1904; Edward J. Balleisen, *Navigating Failure: Bankruptcy and Commercial Society in Antebellum America* (Chapel Hill: University of North Carolina Press, 2001), 173–176.
31. "Sully Corner Suits To Be Compromised," *New York Times*, June 26, 1907.
32. "New York City," *Fibre and Fabric* XL, no. 1039 (January 28, 1905), p. 17; "New York City," *Fibre and Fabric* XLIII, no. 1109 (June 2, 1906), p. 22.
33. "Told 'Round the Ticker," New York *Times*, October 30, 1904, p. 13.
34. "Oldest Cotton Exchange in the World Is Ours," *New York Times*, December 4, 1904.
35. Department of Commerce, Bureau of the Census. *Bulletin 125. Cotton Production, 1913* (Washington, D.C.: GPO, 1914), table 1, p. 7.
36. "Hold The Cotton, Brown Advises," *Atlanta Constitution*, December 6, 1904.
37. Quoted in James C. Giesen, *Boll Weevil Blues: Cotton, Myth, and Power in the American South* (Chicago: University of Chicago Press, 2011), iii, 1.
38. Fabian Lange, Alan L. Olmstead, and Paul W. Rhode, "The Impact of the Boll Weevil, 1892–1932," (Working Paper: February 2008), 3–4. www.econ.ucdavis.edu/faculty/alolmstead/Working_Papers/BOLL%20WEEVIL%20.pdf (accessed July 29, 2012).
39. Bruno Latour, *Reassembling the Social: An Introduction to Actor-Network-Theory* (New York: Oxford University Press), 68.
40. Giesen, *Boll Weevil Blues;* Elizabeth Sanders, *Roots of Reform: Farmers, Workers, and the American State, 1877–1917* (Chicago: University of Chicago Press, 1999).
41. Theodore Saloutos, "The Southern Cotton Association, 1905–1908," *Journal of Southern History* 13, no. 4 (Nov. 1947), 493. The organization is called the "Southern Cotton Growers' Association" in Willard Lee Hoing, "James Wilson as Secretary of Agriculture, 1897–1913 (PhD diss., University of Wisconsin, 1964), 168. Jonathan Robins provides a history and genealogy for the SCA that differs from ours in "The Cotton Crisis: Globalization and Empire in the Atlantic World, 1902–1920" (PhD diss., University of Rochester, 2010), 261–264. Likewise, Jamie L. Pietruska, views the farmers' movements and acreage reduction efforts as "statistical resistance" to crop estimates that worked against their interests, in her " 'Cotton Guessers': Crop Forecasters and the Rationalizing of Uncertainty in American Cotton Markets, 1890–1905," in Hartmut Berghoff, Philip Scranton, and Uwe Spiekermann, eds. *The Rise of Marketing and Market Research* (New York: Palgrave MacMillan, 2012): 49–72.
42. "The Boll Weevil Convention," Dallas *Southern Mercury*, November 12, 1903, p. 2.
43. "May Train Guns on Boll Weevil," Atlanta *Constitution*, November 14, 1905, p. 3; *Proceedings of the Boll Weevil Convention called by Governor W. W. Heard in New Orleans, Louisiana, Nov. 30th and Dec. 1st, 1903* (Baton Rouge: Bureau of Agriculture and Immigration, 1903), n.p.; "Boll Weevil To Be Fought By Cotton Men," *Atlanta Constitution*, December 4, 1904, p. B1.
44. "Hold To Cotton Advises Jordan," *Atlanta Constitution*, December 8, 1904.
45. "To Rout Bears While Killing Boll Weevil," *Atlanta Constitution*, December 13, 1904.
46. "Cotton Men Harmonize," Boston *Evening Transcript*, January 25, 1905, p. 10.

47. "Farmers Stand As Solid Unit," *Atlanta Constitution*, February 16, 1905, p. 7.
48. Daniel W. Hollis, "'Cotton Ed Smith': Showman or Statesman?" *South Carolina Historical Magazine* 71, no. 4 (Oct. 1970), 238–239 (quotation 239); "Cotton Men Harmonize," Boston *Evening Transcript*, January 25, 1905, p. 10.
49. Barbara Hahn, *Making Tobacco Bright: Creating an American Commodity, 1617–1937* (Baltimore: Johns Hopkins University Press, 2011), 106.
50. "Would Have Trustees For Cotton Reserve," *New York Times*, January 2, 1905.
51. "Name Selected By Cotton Men," *Atlanta Constitution*, February 1, 1905, p. 3.
52. "Harvie Jordan Roasted By Hon. Thomas Watson," *Atlanta Constitution*, May 1, 1907, p. 6.

CHAPTER 6

1. Thomas K. McCraw, *Prophets of Regulation: Charles Francis Adams, Louis D. Brandeis, James M. Landis, Alfred E. Kahn* (Cambridge, Mass.: Belknap Press of Harvard University Press, 1984), 17–26, 31.
2. Willard Lee Hoing, "James Wilson as Secretary of Agriculture, 1897–1913" (PhD diss., University of Wisconsin, 1964), 1, 7–8, 167.
3. "Wilson Talks On Cotton," *New York Times*, August 21, 1903, p. 1.
4. Ann Fabian, *Card Sharps and Bucket Shops: Gambling in Nineteenth-Century America* (New York: Routledge, 1999), 23, 154–170; Walter Friedman, *Fortune Tellers: The Story of America's First Economic Forecasters* (Princeton, N.J.: Princeton University Press, 2013); Jonathan Ira Levy, "Contemplating Delivery: Futures Trading and the Problem of Commodity Exchange in the United States, 1875–1905," *American Historical Review* 111, no. 2 (April 2006): 307–335.
5. "Cotton Corner Criticism," *New York Times*, August 25, 1903, p. 8. The Senator was M. C. Butler.
6. "Snubbed a Cabinet Officer," *New York Times*, October 30, 1903, p. 1.
7. Emmanuel Didier, "Do Statistics 'Perform' the Economy?" in Donald MacKenzie, Fabian Muniesa, and Lucia Siu, eds., *Do Economists Make Markets? On the Performativity of Economics*, ed. (Princeton, N.J.: Princeton University Press, 2007), 279.
8. James L. Watkins, *The Cotton Crop of 1899–1900*, US Department of Agriculture, Division of Statistics, Miscellaneous Series—Bulletin No. 19 (Washington, D.C.: GPO, 1901), 29.
9. "The Crop Reporting Service of the Division of Statistics of the Department of Agriculture," *Crop Reporter* 3, no. 3 (July 1901), 4; Hoing, "James Wilson," 167; Jonathan Robins, "The Cotton Crisis: Globalization and Empire in the Atlantic World, 1902–1920" (PhD diss., University of Rochester, 2010), 287–288.
10. "Lipton's Irish Bacon From American Hogs," *New York Times*, January 17, 1904, p. 5; "Department Stirred By Story of Cotton Leak," *New York Times*, September 4, 1904, p. 6; "As To the Cotton Leak," *New York Times*, September 13, 1904, p. 16.
11. "Department Stirred By Story of Cotton Leak," *New York Times*, September 4, 1904, p. 6.
12. Hoing, "James Wilson," 164; Richard White, "Information, Markets, and Corruption: Transcontinental Railroads in the Gilded Age," *Journal of American History* 90, no. 1 (June 2003): 19–43.
13. "Cotton Leak Big Bonanza For Holmes," *Atlanta Constitution*, July 9, 1905. The case was also reported heavily in the *Washington Post* between June 11 and July 4, 1907; see Hoing, "James Wilson," 169n22–23.
14. "Secretary Wilson's Troubles," *New York Times*, July 11, 1905, p. 6.
15. "Cotton Leak Will Result In Scandal," *Atlanta Constitution*, July 8, 1905, p. 1; "Edwin S. Holmes, Cotton Grafter," Atlanta Constitution, July 29, 1905, p. 1.
16. Hoing, "James Wilson," 169–170; "Holmes, Cotton Report Juggler, Is Dismissed," *New York Times*, July 5, 1905.
17. "Holmes, Cotton Report Juggler, Is Dismissed," *New York Times*, July 5, 1905; "Hyde Sent To Europe To Aid Conspirators," *Atlanta Constitution*, July 9, 1905, p. B2.

18. "Charges Hold, Says Cheatham," *Atlanta Constitution*, June 17, 1905, p. 1 ("old man"); "Cotton Leak Big Bonanza For Holmes," *Atlanta Constitution*, July 9, 1905, p. Bl;, "Secretary Wilson's Troubles," *Atlanta Constitution*, July 11, 1905, p. 6; "Wilson, Faith Shaken, Takes Up New Charges," *New York Times*, July 12, 1905, p. 6.

19. "Criminal Inquiry On In Cotton Leak Case," *New York Times*, July 13, 1905, reprints the letter under the subheading "Demand Full Inquiry," which also names Atwood Violett as the whistle-blowing broker. His locations can be found in William Harris Miller, *History and Genealogies* (Lexington, Ky.: Press of Transylvania Co., 1907), 592.

20. "Criminal Inquiry On In Cotton Leak Case," *New York Times*, July 13, 1905; "Makeshift Revision Angers Cotton Men," *New York Times*, July 26, 1905.

21. Wilson to Roosevelt, July 17, 1905; on p. 69 of #13 of "fourteen letterbooks of 'confidential and private' correspondence of Wilson while he was Secretary . . . in the possession of Mrs. Albert Lehninger"; and Moody to Roosevelt, July 17, 1905 (two letters), in the "manuscript collection of President Theodore Roosevelt . . . on file in the Manuscript Division of the Library of Congress, Washington, D.C." both quoted in Hoing, "James Wilson," 173, 174n34, 281.

22. "Charges Hold, Says Cheatham," *Atlanta Constitution*, June 17, 1905, p. 1; "Cotton Leak Big Bonanza For Holmes," *Atlanta Constitution*, July 9, 1905, p. Bl;, "Secretary Wilson's Troubles," *Atlanta Constitution*, July 11, 1905, p. 6; "Wilson, Faith Shaken, Takes Up New Charges," *New York Times*, July 12, 1905, p. 6.

23. "Criminal Inquiry On In Cotton Leak Case," *New York Times*, July 13, 1905, p. 6.

24. "The 'Quarrel Among Gamblers,'" *New York Times*, July 13, 1905, p. 6; "Cotton Leak Big Bonanza For Holmes," *Atlanta Constitution*, July 9, 1905, p. Bl;, "Secretary Wilson's Troubles," *Atlanta Constitution*, July 11, 1905, p. 6; "Wilson, Faith Shaken, Takes Up New Charges," *New York Times*, July 12, 1905, p. 6.

25. "Wilson, Faith Shaken, Takes Up New Charges," *New York Times*, July 12, 1905, p. 6.

26. In 1914, as a result of the Keep Commission's recommendations, the USDA's Division of Statistics was renamed the Division of Estimates. Jamie L. Pietruska, "'Cotton Guessers': Crop Forecasters and the Rationalizing of Uncertainty in American Cotton Markets, 1890–1905," in Hartmut Berghoff, Philip Scranton, and Uwe Spiekermann, eds. *The Rise of Marketing and Market Research* (New York: Palgrave MacMillan, 2012), 62–66; Emmanuel Didier, "Do Statistics 'Perform' the Economy?" in Donald MacKenzie, Fabian Muniesa, and Lucia Siu, eds., *Do Economists Make Markets? On the Performativity of Economics*, ed. (Princeton, N.J.: Princeton University Press, 2007): 276–310; Hoing, "James Wilson," 185–186.

27. In November 2009, the chairman of the Commodity Futures Trading Commission testified to the Senate Committee on Agriculture that the law "should be amended to make unlawful the misappropriation and trading on the basis of material non-public information from any governmental authority." "We loosely call this the Eddie Murphy rule," the chairman explained, "given the role he played in the movie *Trading Places*." Gary Gensler, "Testimony of Gary Gensler, Chairman, Commodity Futures Trading Commission Before the Senate Committee on Agriculture, November 18, 2009," US Commodity Futures Trading Commission www.cftc.gov/PressRoom/SpeechesTestimony/opagensler-19 (accessed July 30, 2014).

28. "Wilson, Faith Shaken, Takes Up New Charges," *New York Times*, July 12, 1905, p. 6.

29. Wilson to Smith McPherson, August 10, 1905, 136, #12, of Wilson's letterbooks quoted in Hoing, "James Wilson," 183n49.

30. Theodore Roosevelt to William Henry Moody, July 12, 1905, in *The Letters of Theodore Roosevelt*, vol. 4, selected and edited by Elting G. Morison (Cambridge, Mass.: Harvard University Press, 1951), 1273; "'Leak Gang' Hard Rapped By Roosevelt," *Atlanta Constitution*, July 16, 1905, p.Bl.

31. "John Hyde Forced To Quit His Place By Cotton Scandal," *Atlanta Constitution*, July 19, 1905, p. 1; "Holmes Pays Big Fine," *Washington Post*, June 30, 1910, p. 16

32. "John Hyde Forced To Quit His Place By Cotton Scandal," *Atlanta Constitution*, July 19, 1905, p. 1.

33. Didier, "Do Statistics 'Perform' the Economy?," 285–286; Thomas K. McCraw, *Prophets of Regulation: Charles Francis Adams, Louis D. Brandeis, James M. Landis, Alfred E. Kahn* (Cambridge, Mass.: Belknap Press of Harvard University Press, 1986).

34. "Cotton Is Opening Rapidly," *Atlanta Constitution*, September 3, 1906, p. 6.

35. For an overview of the storm, see E. B. Garriott, "The West Indian Hurricanes of September, 1906," *Monthly Weather Review* (September 1906), 418–423.

36. "Mobile Mangled," *Atlanta Constitution*, September 29, 1906, p. 1; "Fierce Hurricane Sweeps The Gulf States," *Atlanta Constitution*, September 28, 1906, p. 1; "Cotton Torn Out Of Bolls By Hurricane," *Atlanta Constitution*, September 29, 1906, p. 2; "Cotton Cut Down About One-Third," *Atlanta Constitution*, October 4, 1906, p. 4; "Damage Done To The Cotton," *Atlanta Constitution*, September 30, 1906, p. 3;. "Gloomy Reports On Cotton Crop," *Atlanta Constitution*, October 8, 1906, p. 2.

37. "Gloomy Reports On Cotton Crop," *Atlanta Constitution*, October 8, 1906, p. 2.

38. United States, Bureau of Corporations, *Report of the Commissioner of Corporations on Cotton Exchanges*, Part 1 (Washington, D.C.: GPO, 1908), xv.

39. United States, Bureau of Corporations, *Report of the Commissioner of Corporations on Cotton Exchanges*, Part 1, 116–148.

40. United States, Bureau of Corporations, *Report of the Commissioner of Corporations on Cotton Exchanges*, Part 1, 144.

41. Wayne E. Fuller, *Morality and the Mail in Nineteenth-Century America* (Urbana: University of Illinois Press, 2003), 202; "Charge Fraud Against N.Y. Cotton Exchange," *New York Times*, January 3, 1907, p. 1; "Can't Bluff Me—Livingston," *New York Times*, January 5, 1907, p. 5.

42. "Phenomenal Demand for Cotton Throughout 1906," *New York Times*, January 6, 1907, p. AFR22.

43. "Cotton Exchange's Defense," *New York Times*, January 6, 1907.

44. "Cotton Exchange's Foes Ask Action By House," *New York Times*, January 27, 1907; *Congressional Record*, House, 59th Cong., 2nd sess., Jan. 26, 1907, 1783; Elizabeth Sanders, *Roots of Reform: Farmers, Workers, and the American State, 1877–1917* (Chicago and London: University of Chicago Press, 1999), 275; "For Cotton Investigation," *New York Times*, February 4, 1907, p. 4; "For a Cotton Inquiry," February 5, 1907, p. 4; *Congressional Record*, House, 59th Cong., 2nd sess., Feb. 4, 1907, 2225–2230.

45. United States, Bureau of Corporations, *Report of the Commissioner of Corporations on Cotton Exchanges*, Part 1, 10–13, 101–116.

46. United States, Bureau of Corporations, *Report of the Commissioner of Corporations on Cotton Exchanges*, Part 1, 17.

47. United States, Bureau of Corporations, *Report of the Commissioner of Corporations on Cotton Exchanges*, Part 1, 19. Fuller details of the November 1906 revision committee scandal are found in pp. 116–147, 193–232.

CHAPTER 7

1. Charles A. Daney, "Calm in Cotton Market," *New York Times*, December 5, 1909.

2. Arthur R. Marsh, "The Economic Status of Cotton," *New York Times*, January 9, 1910.

3. Marsh, "The Economic Status of Cotton."

4. Marsh, "The Economic Status of Cotton."

5. Robey Wentworth Harned, "Boll Weevil in Mississippi, 1909," *Mississippi Agricultural Experiment Station, Bulletin No. 139* (Agricultural College, Mississippi, March 1910), 15.

6. Charles A. Daney, "Sixteen Cent Cotton Added to the Cheer," *Atlanta Constitution*, December 26, 1909.

7. Robey Wentworth Harned, "Boll Weevil in Mississippi, 1909," Mississippi Agricultural Experiment Station, Bulletin No. 139 (Agricultural College, Mississippi, March 1910), 15.

8. Daney, "Sixteen Cent Cotton Added to the Cheer."

9. Charles C. Cowan, "Time for the South to Unite in Fighting Cotton Bears," *Atlanta Constitution*, May 1, 1910.

10. Charles T. Plunkett, "President's Address [to the Meeting of the National Association of Cotton Manufacturers, Apr. 28–29, 1909]," *Textile World Record* 37, no. 2 (May 1909), p. 93.

11. This was not so far out of line with usual production: the crop brought into sight by that time of year had been 3.1 million bales in 1906 and 3.6 in 1907."The Cotton Market," *Textile World Record* 37, no. 4 (July 1909), 191.

12. "The Cotton Market," *Textile World Record* 37, no. 4 (July 1909), 191.

13. Cowan, "Time for the South to Unite in Fighting Cotton Bears."

14. Cowan, "Time for the South to Unite in Fighting Cotton Bears."

15. "Synopsis of the Matters Contained in the Several Counts," *United States v. James A. Patten, et al.,* Circuit Court of the United States for the Southern District of New York, July Term 1910, Court File 3-71, Criminal Case Files, RG 21: Records of District Courts of the United States, 1685-2004, NARA New York.

16. "Patten Indicted with Cotton Pool," *New York Times,* June 18, 1910; "Sues for $36,000 for 'Saving' Broker," *New York Times,* August 17, 1919; Stuart Rockoff, "Woodville, Mississippi," *Encyclopedia of Southern Jewish Communities,* www.msje.org/history/archive/ms/woodville. htm (accessed October 31, 2011); Passport Application, *Passport Applications, January 2, 1906–March 31, 1925,* NARA Microfilm Publication M1490, Roll 0015, Certificate 17115; Charles B. Bernstein, *The Rothschilds of Nordstetten: Their History and Genealogy* (Chicago: C. B. Bernstein, 1989).

17. "The Ups and Downs of a Plunger in Cotton," *New York Times,* January 23, 1910; "Patten Indicted with Cotton Pool," *New York Times,* June 18, 1910; "July & Aug. '03 Pool," Folder 9, Box 2, Brown Papers; "Eugene G. Scales, Grain Trader, Dies," *New York Times,* June 6, 1928; 1900 US Census, Texas, Bell County, Temple Ward 2, E.D. 29, p. 7; 1910 US Census, Texas, Dallas County, Dallas Ward 4, p. 33; 1910 US Census, New York, New York County, Manhattan Ward 21, E.D. 1268, p. 5. Though some sources indicate he was born in Louisiana, his obituary in the *New York Times,* June 6, 1928, supports this version of his story.

18. "Cotton Leaps to Sixteen Cents," *Atlanta Constitution,* December 24, 1909, p. 1; "The Ups and Downs of a Plunger in Cotton," *New York Times,* January 23, 1910; "Patten Indicted with Cotton Pool," *New York Times,* June 18, 1910; "May Oats Corner Closed," *New York Times,* June 1, 1902, p. 18; "Corn Corner; Delerium," Spokane *Spokesman-Review,* May 28, 1908, p. 2; "Pandemonium Reigned In Corn Pit," *Meriden (Conn.) Morning Record,* May 27, 1908, p. 1; Jan Olsson, "Trading Places: Griffith, Patten and Agricultural Modernity," *Film History* 17, no. 1 (2005): 39–65.

19. William James McKnight, *Jefferson County, Pennsylvania: Her Pioneers and People,* vol. 2 (Chicago: J. H. Beers & Co., 1917), 144; F. B. Howard-White, *Nickel: An Historical Review* (London: Methuen, 1963), 126–128; "Patten Indicted with Cotton Pool," *New York Times,* June 18, 1910.

20. Daney, "Calm in Cotton Market"; Cowan, "Time for the South to Unite in Fighting Cotton Bears."

21. Daney, "Calm in Cotton Market."

22. "Cotton Output is Smaller," *New York Times,* December 9, 1909.

23. Charles A. Daney, "Sixteen Cent Cotton Added to the Cheer," *Atlanta Constitution,* December 26, 1909; "Brown at Head Bull Movement," *Atlanta Constitution,* December 19, 1909.

24. Charles A. Daney, "Horns Still Locked in Cotton Fight," *Atlanta Constitution,* January 30, 1910.

25. "Higher Prices Sure for Cotton," *Atlanta Constitution,* January 16, 1910.

26. "Farmers Urged to Hold Cotton," *Atlanta Constitution,* January 20, 1910; "Higher Prices Sure for Cotton," *Atlanta Constitution,* January 16, 1910.

27. Marsh, "The Economic Status of Cotton."

28. *Atlanta Constitution,* January 9, 1910.

29. Cowan, "Time for the South to Unite in Fighting Cotton Bears."

30. Cowan, "Time for the South to Unite in Fighting Cotton Bears."

31. "Cotton Slump Costs Scales $6,000,000," *New York Times*, January 15, 1910.
32. Charles A. Daney, "Spot Cotton Holders Should Remain Firm," *Atlanta Constitution*, January 16, 1910.
33. "Cotton Slump Costs Scales $6,000,000," *New York Times*, January 15, 1910; "The Ups and Downs of a Plunger in Cotton," *New York Times*, January 23, 1910; "Cotton Pool Bulls Clashing in Court," *New York Times*, December 18, 1910; "Patten Indicted with Cotton Pool," *New York Times*, June 18, 1910.
34. Daney, "Spot Cotton Holders Should Remain Firm." They arrived on Monday morning, January 10, 1910.
35. "Twenty Cent Cotton Soon to Arrive," *Atlanta Constitution*, January 30, 1910.
36. Daney, "Spot Cotton Holders Should Remain Firm"; "Twenty Cent Cotton Soon to Arrive," *Atlanta Constitution*, January 30, 1910.
37. "James A. Patten Dies at Age of 76," *New York Times*, December 9, 1928; Jan Olsson, "Trading Places: Griffith, Patten and Agricultural Modernity," *Film History* 17, no. 1 (2005): 39–65.
38. "James A. Patten Dies at Age of 76," *New York Times*, December 9, 1928.
39. Item without headline, datelined London, March 12, *New York Times*, March 13, 1910, p. C4.
40. "'Wheat King' and 'Cotton Bull'," Hawera and Normanby (New Zealand) *Star*, Haratua [May] 2, 1910, p. 6.
41. Cowan, "Time for the South to Unite in Fighting Cotton Bears."
42. US House Committee on Expenditures in the Department of Justice, *Hearings Before the Committee on Expenditures in the Department of Justice, House of Representatives, on House Resolution No. 103, To Investigate the Expenditures in the Department of Justice*, 62nd. Cong., 1st Sess., Vol. 2, June 10, 1911, pp. 112–114; Deborah S. Gardner, *Cadwalader, Wickersham, & Taft: A Bicentennial History, 1792–1992*, (New York: Cadwalader, Wickersham & Taft, 1994), 11.
43. Henry W. Taft, *A Century and a Half at the New York Bar* (New York: privately printed, 1938), 284–285; Gardner, *Cadwalader, Wickersham, & Taft*, 10–11, and the captions to figures 18 & 19 tipped in between those pages.
44. Gerald Gunther, *Learned Hand: The Man and the Judge* (New York: Knopf, 1994), 129–130.
45. Gardner, *Cadwalader, Wickersham, & Taft*, 10–11, and the captions to figures 18 & 19 tipped in between those pages.
46. "Cotton Investigation," *Wall Street Journal*, April 20, 1910.
47. US House Committee on Expenditures in the Department of Justice, *Hearings Before the Committee on Expenditures in the Department of Justice, House of Representatives, on House Resolution No. 103, To Investigate the Expenditures in the Department of Justice*, 62nd. Cong., 1st Sess., Vol. 2, June 10, 1911, 103–105, 112–113; "Cotton Pool Row Turns Into Politics," *New York Times*, April 21, 1910.
48. "The Sully Cotton Failure," *Fibre and Fabric: A Record of American Textile Industries in the Cotton and Woolen Trade* 39: 995 (March 25, 1904), 73; "David H. Miller and Henry W. Taft," notice, *Fibre and Fabric: A Record of American Textile Industries in the Cotton and Woolen Trade* 39: 996 (April 2, 1904), 88. When Miller was suggested on his own "this not being satisfactory to the creditors," creditors "met at the Cotton Exchange March 22," and the two men "took charge of affairs" March 23 "having filed bonds of $200,000."
49. Henry W. Taft to Theodore Roosevelt, December 1, 1904, in the possession of Cadwalader Wickersham and Taft. Thanks to Claudia Freeman in the Public Relations Department of that firm for this source.
50. "Cotton Pool Row Turns Into Politics," *New York Times*, April 21, 1910.
51. "Overt Act 6," February 26, 1910, pp. 15–18 (quotation 16), *United States v. James A. Patten, et al.*, Circuit Court of the United States for the Southern District of New York, July Term 1910, Court File 3–71, Criminal Case Files, RG 21: Records of District Courts of the United States, 1685-2004, NARA New York.

52. US House Committee on Expenditures in the Department of Justice, *Hearings Before the Committee on Expenditures in the Department of Justice, House of Representatives, on House Resolution No. 103, To Investigate the Expenditures in the Department of Justice*, 62nd. Cong., 1st Sess., Vol. 1, May 31, 1911, 42.
53. "Overt Act 1," February 19, 1910, p. 11, *United States v. James A. Patten, et al.*
54. "Overt Act 6," February 26, 1910, pp. 15–16, *United States v. James A. Patten, et al.*
55. "Twenty Cent Cotton Soon to Arrive," *Atlanta Constitution*, January 30, 1910.
56. "Lewis W. Parker Dead," *New York Times*, Apr. 12, 1916; "Lewis W. Parker, Greenville, SC," http://textilehistory.org/LewisWParker.html (accessed Sept. 17, 2012); W. M. McLaurine, *James William Cannon (1852–1921): His Plants, His People, His Philosophy* (New York: Newcomen Society, 1951); Helen Arthur-Cornett, *Remembering Kannapolis: Tales from Towel City* (Charleston, S.C.: History Press, 2006), 20–27; Gary N. Mock, "Fuller E. Callaway" www.textilehistory.org/FullerECallaway.html (accessed October 29, 2012).
57. Statement of Lewis W. Parker, in *Regulation of Cotton Exchanges: Hearings before the Committee on Agriculture, House of Representatives, Sixty-Third Congress, Second Session, Regarding Various Bills Relative to the Regulation of Cotton Exchanges, April 22 to 25, 1914* (Washington, D.C.: GPO, 1914), 4.
58. David L. Carlton argued that textile mills in the South were built largely by local money, in contrast to an earlier generation of scholarship that thought of the mills as built by outside capital. See David L. Carlton, *Mill and Town in South Carolina, 1880–1920* (Baton Rouge: Louisiana State University Press, 1982).
59. W. B. Tanner, affidavit, May 7, 1910, in House of Representatives, *Hearings Before the Committee on Expenditures in the Department of Justice*, vol. 2, June 10, 1911, pp. 116–117.
60. Montgomery Cotton Mills to Craig & Jenks, March 7, 1910, Exhibit A in in House of Representatives, *Hearings Before the Committee on Expenditures in the Department of Justice*, vol. 2, June 10, 1911, pp. 120–121.
61. Craig & Jenks to W. B. Tanner, March 10, 1910, Exhibit B in in House of Representatives, *Hearings Before the Committee on Expenditures in the Department of Justice*, vol. 2, June 10, 1911, pp. 121–122.
62. [W. B. Tanner] to Craig & Jenks, April 6, 1910, Exhibit O; Craig & Jenks to W. B. Tanner, April 7, 1910, telegram, Exhibit P; Craig & Jenks to W. B. Tanner, April 16, 1910, telegram, Exhibit S; all in House of Representatives, *Hearings Before the Committee on Expenditures in the Department of Justice*, vol. 2, June 10, 1911, pp. 125–127.
63. W. B. Tanner, affidavit, May 7, 1910, in House of Representatives, *Hearings Before the Committee on Expenditures in the Department of Justice*, vol. 2, June 10, 1911, pp. 116–117.
64. W. B. Tanner, affidavit, May 7, 1910, in House of Representatives, *Hearings Before the Committee on Expenditures in the Department of Justice*, vol. 2, June 10, 1911, p. 119.
65. *Regulation of Cotton Exchanges: Hearings before the Committee on Agriculture, House of Representatives, Sixty-Third Congress, Second Session, Regarding Various Bills Relative to the Regulation of Cotton Exchanges, April 22 to 25, 1914* (Washington, D.C.: GPO, 1914), 108–109.
66. House of Representatives, *Hearings Before the Committee on Expenditures in the Department of Justice*, vol. 2, June 10, 1911, pp. 103–105.
67. "Government Blow at Option Trading," *New York Times*, April 20, 1910; "Cotton Pool Row Turns Into Politics," *New York Times*, April 21, 1910, p. 1; "Dear Cotton Hits Big Firm," *New York Times*, April 22, 1910, p. 1; "Dick Contradicts Patten," *New York Times*, April 23, 1910, p. 2; "The Cotton Conspiracy," *New York Times*, June 19, 1910.
68. "No May Settlement," *New York Times*, April 24, 1910, p. 4
69. "Government Blow at Option Trading," *New York Times*, Apr. 20, 1910.

CHAPTER 8

1. "Cotton Market of the World on Keen Edge," *Atlanta Constitution*, April 24, 1910.
2. "Cotton Bulls Stand Shock of Deliveries," *New York Times*, April 30, 1910, p. 2.

3. The calculation assumed they paid nine cents a pound at 500 pounds to the bale, for 202,000 bales, bringing their total costs to $9.09 million. Some sources report deliveries of 225,000 bales, which probably represents the total deliveries for the month, not just the single staggering day.
4. "Cotton Inquiry Centres on Patten," *New York Times*, May 6, 1910, p. 6.
5. "Cotton Market of the World on Keen Edge," Atlanta *Constitution*, April 24, 1910.
6. "Dear Cotton Hits Big Firm," *New York Times*, April 22, 1910.
7. "Firm Declines Information," and "Expect No Big Loss Here," *New York Times*, April 23, 1910, p. 2.
8. "Firm Declines Information," and "Expect No Big Loss Here," *New York Times*, April 23, 1910, p. 2.
9. "Cotton Fraud Suit Involves $4,500,000," *New York Times*, February 3, 1913.
10. It was the revelation of a similar scheme involving Chinese cotton in 1864 that contributed to the recognition in Liverpool of short selling, and the development of formal futures out of existing sales of cotton in advance of its delivery in that city's cotton brokers association; see A.W.B. Simpson, "The Origins of Futures Trading in the Liverpool Cotton Market," in Peter Cane and Jane Stapleton, eds. *Essays for Patrick Atiyah* (Oxford: Clarendon Press, 1991), 194.
11. "Cotton Fraud Trial," *New York Times*, April 2, 1911; "Cotton Fraud Suit Involves $4,500,000," *New York Times*, February 3, 1913; George W. Neville, "The Bill of Lading Controversy," *New York Times,* January 8, 1911.
12. "Cotton Market of the World on Keen Edge," *Atlanta Constitution*, April 24, 1910.
13. "Cotton Bulls Stand Shock of Deliveries," *New York Times*, April 30, 1910, p. 2.
14. "Bull Pockets Begin to Bulge," *Atlanta Constitution*, May 1, 1910.
15. "Cotton Bears Raid Market," *New York Times*, June 1, 1910.
16. Article without headline, datelined New Orleans, June 2, 1910, *New York Times*, June 3, 1910; "Cotton Crop Report Out," *New York Times*, June 3, 1910; "Commodities Markets: Cotton," *New York Times*, June 3, 1910.
17. "Cotton Bears Raid Market," *New York Times*, June 1, 1910.
18. Article without headline, datelined New Orleans, June 2, 1910, *New York Times*, June 3, 1910; "Cotton Crop Report Out," *New York Times*, June 3, 1910; "Commodities Markets: Cotton," *New York Times*, June 3, 1910.
19. "Commodities Markets: Cotton," *New York Times*, June 5, 1910.
20. "The Commodities Markets: Cotton," *New York Times,* June 17, 1910; also June 10, June 12, June 16, and June 18, 1910.
21. "Patten Indicted with Cotton Pool," *New York Times*, June 18, 1910, p. 1.
22. "Cotton 'Corner' Up to High Court," *Atlanta Constitution*, October 24, 1912; "Spooner, John Coit (1843–1919)," *Biographical Directory of the U.S. Congress,* http://bioguide.congress.gov/ (accessed September 1, 2011).
23. Documents, December 20, 1910, *United States v. James A. Patten, et al.*, Circuit Court of the United States for the Southern District of New York, July Term 1910, Criminal Case Files, RG 21: Records of District Courts of the United States, 1685-2004, NARA New York.
24. "Cotton Pool Row Turns Into Politics," *New York Times*, April 21, 1910; "Dear Cotton Hits Big Firm," *New York Times*, April 22, 1910.
25. "Cotton Pool Row Turns Into Politics," *New York Times*, April 21, 1910, p. 1.
26. "No May Settlement," *New York Times*, April 24, 1910, p. 4.
27. "Cotton Inquiry Centers on Patten," *New York Times*, May 6, 1910, p. 6; US House Committee on Expenditures in the Department of Justice, *Hearings Before the Committee on Expenditures in the Department of Justice, House of Representatives, on House Resolution No. 103, To Investigate the Expenditures in the Department of Justice*, 62nd. Cong., 1st Sess., Vol. 2, June 10, 1911, 94, 104.
28. US House Committee on Expenditures in the Department of Justice, *Hearings Before the Committee on Expenditures in the Department of Justice*, Vol. 7, July 19 and 21, 1911, 359.

29. US House Committee on Expenditures in the Department of Justice, *Hearings Before the Committee on Expenditures in the Department of Justice*, Vol. 2, June 10, 1911, 88.
30. "Lawyers and Legal Events," 17 Bench and B., o.s. 40 (1909), http://heinonline.org/HOL/LandingPage?collection=journals&handle=hein.journals/babl7&div=10&id=&page= (accessed September 22, 2012).
31. "Wise Will Take Stimson's Place," New York *Times*, March 24, 1909; "Lawyers and Legal Events," 17 Bench and B., o.s. 40 (1909), http://heinonline.org/HOL/Landing Page?collection=journals&handle=hein.journals/babl7&div=10&id=&page= (accessed September 22, 2012).
32. "Wise Will Take Stimson's Place," *New York Times*, March 24, 1909; "Lawyers and Legal Events," 17 Bench and B., o.s. 40 (1909), http://heinonline.org/HOL/LandingPage?collection=journals&handle=hein.journals/babl7&div=10&id=&page= (accessed September 22, 2012).
33. US House Committee on Expenditures in the Department of Justice, *Hearings Before the Committee on Expenditures in the Department of Justice*, Vol. 1, May 31, 1911, 50.
34. "The Cotton Conspiracy," *New York Times*, June 19, 1910, p. 10.
35. US House Committee on Expenditures in the Department of Justice, *Hearings Before the Committee on Expenditures in the Department of Justice*, Vol. 2, June 10, 1911, 98.
36. US House Committee on Expenditures in the Department of Justice, *Hearings Before the Committee on Expenditures in the Department of Justice*, Vol. 1, May 31, 1911, 40, 43.
37. US House Committee on Expenditures in the Department of Justice, *Hearings Before the Committee on Expenditures in the Department of Justice*, Vol. 1, May 31, 1911, 45.
38. US House Committee on Expenditures in the Department of Justice, *Hearings Before the Committee on Expenditures in the Department of Justice*, Vol. 1, May 31, 1911, 40, 43.
39. US House Committee on Expenditures in the Department of Justice, *Hearings Before the Committee on Expenditures in the Department of Justice*, Vol. 2, June 10, 1911, 99.
40. "Reply in Cotton Cases," *Wall Street Journal*, June 30, 1910; "Patten Indicted with Cotton Pool," *New York Times*, June 18, 1910, p. 1.
41. US House Committee on Expenditures in the Department of Justice, *Hearings Before the Committee on Expenditures in the Department of Justice*, Vol. 2, June 10, 1911, 88; US House Committee on Expenditures in the Department of Justice, *Hearings Before the Committee on Expenditures in the Department of Justice*, Vol. 3, 131. According to Wise, the second indictment was delayed because the defendants were out of town, and the holding of a second indictment in anticipation of the failure of a first one was not uncommon.
42. Document 20, February 9, 1911. *United States v. James A. Patten, et al.*
43. "Patten Indicted with Cotton Pool," *New York Times*, June 18, 1910.
44. "The Commodities Markets: Cotton," *New York Times*, July 2, 1910.
45. "The Commodities Markets: Cotton," *New York Times*, July 11, 1910; this had been predicted in the same column for July 1, 1910.
46. "The Commodities Markets: Cotton," *New York Times*, July 11, 1910; July 12, 1910.
47. "Cotton," *New York Times*, July 15, 1910.
48. "Not Done with Cotton Pool," *New York Times*, July 16, 1910.
49. "Brokers in a Fist Fight," *New York Times*, July 21, 1910.
50. *The Handbook of Texas Online*, s.v. Fleming, Lamar Jr. www.tshaonline.org/handbook/online/articles/ffl09 (accessed September 23, 2012).
51. "Brokers in a Fist Fight," *New York Times*, July 21, 1910.
52. "Rush of July Cotton," *Boston Evening Transcript*, July 28, 1910.
53. This came after a "very short crop last year" of only 10.35 million bales. "Cotton Condition Shows a Decline," *New York Times*, August 3, 1910.
54. "20-Cent Cotton for This Season, Say Bull Leaders," *Atlanta Constitution*, August 30, 1910; "The Range of Cotton Options," *Atlanta Constitution*, August 30, 1910, p. 9.
55. "Cotton, 2,302,211 Bales," *New York Times*, October 4, 1910.
56. "Commodity Markets," *New York Times*, November 28, 1910.

57. "Millions in Cotton Frauds," *New York Times*, November 25, 1910; "Cotton Fraud Trial," *New York Times*, April 2, 1911. It was the post office inspectors who provided evidence and indictment of John W. Knight, among others; "Guaranteeing Cotton Bills," *New York Times*, December 10, 1910.

58. "Cotton Men Face Problem," *New York Times*, September 1, 1910.

59. "Bertilloned Cotton Bills," *New York Times*, September 12, 1910.

60. "The Cotton Bill Problem," *New York Times*, September 16, 1910; "Won't Certify Cotton Bills," *New York Times*, October 7, 1910.

61. "The Cotton Bill Problem," *New York Times*, October 16, 1910.

62. "Bankers Go Ahead Without Cotton Men," *New York Times*, October 16, 1910.

63. "To Block Cotton Plan," *New York Times*, October 22, 1910.

64. "Guaranteeing Cotton Bills," *New York Times*, December 10, 1910.

65. "The Commodities Markets: Cotton," *New York Times*, September 26, 1910.

66. "Cotton Pool Bulls Clashing in Court," *New York Times*, December 18, 1910.

67. *US v. James A. Patten et al.*, File #22,654, Supreme Court of the United States #282, October 1912. *United States v. James A. Patten, et al.*

68. "Patten Cotton Corner Is Held to Be Clearly Against the Law," *Wall Street Journal*, January 1, 1913.

69. "Other Members of Pool Will Not Plead Guilty," *Atlanta Constitution* February 12, 1913; "Cotton Pool Indictments," *Wall Street Journal*, July 2, 1913; "Members of 1909 Cotton Pool Plead Nolo Contendere," *Wall Street Journal*, December 15, 1913.

70. "Regulation of Cotton Exchanges: Hearings . . ." (GPO, 1914), 91.

71. Roger Shale and G. Carroll Todd, *Decrees and Judgments in Federal Anti-trust Cases, July 2, 1890-Jan. 1, 1918* (Washington, D.C.: US Government Printing Office, 1918), 807.

72. "Government Blow at Option Trading," *New York Times*, April 20, 1910.

CHAPTER 9

1. Carl Parker argues that the timing of these legislative efforts was more a response to general economic crises. See Carl Parker, "Governmental Regulation of Speculation," *Annals of the American Academy of Political and Social Science* 38, no. 2 (September 1911), 141–144. For more on the background of the Cotton Futures Act of 1914, see James C. Malin, "The Background of the First Bills to Establish a Bureau of Markets, 1911–12," *Agricultural History* 6, no. 3 (July 1932), 114–116; I. Newton Hoffman, "The Cotton Futures Act," *Journal of Political Economy* 23, no. 5 (May 1915): 465–489.

2. *Report of the Commissioner of Corporations on Cotton Exchanges. Part IV. Effect of Future Contracts on Prices of Cotton. Part V. Influence of Producers' Organizations on Prices of Cotton. December 6, 1909* (Washington, D.C.: GPO, 1909), 9.

3. *Report of the Commissioner of Corporations on Cotton Exchanges. Part IV.*, 23.

4. John Corrigan Jr., "Cotton Exchange Dealt Hard Blow," *Atlanta Constitution*, December 6, 1909.

5. "Where Cotton Is The Gamble Stake!" *Atlanta Constitution*, December 6, 1909, p. 4.

6. "Our Cotton Exchange," *New York Times*, December 7, 1910, p. 8.

7. "Future System In Cotton Trade," *Atlanta Constitution*, December 15, 1910. See also the detailed and careful explanation in "'Gambling in Futures'—The Real Meaning of the Phrase and the part Played by the Speculator in the Business Life of the Nation," *New York Times*, January 9, 1910, p. SM4.

8. "Farmers' Union To Demand Action Against Gambling," *Atlanta Constitution*, January 2, 1910, p. B8.

9. "Farmers' Union To Demand Action Against Gambling," *Atlanta Constitution*, January 2, 1910, p. B8.

10. "Hearings On Speculation," *New York Times*, January 23, 1910, p. 10. The bills were introduced by J. T. Heflin of Alabama (H.R. 15426, December 15, 1909), Jack Beall of Texas (H.R. 16030, December 20, 1910), and Scott Ferris of Oklahoma (H.R. 18173, January 14, 1910). See *House Journal*, 61st Cong., 2nd Sess., Serial Set Vol. 5581, 79, 95, 168.

11. House of Representatives, United States, *Hearings before the Committee on Agriculture during the Second Session of the Sixty-First Congress, Vol. 2, Hearings on Bills for the Prevention of "Dealing in Futures" on Boards of Trade, Etc.* (Washington, D.C.: GPO, 1910), 24.

12. House of Representatives, United States, *Hearings before the Committee on Agriculture during the Second Session of the Sixty-First Congress, Vol. 2, Hearings on Bills for the Prevention of "Dealing in Futures" on Boards of Trade, Etc.* (Washington, D.C.: GPO, 1910), 603.

13. "Knell Sounding For Gamblers On Cotton Crop," *Atlanta Constitution*, April 6, 1910, p. 1; *House Journal*, 61st Cong., 2nd Sess., Serial Set Vol. 5581, April 5, 1910, p. 529.

14. "W. B. Thompson Opposes Cotton Futures Bill," *Atlanta Constitution*, April 8, 1910, p. 5.

15. W. H. Lawson, "As To Future Dealing," *Atlanta Constitution*, April 16, 1910, p. 6; "Got Them On Run Says Barrett Of Exchanges," *Atlanta Constitution*, February 10, 1910, p. 1; "Pass Cotton Exchange Bill," *New York Times*, June 25, 1910, p. 3; *House Journal*, 61st Cong., 2nd Sess., Serial Set Vol. 5581, June 23, 1910, p. 836; *Senate Journal*, 61st Cong., 2nd Sess., Serial Set Vol. No. 5580, June 24, 1910, p. 495; Anne Firor Scott, "A Progressive Wind from the South, 1906–1913," *Journal of Southern History* 29, no. 1 (February 1963), 59.

16. These were H.R. 14681, 18489, 18587, 18595, 18650, and 19809. See *House Journal*, 62nd Cong., 2nd Sess., Serial Set Vol. No. 6119, 29 (December 6, 1911), 202 (January 22, 1912), 208 (January 22, 1912), 208 (January 23, 1912), 213 (January 24, 1912), 289 (February 9, 1912). Other similar bills included H.R. 18778, H.R. 18779, H.R. 20836, and S. 4104. See *House Journal*, 62nd Cong., 2nd Sess., Serial Set Vol. No. 6119, 221 (January 26, 1912), 221 (January 26, 1912), 364 (February 26, 1912), and *Senate Journal*, 62nd Cong., 2nd Sess., Serial Set Vol. No. 6118, 60 (January 4, 1912), 74 (January 15, 1912). On Heflin, see Ray T. Tucker, "Don Tom of Alabam'," *North American Review* 226, no. 2 (August 1928): 148–157.

17. "Standard Grades For Cotton Trade," *Atlanta Constitution*, January 19, 1912, p. 3; *Senate Journal*, 62nd Cong., 2nd Sess., Serial Set Vol. No. 6118, January 18, 1912, p. 91. Relatively little has been written on Smith; a brief overview is Daniel W. Hollis, "'Cotton Ed Smith': Showman or Statesman?" *South Carolina Historical Magazine* 71, no. 4 (October 1970): 235–256.

18. Arthur R. Marsh, "Cotton Exchanges and Their Economic Functions," *Annals of the American Academy of Political and Social Science* 38, no. 2 (September 1911), 280.

19. "Federal Control Of The Exchanges," *Atlanta Constitution*, April 10, 1912, p. 5.

20. *House Reports*, 62nd Cong., 2nd Sess., No. 602, April 25, 1912, "Interference With Commerce Among the States, Etc.," 1; "Cotton Gambling Placed Under Ban," *Atlanta Constitution*, July 17, 1912, p. 12; *House Journal*, 62nd Cong., 2nd Sess., Serial Set Vol. No. 6119, July 16, 1912, p. 868.

21. G. Wright Hoffman, *Future Trading upon Organized Commodity Markets in the United States* (Philadelphia: University of Pennsylvania Press, 1932), 115. The decision was *Christie Grain and Stock Co., et al., v. Board of Trade of the City of Chicago* (798 US 236). This case is at the heart of Jonathan Ira Levy, "Contemplating Delivery: Futures Trading and the Problem of Commodity Exchange in the United States, 1875–1905," *American Historical Review* 111, no. 2 (Apr. 2006): 307–335.

22. *Senate Journal*, 62nd Cong., 2nd Sess., 461 (July 17, 1912), 426 (June 17, 1912), 444 (July 4, 1912); *Senate Manual* (Washington, D.C.: GPO, 1913), 11–12.

23. Kenneth W. Hechler, *Insurgency: Personalities and Politics of the Taft Era* (New York: Columbia University Press, 1940), 14, 27–82; James Holt, *Congressional Insurgents and the Party System, 1909–1916* (Cambridge, Mass.: Harvard University Press, 1967), 40–43.

24. Shanon Ashley Hays, "Progressivism, Southern Style: The Congressional Career of Asbury Francis Lever, 1901–1919" (MA thesis, Clemson University, 1998), 5, 10, 32, 34.

25. "Cotton Boards To Join Forces," *Atlanta Constitution*, January 7, 1913, p. 1; "To Federate Cotton Exchanges," Schulenburg (Tex.) *Sticker*, January 10, 1913.

26. Arthur Kuffler, "Report on the Liverpool Conference with American and European Cotton Exchanges," in *The Ninth International Congress of Delegated Representatives of Master*

Cotton Spinners' and Manufacturers' Associations, Held in the Kurhaus, Scheveningen, June 9th, 10th, and 11th, 1913 (Manchester: Taylor, Garnett, Evans, and Co., n.d.), 52.

27. Kuffler, "Report on the Liverpool Conference with American and European Cotton Exchanges," 542, 544 (quotation).

28. "Cotton Exchanges Plan Association," *Atlanta Constitution*, October 28, 1913, p. 14; "Uniformity In Grades Of Southern Cotton," *Atlanta Constitution*, October 29, 1913, p. 10.

29. *Atlanta Constitution*, March 12, 1914.

30. John Corrigan Jr., "Wilson To Solve Cotton Problem," *Atlanta Constitution*, September 19, 1913, p. 5.

31. John Corrigan Jr., "Wilson To Solve Cotton Problem," *Atlanta Constitution*, September 19, 1913, p. 5; *Senate Journal*, 63rd Cong., 1st Sess., Serial Set Vol. No. 6508, April 7, 1913, p. 7; "Trading in Cotton Futures," 63rd Cong., 2nd Sess., Sen. Rep. 289 (February 26, 1914), p. 4; *Senate Journal*, 63rd Cong., 2nd Sess., Serial Set Vol. No. 6550, February 26, 1914, p. 143; *Senate Journal*, 63rd Cong., 2nd Sess., Serial Set Vol. No. 6550, March 28, 1914, p. 203; *House Journal*, 63rd Cong., 2nd Sess., Serial Set Vol. No. 6551, March 28, 1914, p. 370; *House Journal*, 63rd Cong., 2nd Sess., Serial Set Vol. No. 6551, April 1, 1914, p. 386.

32. *Regulation of Cotton Exchanges: Hearings before the Committee on Agriculture, House of Representatives, Sixty-Third Congress, Second Session, Regarding Various Bills Relative to the Regulation of Cotton Exchanges, April 22 to 25, 1914* (Washington, D.C.: GPO, 1914), 3.

33. *House Journal*, 63rd Cong., 2nd Sess., Serial Set Vol. No. 6551, April 2, 1914, p. 392.

34. *Regulation of Cotton Exchanges: Hearings before the Committee on Agriculture, House of Representatives, Sixty-Third Congress, Second Session, Regarding Various Bills Relative to the Regulation of Cotton Exchanges, April 22 to 25, 1914* (Washington, D.C.: GPO, 1914), 22.

35. *Regulation of Cotton Exchanges: Hearings before the Committee on Agriculture, House of Representatives, Sixty-Third Congress, Second Session, Regarding Various Bills Relative to the Regulation of Cotton Exchanges, April 22 to 25, 1914* (Washington, D.C.: GPO, 1914), 25–49 (quotation 36), 96–101.

36. "Trading in Cotton Futures," 63rd Congress, 2nd Session, House Report No. 765, June 4, 1914, pp. 18–20.

37. *Senate Journal*, 63rd Cong., 2nd Sess., Serial Set Vol. No. 6550, Jun. 30, 1914, p. 368–369; *House Journal*, 63rd Cong., 2nd Sess., Serial Set Vol. No. 6551, Jun. 30, 1914, p. 718; *Senate Journal*, 63rd Cong., 2nd Sess., Serial Set Vol. No. 6550, August 19, 1914, p. 470.

CONCLUSION

1. "Cotton Exchange Closed Because of Heavy Slump," New York *Evening World*, July 31, 1914, p. 3.

2. "Stock Exchanges of U.S. Close," *Ogden (Utah) Standard*, July 31, 1914, p. 5.

3. "Cotton Exchange To Remain Closed," New York *Sun*, August 4, 1914, p. 12.

4. Arthur S. Link, "The Cotton Crisis, the South, and Anglo-American Diplomacy, 1914–1915," in J. Carlyle Sitterson, ed., *Studies in Southern History.* James Sprunt Studies in History and Political Science, vol. 39 (Chapel Hill: University of North Carolina Press, 1957), 122.

5. James L. McCorkle Jr., "The Louisiana 'Buy-a-Bale' of Cotton Movement, 1914," *Louisiana History* 15, no. 2 (Spring 1974), 136.

6. Arthur S. Link, "The Cotton Crisis, the South, and Anglo-American Diplomacy, 1914–1915." In J. Carlyle Sitterson, ed., *Studies in Southern History.* James Sprunt Studies in History and Political Science, vol. 39, (Chapel Hill: University of North Carolina Press, 1957), 126 (quotation), 129.

7. "$1,500,000 Is Ready For Cotton Brokers," *New York Times*, November 3, 1914, p. 14.

8. "Cotton Exchange To Open Monday," *New York Times*, November 14, 1915, p. 15.

9. Arthur S. Link, "The Cotton Crisis, the South, and Anglo-American Diplomacy, 1914–1915," in J. Carlyle Sitterson, ed., *Studies in Southern History.* James Sprunt Studies in History and Political Science, vol. 39 (Chapel Hill: University of North Carolina Press, 1957), 138.

10. "Cotton Futures Act Called Void," *New York Times*, October 14, 1915, p. 4.
11. "No Cotton-Act Appeal Yet," *New York Times*, October 15, 1915, p. 16.
12. "History of the CFTC" www.cftc.gov/about/historyofthecftc/index.htm (accessed November 22, 2012).
13. "History of the CFTC" www.cftc.gov/About/HistoryoftheCFTC/history_precftc (accessed October 1, 2012).
14. *U.S. v. American Tobacco,* 221 U.S. 179 (1911), quoted in Elizabeth Sanders, *Roots of Reform: Farmers, Workers, and the American State, 1877–1917* (Chicago and London: University of Chicago Press, 1999), 277n41.
15. Audrey Sherman, "The History of the New Orleans Cotton Exchange, 1871–1914," (MA thesis, Tulane University, 1934), 84–85; Henry E. Chambers, *A History of Louisiana: Wild erness-Colony-Province-Territory-State-People* (American Historical Society, 1925), 3:382, s.v. "Franklin Brevard Hayne."
16. Donald A. Gill, *Stories Behind New Orleans Street Names* (Chicago: Bonus Books, 1992), 112.
17. Paula A. Fortier, "Behind the Banner of Patriotism: The New Orleans Chapter of the American Red Cross and Auxiliary Branches 6 and 11 (1914–1917)" (MA thesis, University of New Orleans, 2010), 21.
18. Alcée Fortier, *Louisiana: Comprising Sketches of Parishes, Towns, Events, Institutions, and Persons, Arranged in Cyclopedic Form,* (Madison, Wisc.: Century Historical Association, 1914), 3:761, s.v. "Hayne, Franklin B."
19. "Daniel Sully, Cotton King, Dies in West," *Miami Daily News*, Sept. 20, 1930, p. 3.
20. "'Dan' Sully, Ex-Cotton King, A Boarding House Keeper," *New York Times*, July 14, 1912.
21. "Mrs. D. J. Sully, Wife of Cotton King, Is Dead," *New London (Conn.) Day*, May 26, 1911 [afternoon edition], p. 1.
22. "Daniel Sully, Cotton King, Dies in West," *Miami Daily News*, Sept. 20, 1930, p. 3.
23. "William P. Brown, Noted Cotton Man, Dies In His Home, " *New Orleans Times-Picayune*, Oct. 6, 1914.
24. William Garrott Brown, *The South At Work: Observations from 1904*, Bruce E. Baker, ed. (Columbia: University of South Carolina Press, 2014).
25. W.E.B. Du Bois, *The Quest of the Silver Fleece* (New York: A. C. McClurg & Co., 1911), chapter 18.
26. C. Vann Woodward, *Origins of the New South: 1877–1913* (Baton Rouge: Louisiana State University Press, 1951); Claire Strom, *Making Catfish Bait Out of Government Boys: The Fight Against Cattle Ticks and the Transformation of the Yeoman South* (Athens: University of Georgia Press, 2009).
27. *Regulation of Cotton Exchanges: Hearings before the Committee on Agriculture, House of Representatives, Sixty-Third Congress, Second Session, Regarding Various Bills Relative to the Regulation of Cotton Exchanges, April 22 to 25, 1914* (Washington, D.C.: GPO, 1914), 27.

ESSAY ON SOURCES

1. Jonathan Robins, "The Cotton Crisis: Globalization and Empire in the Atlantic World, 1902–1920" (PhD diss., University of Rochester, 2010).
2. A good example of the rather muddled nature of accounts of Patten's role is Jerry W. Markham, *A Financial History of the United States: Vol. II, From J. P. Morgan to the Institutional Investor (1900–1970)* (Armonk, N.Y.: M. E. Sharpe, 2002), 40, which suggests that the Supreme Court ruling related to Patten's wheat corner and that he tried to cor- ner cotton in 1913.
3. "W. P. Brown Fined," *New Orleans Item*, December 6, 1902, p. 2.
4. M. B. Hammond, *The Cotton Industry: An Essay in American Economic History* (New York: Macmillan, 1897).
5. Eugene W. Hilgard, *Report on Cotton Production in the United States* (Washington, D.C.: GPO, 1884); Bureau of the Census, *Bulletin 125: Cotton Production, 1913* (Washington, D.C.: GPO, 1914).

6. John A. Todd, *The Marketing of Cotton: From the Grower to the Spinner* (London: Sir I. Pitman & Sons, 1934); Alston Hill Garside, *Cotton Goes To Market: A Graphic Description of a Great Industry* (New York: Frederick A. Stokes Co., 1935); James E. Boyle, *Cotton and the New Orleans Cotton Exchange: A Century of Commercial Evolution* (Garden City, N.Y.: Country Life Press, 1934); Audrey Sherman, "The History of the New Orleans Cotton Exchange, 1871–1914" (MA thesis, Tulane University, 1934).

7. Harold D. Woodman, "Introduction to Southern Classics Series Edition," *King Cotton and His Retainers: Financing and Marketing the Cotton Crop of the South, 1800–1925* (Columbia: University of South Carolina Press, 1990 [1968]), ix.

8. The literature on the economic development of the New South, and particularly the development of agriculture and land tenure in this period, is vast. A good starting point is the collection of essays looking back at Woodward's book after half a century: John B. Boles and Bethany L. Johnson, eds., *Origins of the New South Fifty Years Later: The Continuing Influence of a Historical Classic* (Baton Rouge: Louisiana State University Press, 2003). This body of scholarship itself reaches back in many ways to the 1938 Report on Economic Conditions in the South. See David L. Carlton and Peter A. Coclanis, eds., *Confronting Southern Poverty in the Great Depression: The Report on Economic Conditions in the South with Related Documents* (Boston: Bedford, 1996).

9. L. Tuffly Ellis, "The Texas Cotton Compress Industry: A History" (PhD diss., University of Texas, 1964); L. Tuffly Ellis, "The Round Bale Cotton Controversy," *Southwestern Historical Quarterly* 71, no. 2 (October 1967): 194–225; L. Tuffly Ellis, "The Revolutionizing of the Texas Cotton Trade, 1865–1885," *Southwestern Historical Quarterly* 73, no. 4 (April 1970): 478–508.

10. Abigail Curlee Holbrook, "Cotton Marketing in Antebellum Texas," *Southwestern Historical Quarterly* 63 (Apr. 1970): 431–455; Ronnie C. Tyler, "Cotton on the Border, 1861–1865," *Southwestern Historical Quarterly* 63 (Apr. 1970): 456–477; L. Tuffly Ellis, "The Revolutionizing of the Texas Cotton Trade, 1865–1885," *Southwestern Historical Quarterly* 63 (Apr. 1970): 478–508; John R. Killick, "Risk, Specialization and Profit in the Mercantile Sector of the Nineteenth Century Cotton Trade: Alexander Brown & Sons, 1820–80," *Business History* 16 (Jan. 1974): 1–16; John R. Killick, "The Cotton Operations of Alexander Brown and Sons in the Deep South, 1820–1880," *Journal of Southern History* 43 (May 1977): 169–194; John R. Killick, "The Transformation of Cotton Marketing in the Late Nineteenth Century: Alexander Sprunt and Son of Wilmington, N.C., 1884–1956," *Business History Review* 55 (Summer 1981): 143–169.

11. Mark Kurlansky, *Salt: A World History* (New York: Walker and Co., 2002); Mark Kurlansky, *Cod: A Biography of the Fish That Changed the World* (New York: Walker and Co., 1997); Michael Redclift, *Chewing Gum: The Fortunes of Taste* (New York: Routledge, 2004).

12. Sven Beckert, "Emancipation and Empire: Reconstructing the Worldwide Web of Cotton Production in the Age of the American Civil War," *American Historical Review* 109, no. 5 (December 2004): 1405–1438; Sven Beckert, "From Tuskegee to Togo: The Problem of Freedom in the Empire of Cotton," *Journal of American History* 92, no. 2 (September 2005): 498–526; Sven Beckert, *Empire of Cotton: A Global History* (New York: Knopf, 2014); Andrew Zimmerman, *Alabama in Africa: Booker T. Washington, the German Empire, and the Globalization of the New South* (Princeton, N.J.: Princeton University Press, 2010); Giorgio Riello, *Cotton: The Fabric That Made the Modern World* (Cambridge: Cambridge University Press, 2013).

13. L. Tuffly Ellis, "The New Orleans Cotton Exchange: The Formative Years, 1871–1880," *Journal of Southern* History 39, no. 4 (November 1973): 545–564; Robert Bouilly, "The Development of American Cotton Exchanges, 1870–1916" (PhD diss., University of Missouri, 1975); Kenneth J. Lipartito, "The New York Cotton Exchange and the Development of the Cotton Futures Market," *Business History Review* 57, no. 1 (Spring 1983): 50–72.

14. Jeffrey C. Williams, "The Origin of Futures Markets," *Agricultural History* 56, no. 1 (Jan. 1982): 306–316; Jeffery C. Williams, *The Economic Function of Futures Markets* (New York: Cambridge University Press, 1989); *Oxford English Dictionary*, s.v. "bear."

15. Lisa Bernstein, "Private Commercial Law in the Cotton Industry: Creating Cooperation through Rules, Norms, Institutions," *Michigan Law Review* 99, no. 7 (June 2001): 1724–1790; A.W.B. Simpson, "The Origins of Futures Trading in the Liverpool Cotton Market," in *Essays for Patrick Atiyah* (Oxford: Clarendon Press, 1991), 179–208.

16. See, for instance, G. Wright Hoffman, *Future Trading upon Organized Commodity Markets in the United States* (Philadelphia: University of Pennsylvania Press, 1932).

17. Manfred E. Streit, ed., *Futures Markets, Modeling, Managing, and Monitoring Futures Trading* (Oxford: Basil Blackwell, 1983) is a good example of this; the *Journal of Futures Markets* is currently published by Wiley. Scott A. Redenius and David F. Weiman, "Banking on the Periphery: The Cotton South, Systemic Seasonality, and the Limits of National Banking Reform," in Paul Rhode, Joshua Rosenbloom, and David Weiman, eds., *Economic Evolution and Revolution in Historical Time* (Redwood City, Calif.: Stanford University Press, 2011): 214–242.

18. David S. Jacks, "Populists versus Theorists: Futures Markets and the Volatility of Prices," *Explorations in Economic History* 44, no. 2 (2007): 342–346, quotation at 345; Jeffrey Williams, "The Origins of Futures Markets," *Agricultural History* 56, no. 1 (Jan. 1982): 306–316; and Jeffrey Williams, *The Economic Function of Futures Markets* (New York: Cambridge University Press, 1986) emphasizes that fictitious dealings are really borrowing arrangements reminiscent of money markets rather than insurance policies.

19. Michael Rothschild and Joseph Stiglitz, "Equilibrium in Competitive Insurance Markets: An Essay in the Economics of Imperfect Information," *Quarterly Journal of Economics* 90, no. 4 (Nov. 1976): 629–648; Bruce C. Greenwald and Joseph Stiglitz, "Externalities in Economies with Imperfect Information and Incomplete Markets," *Quarterly Journal of Economics* 101, no. 2 (1986): 229–264.

20. James Gleick, *The Information: A History, a Theory, a Flood* (New York: Pantheon, 2011); L. Ellis and F. L. Kinder, eds., *Travel, Communication and Geography in Late Antiquity: Sacred and Profane* (Aldershot: Ashgate, 2004); Daniel Rosenberg, "Early Modern Information Overload," *Journal of the History of Ideas* 64, no. 1 (Jan. 2003): 1–9. Richard D. Brown, *Knowledge Is Power: The Diffusion of Information in Early America, 1700–1865* (New York: Oxford University Press, 1989).

21. Daniel Walker Howe, *What Hath God Wrought: The Transformation of America, 1815–1848* (Oxford: Oxford University Press, 2007), 1.

22. Richard T. Stillson, *Spreading the Word: A History of Information in the California Gold Rush* (Lincoln: University of Nebraska Press, 2006); Yael A. Sternhell, "Communicating War: The Culture of Information in Richmond During the American Civil War," *Past and Present* 202 (Feb. 2009): 175–205; Richard R. John, *Network Nation: Inventing American Telecommunications* (Cambridge, Mass.: Belknap Press of the Harvard University Press, 2010).

23. Daniel J. Headrick, *When Information Came of Age: Technologies of Knowledge in the Age of Reason and Revolution, 1700–1850* (New York: Oxford University Press, 2002).

24. Thomas K. McCraw, *Prophets of Regulation* (Cambridge, Mass.: Belknap Press of the Harvard University Press, 1984); Robert H. Wiebe, *Businessmen and Reform: A Study of the Progressive Movement* (Cambridge, Mass.: Harvard University Press, 1962); Gabriel Kolko, *The Triumph of Conservatism: A Re-interpretation of American History* (New York: Simon and Schuster, 1963); Jack C. High, ed., *Regulation: Economic Theory and History* (Ann Arbor: University of Michigan Press, 1991). The classic text on government statistics remains valuable: Henry C. Taylor and Anne Dewees Taylor, *The Story of Agricultural Economics in the United States, 1840–1932: Men, Services, Ideas* (Ames: Iowa State College Press, 1952).

25. Jonathan Lurie, *The Chicago Board of Trade, 1859–1905: The Dynamics of Self-Regulation* (Urbana: University of Illinois Press, 1979); Jonathan Lurie, "Commodities Exchanges, Agrarian 'Political Power,' and the Antioption Battle, 1890–1894," *Agricultural History* 48, no. 1 (January 1974): 115–125; David F. McFarland, "The Ingalls Amendment to

the Sherman Anti-Trust Bill," *Kansas Historical Quarterly* 11, no. 2 (May 1942): 174–198. Elizabeth Sanders, *Roots of Reform: Farmers, Workers, and the American State, 1877–1917* (Chicago: University of Chicago Press, 1999); Charles Postel, *The Populist Vision* (New York: Oxford University Press, 2012).

26. Caitlin Zaloom, *Out of the Pits: Traders and Technology from Chicago to London* (Chicago: University of Chicago Press, 2006) discusses this transition.

27. Jonathan Ira Levy, "Contemplating Delivery: Futures Trading and the Problem of Commodity Exchange in the United States, 1875–1905," *American Historical Review* 111, no. 2 (April 2006): 307–335; Jonathan Levy, *Freaks of Fortune: The Emerging World of Capitalism and Risk in America* (Cambridge, Mass.: Harvard University Press, 2012), Ch. 7. See also a forthcoming book by Alexander Engel, *Birth of the Risk Economy: An Economic and Cultural History of Futures Trading in the 19th and 20th Centuries*.

28. Alexander Engel, *Birth of the Risk Economy: An Economic and Cultural History of Futures Trading in the 19th and 20th Centuries* (forthcoming); Julia Laura Rischbieter, *Mikro-Ökonomie der Globalisierung: Kaffee, Kaufleute und Konsumenten im Kaiserreich 1870–1914* (Köln: Böhlau Verlag, 2011), 132–182; Steven Lestition, "Historical Preface to Max Weber, 'Stock and Commodity Exchanges,'" *Theory and Society* 29, no. 3 (June 2000): 289–304.

29. Michael Zakim and Gary J. Kornblith, eds., *Capitalism Takes Command: The Social Transformation of Nineteenth-Century America* (Chicago: University of Chicago Press, 2012); Charles G. Sellers, *The Market Revolution in America, 1815–1846* (New York: Oxford University Press, 1994); Daniel Walker Howe, *What Hath God Wrought: The Transformation of America 1815–1848* (New York: Oxford University Press, 2007); James L. Huston, *Calculating the Value of the Union: Slavery, Property Rights, and the Economic Origins of the Civil War* (Chapel Hill: University of North Carolina Press, 2002); Richard Franklin Bensel, *The Political Economy of American Industrialization, 1877–1900* (Cambridge: Cambridge University Press, 2000); David Harvey, *Spaces of Capital: Towards a Critical Geography* (London: Routledge, 2001).

30. Joyce Oldham Appleby, *The Relentless Revolution: A History of Capitalism* (New York: Norton, 2010); Jonathan Ira Levy, "Contemplating Delivery: Futures Trading and the Problem of Commodity Exchange in the United States, 1875–1905," *American Historical Review* 111 (Apr. 2006): 307–335; Fredrik Albritton Jonsson, "Rival Ecologies of Global Commerce: Adam Smith and the Natural Historians," *American Historical Review* 115, no. 5 (December 2010): 1342–1363. For an overview, see William H. Sewell Jr., "A Strange Career: The Historical Study of Economic Life," *History and Theory* 49, no. 4 (December 2010): 146–166. A good example of the less abstract history of capitalism would be Scott Reynolds Nelson, *A Nation of Deadbeats: An Uncommon History of America's Financial Disasters* (New York: Knopf, 2012).

31. David Hochfelder, "'Where the Common People Could Speculate': The Ticker, Bucket Shops, and the Origins of Popular Participation in Financial Markets, 1880–1920," *Journal of American History* 93, no. 2 (Sept. 2006): 335–358.

32. Linda Gordon, *Heroes of Their Own Lives: The Politics and History of Family Violence, Boston, 1880–1960* (New York: Viking, 1988).

33. Peter Novick, *That Noble Dream: The "Objectivity Question" and the American Historical Profession* (Cambridge: Cambridge University Press, 1988); Eric Foner, ed., *The New American History* (Philadelphia: Temple University Press, 1990). However, Ellen Fitzpatrick has pointed out that much of the "new" social history was not as new as its practitioners imagined: *History's Memory: Writing America's Past, 1880–1980* (Cambridge, Mass.: Harvard University Press, 2002).

34. Peter Way, *Common Labor: Workers and the Digging of the North American Canals, 1780–1860* (Baltimore: Johns Hopkins University Press, 1997), 93.

35. Walter Johnson, "On Agency," *Journal of Social History* 37, no. 1 (2003): 113–124; Eric Foner, "Afterword" in *After Slavery*; Brian Kelly, "Review of Steven Hahn, *A Nation under Our Feet: Black Political Struggles in the Rural South, From Slavery to the Great Migration*," *Labor* 1, no. 3 (Fall 2004): 145–147.

36. Joyce E. Chaplin, *An Anxious Pursuit: Agricultural Innovation and Modernity in the Lower South, 1730–1815* (Chapel Hill: University of North Carolina Press, 1993), 92–122. See also J. R. McNeill, *Mosquito Empires: Ecology and War in the Greater Caribbean, 1620–1914* (New York: Cambridge University Press, 2010).

37. Timothy Mitchell, *Rule of Experts: Egypt, Techno-Politics, and Modernity* (Berkeley: University of California Press, 2002), 51.

38. Pekka Hämäläinen, "The Rise and Fall of Plains Indian Horse Cultures," *Journal of American History* 90, no. 3 (December 2003): 833–862 (quotation 834). See also, for instance, Virginia DeJohn Anderson, *Creatures of Empire: How Domestic Animals Transformed Early America* (New York: Oxford University Press, 2004).

39. Bruno Latour and Steve Woolgar, *Laboratory Life: The Social Construction of Scientific Facts* (Beverly Hills, Calif.: Sage Publications, 1979); John Law, "Notes on the Theory of Actor-Network: Ordering, Strategy, and Heterogeneity," *Systems Practice* 5, no. 4 (1992): 379–393.

40. (New York: Oxford University Press, 2005).

41. See, for example, Per H. Hansen, "Networks, Narratives, and New Markets: The Rise and Decline of Danish Modern Furniture Design, 1930–1970," *Business History Review* 80, no. 3 (Autumn 2006): 449–483; also Susie Pak, *Gentlemen Bankers: The World of J. P. Morgan* (Cambridge, Mass.: Harvard University Press, 2013).

42. Certainly nothing to match Earle B. Young's *Galveston and the Great West* (College Station: Texas A&M University Press, 1997).

43. Joy Jackson, "Bosses and Businessmen in Gilded Age New Orleans Politics," *Louisiana History* 5, no. 4 (Autumn 1964): 387–400; Joy J. Jackson, *New Orleans in the Gilded Age* (Baton Rouge: Louisiana State University Press, 1969).

44. Burton I. Kaufman, "Organization for Foreign Trade Expansion in the Mississippi Valley, 1900–1920," *Business History Review* 46, no. 4 (Winter 1972): 444–465; Burton I. Kaufman, "New Orleans and the Panama Canal, 1900–1914," *Louisiana History* 14:4 (Autumn 1973): 333–346.

45. Scott P. Marler, "'A Monument to Commercial Isolation': Merchants and the Economic Decline of Postbellum New Orleans," *Journal of Urban History* 36:4 (July 2010): 507–527; Scott P. Marler, *The Merchants' Capital: New Orleans and the Political Economy of the Nineteenth-Century South* (New York: Cambridge University Press, 2013).

46. For example, John Wilds, *James W. Porch and the Port of New Orleans* (New Orleans: International Trade Mart, 1984).

47. Larry Schweikart, *Banking in the American South from the Age of Jackson to Reconstruction* (Baton Rouge: Louisiana State University Press, 1987); George D. Green, *Finance and Economic Development in the Old South: Louisiana Banking, 1804–1861* (Redwood City, Calif.: Stanford University Press, 1972); Linda Kay Murphy, "The Shifting Economic Relationships of the Cotton South: A Study of the Financial Relationships of the South During its Industrial Development, 1864–1913" (PhD diss., Texas A&M University, 1999); Redenius and Weiman, "Banking on the Periphery." 214–242.

GLOSSARY

basis contract   The word "basis" is used in a couple of different ways in futures trading, but for our purposes it means that the cotton futures contract does not specify a particular grade of cotton. The price agreed was the price of middling cotton. Since future contracts were made months ahead they needed to be flexible, and in this regard the flexibility was on the side of the seller, with the various grades of cotton helping the seller fulfill the contract. For this system to work for everyone, it was crucial that the differences between on and off middling ("on" middling meant better grades that cost more than middling cotton, a premium over the cost specified in a basis contract, while "off" middling meant worse grades that cost less and created a discount on the basis contract; these price differences, whether premium or discount, were stipulated by the rules of the cotton exchange where the contract was traded) actually reflected the prices for the various grades in the spot market. If the difference between middling and good ordinary cotton was set at twenty points (a "point" was a hundredth of a cent) but good ordinary was actually selling at fifty points off middling in the spot market, then a broker could exploit this disparity, buying good ordinary cotton in the spot market to deliver and pocketing the thirty-point profit. The buyer was out of luck. Establishing correct differences for futures contracts that matched the differences in the spot market was one of the most important things that made a futures market work fairly for everyone. See also **grades**; **differences**; **commercial differences**; **fixed differences**.

bears, bear traders   In a market, bears are those traders pursuing a strategy to make money on falling prices. Bulls pursue a strategy to make money on rising prices. The terminology seems to date from the mid-nineteenth century, according to the *Oxford English Dictionary*. See also **long/short position**; **bulls**.

bucket shop   A bucket shop was initially a place where customers could come in and buy small quantities of alcohol, carried home in a bucket. The term came to refer to shops, outside of established commodity exchanges, that dealt in small quantities of commodities. Since the standard contract for cotton futures was one hundred bales, for instance, bucket shops would allow contracts for any smaller amount. More importantly, the rules of trading in bucket shops allowed trading in options using "puts" and "calls," unlike the formal exchanges. This, combined with no requirement for actual delivery of the commodity, meant that bucket shops became little more than gambling establishments, where punters watched the prices of commodities (or stocks) relayed from the formal exchanges in much the same way punters in modern betting shops watch horses race on television. Whatever bets they placed had no effect on the actual prices on the exchanges, in the same way that bets placed at a betting shop don't make the horses run faster.

bulls, bull traders   In a market, bulls are traders who seek to raise the price of the commodity for their own profit. The bull does not appear in the *Oxford English Dictionary*, but he was first used in the same sentence as his opposite number, the bear, and the term seems to date from the mid-nineteenth century. See also **long/short position**; **bears**.

call margins   To call a margin means that one party to a contract demands that the other party place the cash for the margin on deposit with the exchange; as long as both parties agree this step can be avoided, but either party to a futures contract has the right to call the margins on that contract. Originally intended to prevent runaway prices that the purchaser has no intention or ability to pay, calling margins can also demand money and thereby limit the resources of the purchaser in making more contracts. There is another definition of a "call" in options trading, where "puts" and "calls" represent the two sides of a transaction, but that definition does not figure in our story. See also **margin**.

commercial differences   Commercial differences meant that the exchange's differences were set to reflect the actual differences on the spot market, updated whenever changes in the spot market required it, even daily. The differences in the spot market appeared due to changes in supply of the various grades: more cotton off middling than usual would mean higher prices for better grades of cotton. A bigger supply of better cotton would mean the price difference between middling cotton and cotton delivered "on middling" (or above the middling grade) would not be as high as it would if less high-quality cotton were available. To set commercial differences, however, an exchange had to have a large enough spot market to enable the exchange officials to get quotes on actual trades of many grades of cotton. If there were not enough trades of actual cotton occurring, using commercial differences to establish the value of futures contracts became impracticable. See also **grades**; **differences**; **fixed differences**.

corner　To corner a market is to buy more contracts for future delivery than will actually exist, and then to force the sellers of those contracts to settle the contracts at whatever price the buyer demands. A corner differs from a squeeze in its extent: ordinarily, because there are as many contracts to buy as there are contracts to sell (no more and no less—anyone who buys a contract for future delivery buys it from someone who has sold the same contract), the shortfall lasts only a few days and creates only a squeeze. A true corner takes considerably longer and often runs for many months on end, and it requires the purchase of any new contracts offered while paying for deliveries, as advancing prices will often produce surprising supplies from invisible sources. For these reasons running a corner requires an awareness of market conditions and an impending shortfall in supplies, but also considerable financial resources, and the existence of a ready demand for the commodity delivered, which will otherwise lower prices as its owners seek to dispense with it.

differences　Most cotton futures contracts were basis contracts; that is, the price of the contract represented the price of middling cotton, but any grade of cotton could be tendered to fulfill the contract. For that reason, the cotton exchanges that supported futures contracts had a system to establish how the price of the contract should vary depending on the grade of cotton actually delivered. Differences referred to the prices for various grades of cotton "on" (above) or "off" (below) middling that were officially set by a cotton exchange and that were to be used to establish the precise value of contracts when cotton was delivered.

fixed differences   Fixed differences meant that the value of a futures contract (a basis contract), adjusted for the grade of cotton actually delivered, was fixed by fiat. For example, the "revision committee" of the New York Cotton Exchange met at prescribed times and set the exchange's differences, which would be used to settle future contracts until the next revision. From 1888 to 1897 the revision committee met nine times a year, but after that it met only twice a year, in September and November, near the beginning and toward the end of the picking season. Inevitably, the fixed differences set by NYCE were frequently out of line with the actual differences in the spot market, and those trading in cotton futures there learned to lower the price they were willing to pay accordingly. Southern cotton producers complained that this was yet another way for NYCE to drive down the price of cotton, helping spinners a little but mostly helping bear speculators on NYCE at the expense of southern farmers.

future contract, future delivery, futures   A contract between a buyer and a seller for the delivery of a specified quantity of a commodity at a specified price and future date. Futures contracts tend to be governed by the rules of the exchanges upon which they are traded, but in general they impose both a right and an obligation for the seller to deliver the commodity and a right and an obligation on the buyer to pay for it. Cotton futures contracts, in the period this book discusses, were generally traded no more than twelve months before they matured; that is, contracts that came due or "matured" in June 1903 would begin to be traded in June 1902. Futures contracts are often described in terms of the month in which they mature, for example "June contracts" or "June cotton."

gin   The cotton gin (from "engine") is the device that gets the seed out of cotton. In the period of our story, cotton came out of the gin in bales weighing five hundred pounds each, wrapped in a cloth covering (usually jute), and secured with metal bands. Gins also were part of the network of crop reporting employed by the federal government, providing information about the crop passing through their facilities to the US Department of Agriculture and the US Census Bureau.

gold standard   A managed economic system in which the central banks (or governments) of participating nations set exchange rates by making national currencies convertible into gold at fixed rates. The US and England both adhered to the gold standard for the period covered by our story.

grades   Cotton was graded, or classed, according to a variety of factors, primarily the amount of foreign matter mixed in with the fiber and also the color, which could be pure white or "tinged" or "stained." Different kinds of cotton manufacturing required different grades of cotton. A wide range of other factors—especially the length of the fibers (called "staple")—also influenced the quality of cotton but did not enter directly into the grading.

hedging   At its simplest, hedging means that a trader makes an additional transaction to offset the risk of an original transaction. When a futures market was working properly, futures trading could be used to hedge risk. Imagine that in June, Spinner Sam needs to buy one hundred bales of upland middling cotton at 9¢ for delivery in November in order to fulfill his orders. Broker Brown agrees to supply this, and they sign a futures contract for this, the "spinning cotton." If the spot price goes to 11¢ by November then Brown has a problem, since he needs to sell the cotton at 9¢ and would lose 2¢ per pound. To protect himself against the risk of a higher price, and to do so in a way that will protect him equally well in case the price goes down, as soon as Brown makes a contract to deliver one hundred bales of cotton to Sam in November, he himself buys a future contract to purchase one hundred bales for delivery in November at 9¢. When he gets to November, if the cotton he must deliver to Sam now costs him 11¢ on the spot market, then the loss is cancelled out by the profit he makes on the cotton he has purchased on the future contract at 9¢, cotton that he can immediately sell on the spot market for a 2¢ per pound profit. Similarly, if the spot price in November has declined to 7¢, then the cotton that Brown has to buy on the spot market is cheaper than he expected, though the savings there is canceled out by the 2¢ per pound loss he makes on the cotton he buys on his hedge. Brown never intended to complete the hedge contract; he bought cotton in expectation of settling the contract for cash, which offset the original trade in actual cotton. This is why so many futures contracts never resulted in delivery, why so many more contracts were traded than could actually be fulfilled with actual cotton, and why futures markets looked illegitimate while fulfilling their primary function—allowing cotton's consumers to smooth out price volatility.

liquidate   See under **long/short position.**

long/short position   A long position indicates its holder believes prices will rise; a short position indicates that its holder believes prices will fall.

In futures trading, where so many contracts are to hedge rather than to deliver, a "long" position means that a trader has more contracts promising to buy cotton for a particular month than contracts to sell. If all those contracts come to maturity without settlement, the trader will need to pay money to fulfill the terms of contracts. In contrast, a "short" position means that a trader has more contracts binding him to sell cotton for a particular month than contracts to buy. In that case, if the buyers demand delivery, the trader needs not money, but cotton. "Closing a position" means getting back to a position of equilibrium for a given future month, so the trader is neither long nor short. He no longer has any cotton to receive that will have to be paid for and then sold on the spot market, and he also has no contracts open that might require him to deliver cotton. "Liquidate" means much the same thing as closing a long position, but it occurs only for a long position, since for a short position there is nothing to be sold or liquidated.

margin   1) To buy on the margin means to buy on credit, with a portion of the purchase price deposited to guarantee the full payment. Many exchanges have rules concerning their members' purchases on credit designed to keep prices from exceeding the trader's ability to pay. Margins are deposits that function as collateral security on the contractors. 2) The term "margin" is also sometimes used to mean the difference between the futures price and the spot price. As the date of maturity approaches for futures contracts for any particular month the price of new contracts for that month should converge toward the spot price, though remaining slightly higher to account for the cost of delivering the cotton according to the rules of the exchange.

pit   See under **ring**.

points   Cotton prices in Liverpool were traditionally quoted in fractions of a penny, for example 6 3/16d. This style was carried over into the American market, where prices were commonly quoted on fractions of a cent. Decimalization of cotton prices in US markets began sometime in the late nineteenth century, though well into the period we discuss prices are often still quoted in fractions, depending on the source (we have translated all fractions into decimals). A "point" was one hundredth of a cent.

position   See **long/short position**.

pro forma deliveries   This was a method by which NYCE sellers told buyers that their cotton was in the warehouse but forced them to wait as much as two months to actually get their hands on the physical cotton while it was recertificated, since individual bales were not separately graded and tagged.

profit-taking   See **realizing, profit-taking**.

realizing, profit-taking   Both of these terms refer to a trader selling off part or all of a long position. If prices are trending upward, a trader with a long position might want to keep waiting to see how much higher prices will go. On the other hand, he might want to sell off part or all of the contracts he holds to get the profits at that price. Contracts are easier to sell when prices are rising since more people want to buy than when prices are falling—if the price is falling, why make a contract to buy? The price will be lower tomorrow. If the trader waits until the price has peaked and it then begins to decline, it becomes harder to sell, so the canny trader will sell at the last possible moment before the price crests but before it starts to decline again. Figuring out when that moment comes is the hard part for the trader.

ring   Until the advent of computerized trading in the quite recent past, commodities trading was conducted under the "open outcry" system, meaning that traders actually stood around and called out offers to buy and sell (also using elaborate hand signals). In order to bring some sort of order to the trading and to maximize the visibility of traders to one another, trading was usually conducted around a ring, which was a sort of waist-high railing. In some cases trading was conducted in a **pit**, which essentially is a series of concentric circles at different levels, which increases the number of traders visible to one another at any given time.

spots, spot sales   The sale of a commodity on the spot. The buyer pays the money and receives the goods from the seller. Most cotton actually traded hands this way rather than as the result of futures contracts maturing.

squeeze   A squeeze was generally a brief rise in price caused by a shortage of supply—not quite a **corner**, to use the terminology of the trade. To pull off a squeeze a broker (or group of brokers) had to know that conditions—the supply of cotton arriving to a particular market, the level of trade and the market positions of other brokers on the exchange—would mean that for a brief period of time, perhaps only two or three days, sellers would be unable to actually put their hands on enough cotton to meet their contracts, promises made earlier to deliver at a particular price. By buying contracts for just a bit more cotton than would actually be available at the crucial moment, brokers executing a squeeze could insist on extravagant payment from those who had promised to deliver cotton but could not. Remember, defaulting on a contract risked a broker's membership on the exchange, and thus his livelihood. A squeeze required good judgment and a steady nerve, but it did not require the extensive resources that a full-blown corner required.

stopping notices   In futures trading, "stopping notices" or "stopping notices of delivery" has a slightly counterintuitive meaning. While most futures contracts never actually mature, if one does, the seller is required to give the buyer notice that he is going to deliver the commodity. "Stopping" such a notice simply means accepting delivery and paying for the commodity.

tender day   Futures contracts were traded by month, so a July contract, whenever it was created, would mature in July. Most futures contracts never actually matured; that is, cotton and money did not actually change hands, because the contracts were bought and sold as hedges rather than as a mechanism for distributing actual cotton. However, what made futures contracts work as a form of hedging was precisely the possibility that they could mature and that cotton would be delivered and paid for. The rules of the exchanges stipulated that if either party was going to insist that a contract be completed, notice had to be given within a certain period, usually five trading days, before the end of the month in which the contract matured. This allowed the seller to acquire the cotton to deliver or for the buyer to get together the money to pay for the cotton (and figure out where to put it). The last possible day to give these notices was called "tender day."

visible supply   The visible supply of cotton is the amount of cotton at any given time that has been brought to market and is available for purchase. It consists, as the Department of Agriculture described it in 1900, of "the stocks at American ports and interior towns, the European stocks, and the amounts on shipboard *en route* from the United States, India, Egypt, Brazil, and other countries to the various European ports." Reports on the cotton supply often refer to how much cotton has "come into sight," and this is a good way of thinking about visible supply. Cotton that is still in the field waiting to be harvested or in a shed waiting to be ginned is not part of the visible supply (though it could be referred to as the "invisible supply") since it is not available for purchase. Likewise, cotton held by mills usually is not part of the visible supply, but if the price goes high enough, as it did in summer 1903, those mills could actually sell the bales of cotton they had bought to use, so cotton held by mills would become part of the visible supply. On the other hand, a large invisible supply would drive prices down, since mills holding cotton would need less of the fiber, decreasing demand.

BIBLIOGRAPHY

BOOKS, JOURNALS, MAGAZINES

"American 'Cotton Corner' and Other Nations, The." *The Christian Advocate*, vol. 79, (September 22, 1904), 1532.

Anderson, Virginia DeJohn. *Creatures of Empire: How Domestic Animals Transformed Early America*. New York: Oxford University Press, 2004.

Appleby, Joyce Oldham. *The Relentless Revolution: A History of Capitalism*. New York: Norton, 2010.

Arthur-Cornett, Helen. *Remembering Kannapolis: Tales from Towel City*. Charleston, S.C.: History Press, 2006.

Balleisen, Edward J. *Navigating Failure: Bankruptcy and Commercial Society in Antebellum America*. Chapel Hill: University of North Carolina Press, 2001.

Bernstein, Charles B. *The Rothschilds of Nordstetten: Their History and Genealogy*. Chicago: C. B. Bernstein, 1989.

Beckert, Sven. "Emancipation and Empire: Reconstructing the Worldwide Web of Cotton Production in the Age of the American Civil War." *American Historical Review* 109, no. 5 (December 2004): 1405–1438.

Beckert, Sven. "From Tuskegee to Togo: The Problem of Freedom in the Empire of Cotton." *Journal of American History* 92, no. 2 (September 2005): 498–526.

Beckert, Sven. *Empire of Cotton: A Global History*. New York: Knopf, 2014.

Beckert, Sven. *The Monied Metropolis: New York City and the Consolidation of the American Bourgeoisie, 1850–1896*. New York: Cambridge University Press, 2001.

Bensel, Richard Franklin. *The Political Economy of American Industrialization, 1877–1900*. Cambridge: Cambridge University Press, 2000.

Bernstein, Lisa. "Private Commercial Law in the Cotton Industry: Creating Cooperation through Rules, Norms, and Institutions." *Michigan Law Review* 99, no. 7 (June 2001): 1724–1790.

Beveridge, W. H. *Unemployment: A Problem of Industry*. London: Longmans, Green, and Co., 1909.

Biographical and Historical Memoirs of Mississippi. Vol. 2, Part 2. Chicago: Goodspeed Publishing Co, 1891.

Bjerg, Ole. *Poker: The Parody of Capitalism*. Ann Arbor: University of Michigan Press, 2011.

Boles, John B., and Bethany L. Johnson, eds. *Origins of the New South Fifty Years Later: The Continuing Influence of a Historical Classic.* Baton Rouge: Louisiana State University Press, 2003.

Bouilly, Robert. "The Development of American Cotton Exchanges, 1870–1916." PhD diss., University of Missouri, 1975.

Boyle, James E. *Cotton and the New Orleans Cotton Exchange: A Century of Commercial Evolution.* Garden City, N.J.: Country Life Press, 1934.

Brown, Aaron. *The Poker Face of Wall Street.* Hoboken, N.J.: Wiley, 2006.

Brown, Richard D. *Knowledge Is Power: The Diffusion of Information in Early America, 1700–1865.* New York: Oxford University Press, 1989.

Brown, William Garrott. *The South At Work: Observations from 1904.* Bruce E. Baker, ed. Columbia: University of South Carolina Press, 2014.

By-Laws and Rules of the New Orleans Cotton Exchange, Embracing All Rules Governing the Spot and Future Contract Cotton Business in the New Orleans Market. Including Revisions Up To November 29th, 1894. New Orleans: L. Graham & Son, 1894.

Carlton, David L. *Mill and Town in South Carolina, 1880–1920.* Baton Rouge: Louisiana State University Press, 1982.

Carlton, David L., and Peter A. Coclanis, eds. *Confronting Southern Poverty in the Great Depression: The Report on Economic Conditions in the South with Related Documents.* Boston: Bedford, 1996.

Carson, Gerald. "Cracker Barrel Store: Southern Style." *Georgia Review* 9, no. 1 (Spring 1955): 27–37.

Chambers, Henry E. *A History of Louisiana: Wilderness-Colony-Province-Territory-State-People.* Chicago: American Historical Society, 1925.

Chaplin, Joyce E. *An Anxious Pursuit: Agricultural Innovation and Modernity in the Lower South, 1730–1815.* Chapel Hill: University of North Carolina Press, 1993.

Charter, Constitution, By-Laws and Rules of the New Orleans Cotton Exchange. New Orleans: L. Graham & Son, 1894.

Charter, Constitution, By-Laws and Rules of the New Orleans Cotton Exchange. New Orleans: L. Graham & Son, 1885.

Chase, John Churchill. *Frenchmen, Desire Good Children, and Other Streets of New Orleans.* 1949. Reprint. Gretna, La.: Pelican Publishing, 2007.

Clark, Thomas D. *Pills, Petticoats and Plows: The Southern Country Store.* Indianapolis: Bobbs-Merrill, 1944.

Coman, Katherine. "The Negro as a Peasant Farmer." *Publications of the American Statistical Association* 9, no. 66 (Jun. 1904): 39–54.

"Cotton Market, The." *Textile World Record* 37, no. 4 (July 1909), 191.

Cummings, John. "The Permanent Census Bureau: A Decade of Work." *Publications of the American Statistical Association* 13, no. 104 (December 1913): 605–638.

"David H. Miller and Henry W. Taft." Notice, *Fibre and Fabric: A Record of American Textile Industries in the Cotton and Woolen Trade* 39, no. 996 (April 2, 1904), 88.

Davis, Lee. *Natural Disasters.* New ed. New York: Facts on File, 2008.

Didier, Emmanuel. "Do Statistics 'Perform' the Economy?" In Donald MacKenzie, Fabian Muniesa, and Lucia Siu, eds. *Do Economists Make Markets? On the Performativity of Economics.* Princeton, N.J.: Princeton University Press, 2007, 276–310.

Douglass, H. Paul. *Christian Reconstruction in the South.* Boston: Pilgrim Press, 1909.

Du Bois, W.E.B. *The Quest of the Silver Fleece.* New York: A. C. McClurg & Co., 1911.

"Effects of the Cotton Corner." *The Standard [Chicago],* 50:52 (August 29, 1903), 1607.

Ellis, L., and F. L. Kinder, eds. *Travel, Communication and Geography in Late Antiquity: Sacred and Profane.* Aldershot: Ashgate, 2004.

Ellis, L. Tuffly. "The New Orleans Cotton Exchange: The Formative Years, 1871–1880." *Journal of Southern History* 39, no. 4 (November 1973): 545–564.

Ellis, L. Tuffly. "The Revolutionizing of the Texas Cotton Trade, 1865–1885." *Southwestern Historical Quarterly* 73, no. 4 (April 1970): 478–508.

Ellis, L. Tuffly. "The Round Bale Cotton Controversy." *Southwestern Historical Quarterly* 71, no. 2 (October 1967): 194–225

Ellis, L. Tuffly. "The Texas Cotton Compress Industry: A History." PhD diss., University of Texas, 1964.

Ellison, Thomas. *The Cotton Trade of Great Britain.* London: Effingham Wilson, Royal Exchange, 1886.

Engel, Alexander. *Birth of the Risk Economy: An Economic and Cultural History of Futures Trading in the Nineteenth and Twentieth Centuries* (forthcoming).

Fabian, Ann. *Card Sharps and Bucket Shops: Gambling in Nineteenth-Century America.* New York: Routledge, 1999.

Fitzpatrick, Ellen. *History's Memory: Writing America's Past, 1880–1980.* Cambridge, Mass.: Harvard University Press, 2002.

Fortier, Alcée. *Louisiana: Comprising Sketches of Parishes, Towns, Events, Institutions, and Persons, Arranged in Cyclopedic Form.* Vol. 3. Madison, Wisc.: Century Historical Association, 1914.

Foner, Eric, ed. *The New American History.* Philadelphia: Temple University Press, 1990.

Fortier, Paula A. "Behind the Banner of Patriotism: The New Orleans Chapter of the American Red Cross and Auxiliary Branches 6 and 11 (1914–1917)." MA thesis, University of New Orleans, 2010.

Friedman, Walter. *Fortune Tellers: The Story of America's First Economic Forecasters.* Princeton, N.J.: Princeton University Press, 2013.

Frost, Meigs O. *"Hester Says-" An Intimate Personal Sketch of the World's Greatest Cotton Authority.* New Orleans: Theo. H. Harvey Press, 1926.

Fuller, Wayne E. *Morality and the Mail in Nineteenth-Century America.* Urbana: University of Illinois Press, 2003.

Gardner, Deborah S. *Cadwalader, Wickersham, & Taft: A Bicentennial History, 1792–1992.* New York: Cadwalader, Wickersham & Taft, 1994.

Garriott, E. B. "The West Indian Hurricanes of September, 1906." *Monthly Weather Review* (September 1906): 418–423.

Garside, Alston Hill. *Cotton Goes To Market: A Graphic Description of a Great Industry.* New York: Frederick A. Stokes Co., 1935.

Gaston, Paul M. *The New South Creed: A Study in Southern Myth-Making.* Montgomery, Ala.: NewSouth Books, 2002.

Giesen, James C. *Boll Weevil Blues: Cotton, Myth, and Power in the American South.* Chicago: University of Chicago Press, 2011.

Gill, Donald A. *Stories Behind New Orleans Street Names.* Chicago: Bonus Books, 1992.

Gleick, James. *The Information: A History, a Theory, a Flood.* New York: Pantheon, 2011.

Goldsmith, G. L. *Columbus in One Hundred Verses: Including a Directory of its Mercantile and Industrial Institutions.* Columbus, Miss.: G. L. Goldsmith, 1889.

Gordon, Linda. *Heroes of Their Own Lives: The Politics and History of Family Violence, Boston, 1880–1960.* New York: Viking, 1988.

Green, George D. *Finance and Economic Development in the Old South: Louisiana Banking, 1804–1861.* Redwood City, Calif.: Stanford University Press, 1972.

Greenwald, Bruce C., and Joseph Stiglitz. "Externalities in Economies with Imperfect Information and Incomplete Markets." *Quarterly Journal of Economics* 101, no. 2 (1986): 229–264.

Gunther, Gerald. *Learned Hand: The Man and the Judge.* New York: Knopf, 1994.

Hahn, Barbara. *Making Tobacco Bright: Creating an American Commodity, 1617–1937.* Baltimore: Johns Hopkins University Press, 2011.

Hämäläinen, Pekka. "The Rise and Fall of Plains Indian Horse Cultures." *Journal of American History* 90, no. 3 (December 2003): 833–862.

Hammond, M. B. *The Cotton Industry: An Essay in American Economic History.* New York: Macmillan, 1897.

Hannah, Leslie. "J. P. Morgan in London and New York before 1914." *Business History Review* 85, no. 1 (Spring 2011): 113–150.

Hansen, Per H. "Networks, Narratives, and New Markets: The Rise and Decline of Danish Modern Furniture Design, 1930–1970." *Business History Review* 80, no. 3 (Autumn 2006): 449–483.

Harned, Robey Wentworth. "Boll Weevil in Mississippi, 1909." *Mississippi Agricultural Experiment Station, Bulletin No. 139* (Agricultural College, Mississippi, March 1910), 15–1.

Harvey, David. *Spaces of Capital: Towards a Critical Geography.* London: Routledge, 2001.

Hays, Shanon Ashley."Progressivism, Southern Style: The Congressional Career of Asbury Francis Lever, 1901–1919." MA thesis, Clemson University, 1998.

Headrick, Daniel J. *When Information Came of Age: Technologies of Knowledge in the Age of Reason and Revolution, 1700–1850.* New York: Oxford University Press, 2002.

Hechler, Kenneth W. *Insurgency: Personalities and Politics of the Taft Era.* New York: Columbia University Press, 1940.

High, Jack C. ed., *Regulation: Economic Theory and History.* Ann Arbor: University of Michigan Press, 1991.

Hirschstein, Hans. "Commodity Exchanges in Germany." *Annals of the American Academy of Political and Social Science* 155 (May 1931): 208–217.

Hochfelder, David. " 'Where the Common People Should Speculate': The Ticker, Bucket Shops, and the Origins of Popular Participation in Financial Markets, 1880–1920." *Journal of American History* 93, no. 2 (Sept. 2006): 335–358.

Hoffman, G. Wright. *Future Trading upon Organized Commodity Markets in the United States.* Philadelphia: University of Pennsylvania Press, 1932.

Hoffman, I. Newton. "The Cotton Futures Act." *Journal of Political Economy* 23, no. 5 (May 1915): 465–489.

Hoing, Willard Lee. "James Wilson as Secretary of Agriculture, 1897–1913." PhD diss., University of Wisconsin, 1964.

Holbrook, Abigail Curlee. "Cotton Marketing in Antebellum Texas." *Southwestern Historical Quarterly* 63 (Apr. 1970): 431–455.

Hollis, Daniel W. " 'Cotton Ed Smith': Showman or Statesman?" *South Carolina Historical Magazine* 71, no. 4 (October 1970): 235–256.

Holt, James. *Congressional Insurgents and the Party System, 1909–1916.* Cambridge, Mass.: Harvard University Press, 1967.

Howard-White, F. B. *Nickel: An Historical Review.* London: Methuen, 1963.

Howe, Daniel Walker. *What Hath God Wrought: The Transformation of America, 1815–1848.* Oxford: Oxford University Press, 2007.

Humphreys, Hubert. "Photographic Views of Red River Raft, 1873." *Louisiana History* 12, no. 2 (Spring 1971): 101–108.

Huston, James L. *Calculating the Value of the Union: Slavery, Property Rights, and the Economic Origins of the Civil War.* Chapel Hill: University of North Carolina Press, 2002.

Jacks, David S. "Populists versus Theorists: Futures Markets and the Volatility of Prices." *Explorations in Economic History* 44, no. 2 (2007): 342–346.

Jackson, Joy J. "Bosses and Businessmen in Gilded Age New Orleans Politics." *Louisiana History* 5, no. 4 (Autumn 1964): 387–400.

Jackson, Joy J. *New Orleans in the Gilded Age.* Baton Rouge: Louisiana State University Press, 1969.

Jervey, Theodore D. "The Hayne Family." *South Carolina Historical and Genealogical Magazine* 5, no. 3 (July 1904): 168–188.

John, Richard R. *Network Nation: Inventing American Telecommunications.* Cambridge, Mass.: Belknap Press of the Harvard University Press, 2010.

Johnson v. Miller, Supreme Court of Arkansas, Nov. 18, 1895, as recorded in *Southwestern Reporter,* vol. 53 (St. Paul, Minn.: West Publishing Co., 1900), pp. 1053–1056.

Johnson, Walter. "On Agency." *Journal of Social History* 37, no. 1 (2003): 113–124.

Jones, Howard J. "Biographical Sketches of Members of the 1868 Louisiana State Senate." *Louisiana History* 19, no. 1 (Winter 1978): 65–110.

Jonsson, Fredrik Albritton. "Rival Ecologies of Global Commerce: Adam Smith and the Natural Historians." *American Historical Review* 115, no. 5 (December 2010): 1342–1363.

Kaufman, Burton I. "New Orleans and the Panama Canal, 1900–1914." *Louisiana History* 14, no. 4 (Autumn 1973): 333–346.

Kaufman, Burton I. "Organization for Foreign Trade Expansion in the Mississippi Valley, 1900–1920." *Business History Review* 46, no. 4 (Winter 1972): 444–465.

Kelly, Brian. "Review of Steven Hahn, *A Nation under Our Feet: Black Political Struggles in the Rural South, From Slavery to the Great Migration.*" *Labor* 1, no. 3 (Fall 2004): 145–147.

Kendall, John. *The History of New Orleans.* Chicago: Lewis Pub. Co., 1922.

Kennan, George. "The Strike in the Lowell Cotton-Mills." *The Outlook* (May 30, 1903): 269–273.

Kennan, George. *E. H. Harriman: A Biography in Two Volumes.* Boston: Houghton Mifflin Company, 1922.

Killick, John R. "The Cotton Operations of Alexander Brown and Sons in the Deep South, 1820–1880." *Journal of Southern History* 43 (May 1977): 169–194.

Killick, John R. "The Transformation of Cotton Marketing in the Late Nineteenth Century: Alexander Sprunt and Son of Wilmington, N.C., 1884–1956." *Business History Review* 55 (Summer 1981): 143–169.

Killick, John R. "Risk, Specialization and Profit in the Mercantile Sector of the Nineteenth Century Cotton Trade: Alexander Brown & Sons, 1820–80." *Business History* 16 (Jan. 1974): 1–16.

Kolko, Gabriel. *The Triumph of Conservatism: A Re-interpretation of American History.* New York: Simon and Schuster, 1963.

Kuffler, Arthur. "Report on the Liverpool Conference with American and European Cotton Exchanges." In *The Ninth International Congress of Delegated Representatives of Master Cotton Spinners' and Manufacturers' Associations, Held in the Kurhaus, Scheveningen, June 9th, 10th, and 11th, 1913* (Manchester: Taylor, Garnett, Evans, and Co., n.d.), 52.

Kurlansky, Mark. *Cod: A Biography of the Fish That Changed the World.* New York: Walker and Co., 1997.

Kurlansky, Mark. *Salt: A World History.* New York: Walker and Co., 2002.

Larson, Erik. *Isaac's Storm: A Man, a Time, and the Deadliest Hurricane in History.* New York: Crown, 1999.

Latham, Alexander & Co. *Cotton Movement and Fluctuations.* Vol. 30. New York: Latham, Alexander & Co., 1903.

Latour, Bruno. *Reassembling the Social: An Introduction to Actor-Network Theory.* New York: Oxford University Press, 2005.

Latour, Bruno, and Steve Woolgar. *Laboratory Life: The Social Construction of Scientific Facts.* Beverly Hills, Calif.: Sage Publications, 1979.

Law, John. "Notes on the Theory of Actor-Network: Ordering, Strategy, and Heterogeneity." *Systems Practice* 5, no. 4 (1992): 379–393.

Law, John, and John Hassard, eds. *Actor Network Theory and After.* Oxford: Wiley-Blackwell, 1999.

Lefèvre, Edwin. "The Great Bull: The Man Who Rose With Cotton While All the Market Fell." *Saturday Evening Post* 170, no. 9 (August 29, 1903), 2.

Lestition, Steven. "Historical Preface to Max Weber, 'Stock and Commodity Exchanges.'" *Theory and Society* 29, no. 3 (June 2000): 289–304.

Levy, Jonathan. *Freaks of Fortune: The Emerging World of Capitalism and Risk in America.* Cambridge, Mass.: Harvard University Press, 2012.

Levy, Jonathan Ira. "Contemplating Delivery: Futures Trading and the Problem of Commodity Exchange in the United States, 1875–1905." *American Historical Review* 111, no. 2 (April 2006): 307–335.

Lincoln, Rixford J. "The City of New Orleans: A Review of the City's Banking and Commercial Interests." *Banker's Magazine* 65, no. 4 (October 1902): 471–480.

Link, Arthur S. "The Cotton Crisis, the South, and Anglo-American Diplomacy, 1914–1915." In J. Carlyle Sitterson, ed., *Studies in Southern History.* James Sprunt Studies in History and Political Science, vol. 39 (Chapel Hill: University of North Carolina Press, 1957), 122–138.

Lipartito, Kenneth J. "The New York Cotton Exchange and the Development of the Cotton Futures Market." *Business History Review* 57, no. 1 (Spring 1983): 50–72.

Lipscomb, W. L. *A History of Columbus, Mississippi, During the 19th Century.* Birmingham, Ala.: Dispatch Printing Co., 1909.

"Lowell and Other Strikes, The." *Literary Digest* 26, no. 15 (April 11, 1903), 528.

Lurie, Jonathan. *The Chicago Board of Trade, 1859–1905: The Dynamics of Self-Regulation.* Urbana: University of Illinois Press, 1979.

Lurie, Jonathan. "Commodities Exchanges, Agrarian 'Political Power,' and the Antioption Battle, 1890–1894." *Agricultural History* 48, no. 1 (January 1974): 115–125.

MacBrayne, Lewis E. "New England's Great Rival." *National Magazine* 18, no. 5 (August 1903): 547–551.

Malin, James C. "The Background of the First Bills to Establish a Bureau of Markets, 1911–12." *Agricultural History* 6, no. 3 (July 1932): 107–129.

Markham, Jerry W. *A Financial History of the United States: Vol. II, From J. P. Morgan to the Institutional Investor, 1900–1970.* Armonk, N.Y.: M. E. Sharpe, 2002.

Marler, Scott P. "Merchants and the Political Economy of Nineteenth-Century Louisiana: New Orleans and Its Hinterlands." PhD diss., Rice University, 2007.

Marler, Scott P. *The Merchants' Capital: New Orleans and the Political Economy of the Nineteenth-Century South.* Cambridge: Cambridge University Press, 2013.

Marler, Scott P. " 'A Monument to Commercial Isolation': Merchants and the Economic Decline of Postbellum New Orleans." *Journal of Urban History* 36, no. 4 (July 2010): 507–527.

Marsh, Arthur R. "Cotton Exchanges and Their Economic Functions." *Annals of the American Academy of Political and Social Science* 38, no. 2 (September 1911): 253–280.

Mayo-Smith, Richmond. "A Permanent Census Bureau." *Political Science Quarterly* 11, no. 4 (December 1896): 589–600.

McCorkle, James L., Jr. "The Louisiana 'Buy-a-Bale' of Cotton Movement, 1914." *Louisiana History* 15, no. 2 (Spring 1974): 133–152.

McCraw, Thomas K. *Prophets of Regulation: Charles Francis Adams, Louis D. Brandeis, James M. Landis, Alfred E. Kahn.* Cambridge, Mass.: Belknap Press of Harvard University Press, 1984.

McFarland, David F. "The Ingalls Amendment to the Sherman Anti-Trust Bill." *Kansas Historical Quarterly* 11, no. 2 (May 1942): 174–198.

McKnight, William James. *Jefferson County, Pennsylvania: Her Pioneers and People.* Vol. 2. Chicago: J. H. Beers & Co., 1917.

McLaurine, W. M. *James William Cannon (1852–1921): His Plants, His People, His Philosophy.* New York: Newcomen Society, 1951.

McManus, James. *Cowboys Full: The Story of Poker.* London: Souvenir Press, 2010.

McNeill, J. R. *Mosquito Empires: Ecology and War in the Greater Caribbean, 1620–1914.* New York: Cambridge University Press, 2010.

Miller, William Harris. *History and Genealogies.* Lexington, Ky.: Press of Transylvania Co., 1907.

Mills, W. Haslam. *Sir Charles W. Macara, Bart.: A Study of Modern Lancashire,* 2nd ed. Manchester: Sherratt & Hughes, 1917.

Mitchell, Timothy. *Rule of Experts: Egypt, Techno-Politics, and Modernity.* Berkeley: University of California Press, 2002.

Mol, Annemarie. "Ontological Politics: A Word and Some Questions." In John Law and John Hassard, eds. *Actor Network Theory and After.* Oxford and Malden, Mass.: Blackwell Publishing and The Sociological Review, 1999, 74–89.

Morison, Elting E., ed. *The Letters of Theodore Roosevelt*. Vol. 4. Cambridge, Mass.: Harvard University Press, 1951.

Morrison, Andrew. *New Orleans and the New South*. New Orleans: Metropolitan Pub. Co., 1888.

"Mr. Chamberlain's Tariff." *Blackwood's Magazine* 174, no. 1057 (November 1903), 720.

Murphy, Linda Kay. "The Shifting Economic Relationships of the Cotton South: A Study of the Financial Relationships of the South during its Industrial Development, 1864–1913." PhD diss., Texas A&M University, 1999.

Nelson, Scott Reynolds. *A Nation of Deadbeats: An Uncommon History of America's Financial Disasters*. New York: Knopf, 2012.

New Orleans City Directory. New Orleans: Soards, 1895–1905.

"New York City." *Fibre and Fabric* XL, no. 1039 (January 28, 1905), p. 17.

"New York City." *Fibre and Fabric* XLIII, no. 1109 (June 2, 1906), p. 22.

New York Cotton Exchange, 1871–1923. New York: New York Cotton Exchange, 1923.

Novick, Peter. *That Noble Dream: The "Objectivity Question" and the American Historical Profession*. Cambridge: Cambridge University Press, 1988.

Nystrom, Justin A. *New Orleans After the Civil War: Race, Politics, and a New Birth of Freedom*. Baltimore: Johns Hopkins University Press, 2010.

O'Connor, Thomas. *History of the Fire Department of New Orleans*. New Orleans: n.p., 1895.

O'Gorman, James F. *H. H. Richardson: Architectural Forms for an American Society*. Chicago: University of Chicago Press, 1987.

Olsson, Jan. "Trading Places: Griffith, Patten and Agricultural Modernity." *Film History* 17, no. 1 (2005): 39–65.

Oxford English Dictionary.

Pak, Susie. *Gentlemen Bankers: The World of J. P. Morgan*. Cambridge, Mass.: Harvard University Press, 2013.

Parker, Carl. "Governmental Regulation of Speculation." *Annals of the American Academy of Political and Social Science* 38, no. 2 (September 1911): 126–154.

Pietruska, Jamie L. "'Cotton Guessers': Crop Forecasters and the Rationalizing of Uncertainty in American Cotton Markets, 1890–1905." In Hartmut Berghoff, Philip Scranton, and Uwe Spiekermann, eds. *The Rise of Marketing and Market Research*. New York: Palgrave MacMillan, 2012, 49–72.

Pizer, Donald. *The Novels of Frank Norris*. Bloomington: Indiana University Press, 1966.

Plunkett, Charles T. "President's Address [to the Meeting of the National Association of Cotton Manufacturers, Apr. 28–29, 1909]," *Textile World Record* 37, no. 2 (May 1909), p. 93.

Porter, Glenn, and Harold C. Livesay. *Merchants and Manufacturers: Studies in the Changing Structure of Nineteenth-Century Marketing*. Baltimore: Johns Hopkins University Press, 1971.

Postel, Charles. *The Populist Vision*. New York: Oxford University Press, 2012.

Redclift, Michael. *Chewing Gum: The Fortunes of Taste*. New York: Routledge, 2004.

Redenius Scott A., and David F. Weiman. "Banking on the Periphery: The Cotton South, Systemic Seasonality, and the Limits of National Banking Reform." In Paul Rhode, Joshua Rosenbloom, and David Weiman, eds. *Economic Evolution and Revolution in Historical Time*. Redwood City, Calif.: Stanford University Press, 2011, 214–242.

Riello, Giorgio. *Cotton: The Fabric That Made the Modern World*. Cambridge: Cambridge University Press, 2013.

Rischbieter, Julia Laura. *Mikro-Ökonomie der Globalisierung: Kaffee, Kaufleute und Konsumenten im Kaiserreich 1870–1914*. Köln: Böhlau Verlag, 2011.

Robins, Jonathan. "The Cotton Crisis: Globalization and Empire in the Atlantic World, 1902–1920." PhD diss., University of Rochester, 2010.

Roeder, Robert Earl. "New Orleans Merchants, 1800–1837." PhD diss., Harvard University, 1959.

Rosenberg, Daniel. "Early Modern Information Overload." *Journal of the History of Ideas* 64, no. 1 (Jan. 2003): 1–9.

Rothschild, Michael, and Joseph Stiglitz. "Equilibrium in Competitive Insurance Markets: An Essay in the Economics of Imperfect Information." *Quarterly Journal of Economics* 90, no. 4 (Nov. 1976): 629–648.

Rules Governing Business in Contracts for the Future Delivery of Cotton in the New Orleans Cotton Exchange, Adopted January 1880. New Orleans: Clark & Hofeline Steam Power Book Printers, 1880.

Saloutos, Theodore. "The Southern Cotton Association, 1905–1908," *Journal of Southern History* 13, no. 4 (November 1947): 492–510.

Sanders, Elizabeth. *Roots of Reform: Farmers, Workers, and the American State, 1877–1917.* Chicago: University of Chicago Press, 1999.

Schindler, Henri. *Mardi Gras Treasures: Costume Designs of the Golden Age.* Gretna, La.: Pelican Publishing Co., 2002.

Schlesinger, Dorothy G., comp. and ed., *New Orleans Architecture: Vol. 7, Jefferson City.* Gretna, La.: Pelican Publishing, 1989.

Schweikart, Larry. *Banking in the American South from the Age of Jackson to Reconstruction.* Baton Rouge: Louisiana State University Press, 1987.

Scott, Anne Firor. "A Progressive Wind from the South, 1906–1913," *Journal of Southern History* 29, no. 1 (February 1963): 53–70.

Sellers, Charles G. *The Market Revolution in America, 1815–1846.* New York: Oxford University Press, 1994.

Sewell, William H. Jr. "A Strange Career: The Historical Study of Economic Life." *History and Theory* 49, no. 4 (December 2010): 146–166.

Shale, Roger, and G. Carroll Todd. *Decrees and Judgments in Federal Anti-trust Cases, July 2, 1890–Jan. 1, 1918.* Washington, D.C.: GPO, 1918.

Shepperson, Alfred B. *Cotton Facts.* New York: Alfred B. Shepperson, 1904.

Shepperson, Alfred B. *The Standard Telegraphic Cipher Code for the Cotton Trade.* New York: Alfred B. Shepperson, 1881.

Sherman, Audrey. "The History of the New Orleans Cotton Exchange, 1871–1914." MA thesis, Tulane University, 1934.

Simpson, A.W.B. "The Origins of Futures Trading in the Liverpool Cotton Market." In Peter Cane and Jane Stapleton, eds. *Essays for Patrick Atiyah.* Oxford: Clarendon Press, 1991.

Snyder, Robert E. "Federal Crop Forecasts and the Cotton Market, 1866–1929." *Journal of Southwest Georgia History* 7 (1989–1992): 40–58.

Sternhell, Yael A. "Communicating War: The Culture of Information in Richmond During the American Civil War." *Past and Present* 202 (Feb. 2009): 175–205.

Stiglitz, Joseph E., and Andrew Weiss, "Credit Rationing in Markets with Imperfect Information." *American Economic Review* 71, no. 3 (June 1981): 393–410.

Stillson, Richard T. *Spreading the Word: A History of Information in the California Gold Rush.* Lincoln: University of Nebraska Press, 2006.

Streit, Manfred E. ed. *Futures Markets, Modeling, Managing, and Monitoring Futures Trading.* Oxford: Basil Blackwell, 1983.

Strom, Claire. *Making Catfish Bait Out of Government Boys: The Fight Against Cattle Ticks and the Transformation of the Yeoman South.* Athens: University of Georgia Press, 2009.

"Sully Cotton Failure, The." *Fibre and Fabric: A Record of American Textile Industries in the Cotton and Woolen Trade* 39, no. 995 (March 26, 1904): 73–74.

Sully, Daniel J. "Is the High Price of Cotton the Result of Manipulation?" *North American Review* 178, no. 567 (February 1904): 194–204.

"Sully Failure, The." *Literary Digest*, March 26, 1904, p. 438.

Sykes, Alan. *Tariff Reform in British Politics, 1903–1913.* Oxford: Clarendon, 1979.

Taft, Henry W. *A Century and a Half at the New York Bar.* New York: privately printed, 1938.

Taylor, Henry C. and Anne Dewees Taylor. *The Story of Agricultural Economics in the United States, 1840–1932: Men, Services, Ideas.* Ames: Iowa State College Press, 1952.

The Book of Louisiana, a Newspaper Reference Work. New Orleans: Dameron Pierson, 1916.

The Picayune's Guide to New Orleans. New Orleans: Picayune, 1903.

Thirty-Fourth Annual Report of the New Orleans Cotton Exchange. New Orleans: L. Graham Co., 1904.

Todd, John A. *The Marketing of Cotton: From the Grower to the Spinner.* London: Sir Isaac Pitman & Sons, 1934.

Todd, John A. *The World's Cotton Crops.* London: A. & C. Black, 1923.

Toledano, Roulhac. *The National Trust Guide to New Orleans: The Definitive Guide to Architectural and Cultural Treasures.* New York: Wiley, 1996.

Tucker, Ray T. "Don Tom of Alabam'." *North American Review* 226, no. 2 (August 1928): 148–157.

Twentieth Annual Report of the New Orleans Cotton Exchange. New Orleans: L. Graham & Son, Printers, 1890.

Twenty-Third Annual Report of the New Orleans Cotton Exchange. New Orleans: L. Graham & Son, Printers, 1893.

Tyler, Ronnie C. "Cotton on the Border, 1861–1865." *Southwestern Historical Quarterly* 63 (Apr. 1970): 456–477.

Watkins, James L. *The Cotton Crop of 1899–1900.* US Department of Agriculture, Division of Statistics, Miscellaneous Series—Bulletin No. 19. Washington, D.C.: GPO, 1901.

Way, Peter. *Common Labor: Workers and the Digging of the North American Canals, 1780–1860.* Baltimore: Johns Hopkins University Press, 1997.

Wetherington, Mark V. *The New South Comes to Wiregrass Georgia, 1860–1910.* Knoxville: University of Tennessee Press, 1994.

White, Richard. "Information, Markets, and Corruption: Transcontinental Railroads in the Gilded Age." *Journal of American History* 90, no. 1 (2003): 19–43.

Who's Who in America I. Chicago: A.N. Marquis & Company, 1906–1907, 1735.

Wiebe, Robert H. *Businessmen and Reform: A Study of the Progressive Movement.* Cambridge, Mass.: Harvard University Press, 1962.

Wilds, John. *James W. Porch and the Port of New Orleans.* New Orleans: International Trade Mart, 1984.

Williams, Jeffrey C. *The Economic Function of Futures Markets.* Cambridge: Cambridge University Press, 1989.

Williams, Jeffrey C. "The Origin of Futures Markets," *Agricultural History* 56, no. 1 (Jan. 1982): 306–316.

Willis, H. Parker. "The Adjustment of Crop Statistics." *Journal of Political Economy* 11, no. 1 (December 1902): 1–54.

Willis, H. Parker. "The Adjustment of Crop Statistics: II." *Journal of Political Economy* 11, no. 3 (June 1903): 363–398.

Willis, H. Parker. "The Adjustment of Crop Statistics: III." *Journal of Political Economy* 11, no. 4 (September 1903): 540–567.

Woodman, Harold D. *King Cotton and His Retainers: Financing and Marketing the Cotton Crop of the South, 1800–1925.* 1968. Reprint, with a new introduction by Harold D. Woodman, Columbia: University of South Carolina Press, 1990.

Woodward, C. Vann. *Origins of the New South, 1877–1913.* Baton Rouge: Louisiana State University Press, 1951.

Young, Earle B. *Galveston and the Great West.* College Station: Texas A&M University Press, 1997.

Zakim, Michael, and Gary J. Kornblith, eds. *Capitalism Takes Command: The Social Transformation of Nineteenth-Century America.* Chicago: University of Chicago Press, 2012.

Zaloom, Caitlin. *Out of the Pits: Traders and Technology from Chicago to London.* Chicago: University of Chicago Press, 2006.

Zimmerman, Andrew. *Alabama in Africa: Booker T. Washington, the German Empire, and the Globalization of the New South.* Princeton, N.J.: Princeton University Press, 2010.

SIGNED NEWSPAPER ARTICLES
Baynes, Fred. "Bad Trade and Distress in Lancashire," *Times* (London), October 13, 1903, p. 9.

Corrigan, John, Jr. "Cotton Exchange Dealt Hard Blow," *Atlanta Constitution*, December 6, 1909.

Corrigan, John, Jr. "Wilson To Solve Cotton Problem," *Atlanta Constitution*, September 19, 1913, p. 5.

Cowan, Charles C. "Time for the South to Unite in Fighting Cotton Bears," *Atlanta Constitution*, May 1, 1910.

Daney, Charles A. "Calm in Cotton Market During the Past Week," *Atlanta Constitution*, December 5, 1909.

Daney, Charles A. "Horns Still Locked in Cotton Fight," *Atlanta Constitution*, January 30, 1910.

Daney, Charles A. "Sixteen Cent Cotton Added to the Cheer," *Atlanta Constitution*, December 26, 1909.

Daney, Charles A. "Spot Cotton Holders Should Remain Firm," *Atlanta Constitution*, January 16, 1910.

Langley, Lee J. "City of New Orleans New Cotton Capital," *Atlanta Constitution*, March 27, 1904.

Langley, Lee J. "Cotton Is Up to Stay Says Expert Brown," *Atlanta Constitution*, February 3, 1904, p. 6.

Marsh, Arthur R. "The Economic Status of Cotton," *New York Times*, January 9, 1910.

Walker, Judy. "Romanesque Romance: The New Owner of a Landmark Uptown Mansion Opens It For the NOMA Tour," New Orleans *Times-Picayune*, April 9, 2011.

NEWSPAPERS
[Providence, RI] *Manufacturers and Farmers Journal*
London *Times*
Adelaide *Morning Advertiser*
Alexandria *Louisiana Democrat*
Atlanta Constitution
Atlanta *Journal*
Baltimore *Sun*
Bankers' Magazine
Boston *Daily Globe*
Boston Evening Transcript
Brooklyn *Citizen*
Charleston *News and Courier*
Chicago *Daily Tribune*
Cincinnati *Enquirer*
Crop Reporter
Dallas *Southern Mercury*
Fort Worth *Daily Gazette*
Lake Providence (La.) *Banner-Democrat*
London Daily Mail
Manchester Guardian
Memphis *Scimitar*
Miami News
Nashville *American*
New Orleans *Daily Picayune*
New Orleans *Daily States*
New Orleans *Stem*
New Orleans *Times Democrat*

New York *American*
New York *Commercial*
New York *Commercial Advertiser*
New York *Evening Post*
New York *Evening Post*
New York *Evening Telegram*
New York Evening World
New York Herald
New York *Mail and Express*
New York *News*
New York Press
New York *Sun*
New York Times
New York Tribune
Perth [Australia] *Sunday Times*
Philadelphia Record
San Francisco Call
St. Louis *Globe Democrat*
St. Louis *Republic*
Sydney Morning Herald
Vernon (Alabama) *Courier*
Vernon (Alabama), *Pioneer*
Wall Street Journal
Washington Post
Washington, D.C. *Star*
Spokane *Spokesman-Review*
Meriden (Connecticut) Morning Record
Hawera and Normanby (New Zealand) *Star*
Schulenburg (Texas) *Sticker*
Ogden (Utah) Standard
New London (Connecticut) Day

ARCHIVAL COLLECTIONS

Egger, Mack, Dale Darnell, and Earlene Egger. *In the Beginning—'Up Home': A History of Caledonia, Lowndes County, Mississippi.* Caldeonia, MS: n.p., 2004. Billups-Garth Archives, Columbus-Lowndes Public Library, Columbus, Miss.

William Perry Brown Papers and Braughn Family Papers, Historic New Orleans Collection, New Orleans.

Henry W. Taft to Theodore Roosevelt, December 1, 1904, in the possession of Cadwalader Wickersham and Taft.

GOVERNMENT PUBLICATIONS

Act of March 6, 1902 Providing for the Establishment of a Permanent Census Office (Washington, D.C.: GPO, 1902), 5.

British Parliamentary Debates, 124: 1026, July 1, 1903.

Christie Grain and Stock Co., et al., v. Board of Trade of the City of Chicago (798 U.S. 236).

Congressional Record, 57th Cong., 1st Sess., Senate, 1804.

Congressional Record, House, 59th Cong., 2nd sess., Jan. 26, 1907, 1783.

Department of Commerce, Bureau of the Census, *Bulletin 125: Cotton Production, 1913* (Washington, D.C.: GPO, 1914), 27, Table 14.

House of Representatives. "Hearings Before the Committee on Expenditures in the Department of Justice." Washington, D.C.: GPO, 1913.

Hilgard, Eugene W. *Report on Cotton Production in the United States.* Washington, D.C.: GPO, 1884.

Passport Application, *Passport Applications, January 2, 1906–March 31, 1925,* NARA Microfilm Publication M1490, Roll 0015, Certificate 17115.

Proceedings of the Boll Weevil Convention called by Governor W. W. Heard in New Orleans, Louisiana, Nov. 30th and Dec. 1st, 1903 (Baton Rouge: Bureau of Agriculture and Immigration, 1903), n.p.

Report of the Commissioner of Corporations on Cotton Exchanges. Part IV. Effect of Future Contracts on Prices of Cotton. Part V. Influence of Producers' Organizations on Prices of Cotton. December 6, 1909 (Washington, D.C.: GPO, 1909), 9.

Report of the Joint Select Committee to Inquire into the Condition of Affairs in the Late Insurrectionary States, Vol. 12, Mississippi, vol. II. Washington, D.C.: GPO, 1872.

US House Committee on Agriculture. *Hearings before the Committee on Agriculture during the Second Session of the Sixty-First Congress, Vol. 2, Hearings on Bills for the Prevention of "Dealing in Futures" on Boards of Trade, Etc.* Washington, D.C.: GPO, 1910.

US House Committee on Agriculture. *Regulation of Cotton Exchanges: Hearings before the Committee on Agriculture, House of Representatives, Sixty-Third Congress, Second Session, Regarding Various Bills Relative to the Regulation of Cotton Exchanges, April 22 to 25, 1914* (Washington, D.C.: GPO, 1914), 130.

US House Committee on Banking and Currency. *Report of the Committee on Banking and Currency.* 60th Cong, 1st Sess., 1908. H. Rept. 1126.

US *House Journal.*

US House. *Interference With Commerce Among the States, Etc.* 62nd Cong., 2nd Sess., 1912. H. Rept. 602.

US House. *Trading in Cotton Futures.* 63rd Congress, 2nd Session, 1914. H. Rept. 765.

US *Senate Journal.*

US *Senate Manual* (Washington, D.C.: GPO, 1913), 11–12.

US Senate. *Trading in Cotton Futures.* 63rd Cong., 2nd Sess., 1914. S. Rept. 289.

United States, Bureau of Corporations. *Report of the Commissioner of Corporations on Cotton Exchanges.* Part 1. Washington, D.C.: GPO, 1908.

United States. Bureau of the Census, *Cotton Production and Distribution, Season of 1914–15.* Washington, D.C.: GPO, 1915.

United States v. James A. Patten, et al. Circuit Court of the United States for the Southern District of New York. July Term 1910. Court File 3–71. Criminal Case Files, RG 21: Records of District Courts of the United States, 1685–2004. NARA New York.

Watkins, James L. *The Cotton Crop of 1899–1900,* US Department of Agriculture, Division of Statistics, Miscellaneous Series—Bulletin No. 19. Washington, D.C.: GPO, 1901.

ONLINE SOURCES

Farnie, D. A. "Ellison, Thomas (1833–1904)," *Oxford Dictionary of National Biography,* Oxford University Press, 2004, http://0-www.oxforddnb.com.catalogue.ulrls.lon. ac.uk/view/article/58116 (accessed April 4, 2011).

"Fleming, Lamar, Jr." *The Handbook of Texas Online,* http://www.tshaonline.org/hand-book/online/articles/ffl09 (accessed September 23, 2012).

Lange, Fabian, Alan L. Olmstead, and Paul W. Rhode. "The Impact of the Boll Weevil, 1892–1932." Working Paper: February 2008. http://www.econ.ucdavis.edu/faculty/alolmstead/Working_Papers/BOLL%20WEEVIL%20.pdf (accessed July 29, 2012).

Hauschild, Henry. "RUNGE, JULIUS." *Handbook of Texas Online* http://www.tshaonline. org/handbook/online/articles/fru26 (accessed September 9, 2012). Published by the Texas State Historical Association.

Hays, Paul. "John Cherry Brown (1833–1877)" http://www.findagrave.com/cgi-bin/fg.cgi?page=gr&GRid=34262215 (accessed May 29, 2012).

"History of the CFTC" http://www.cftc.gov/about/historyofthecftc/index.htm (accessed November 22, 2012).

"History of the CFTC" http://www.cftc.gov/About/HistoryoftheCFTC/history_precftc (accessed October 1, 2012).

"Lawyers and Legal Events," 17 Bench and B., o.s. 40 (1909), http://heinon-line.org/HOL/LandingPage?collection=journals&handle=hein.journals/babl7&div=10&id=&page= (accessed September 22, 2012).

Mock, Gary N. "Fuller E. Callaway" http://www.textilehistory.org/FullerECallaway.html (accessed October 29, 2012).

"Parker, Lewis W. Greenville, SC" http://textilehistory.org/LewisWParker.html (accessed September 17, 2012).

Rockoff, Stuart. "Woodville, Mississippi," *Encyclopedia of Southern Jewish Communities*, http://www.msje.org/history/archive/ms/woodville.htm (accessed October 31, 2011)

"Spooner, John Coit (1843–1919)," *Biographical Directory of the U.S. Congress*, http://bioguide.congress.gov/ (accessed September 1, 2011).

INDEX